MEMOIRS OF A NOT SO DUTIFUL DAUGHTER

Jenni Murray's memoir begins at her sick mother's bedside. She is not, she acknowledges, the only woman to have had a difficult relationship with her mother, yet family history and the times in which they live seem to militate against any prospect of a true reconciliation between them.

Benefiting from the women's movement and the chance to go to university and have a career, Jenni was able to break free from her mother's constraints, but never from her influence. While remaining determined to go her own way, she has always felt a sense of guilt: she has been a 'not so dutiful daughter'.

And then, after she began her memoir, Jenni's life took a distinctly downward turn. Her mother and father died within six months of each other, and she found that she had breast cancer.

This book is a diary of that terrible year—and an extraordinary honest exploration of the eternal triangle of an only daughter, her mother and her father.

MEMOIRS OF A
NOT SO DUTIFUL
DAUGHTER

Jenni Murray

BBC
LARGE
PRINT

First published 2008
by
Bantam Press
This Large Print edition published 2009
by
BBC Audiobooks Ltd
by arrangement with
Transworld Publishers Ltd

UK Hardcover ISBN 978 1 408 41469 9
UK Softcover ISBN 978 1 408 41470 5

This book is a work of non-fiction based on the life,
experiences and recollections of the author. In some limited
cases names of people, places, dates, sequences or the detail of
events have been changed solely to protect the privacy of
others. The author has stated to the publishers that, except in
such minor respects not affecting the substantial accuracy of
the work, the contents of this book are true.

British Library Cataloguing in Publication Data available

Printed and bound in Great Britain by
CPI Antony Rowe, Chippenham, Wiltshire

In loving memory of Alvin and Win Bailey

My thanks to David, the best life support system a woman could wish for, and to my sons, Ed and Charlie, who accept with gracious resignation that, as the American writer Nora Ephron said, 'Life is copy.' I'm especially grateful to my editor, Selina Walker, whose loyalty, patience and judgement have been invaluable through very difficult times.

PHOTOGRAPHS

INTRODUCTION

'I feel I am beginning a love letter. I'm saying things I could not have expressed even a year ago, because there was a barrier between us that's existed for as long as I can remember. It collapses today in hospital when I hold her hand and stroke her hair, and she says, "Do you love me? I've often wondered."

'The words come, barely audible, through the haze of the wicked disease that has taken away the difficult, argumentative, demanding woman who has haunted my life from the moment I was born, driven so much of what I have striven to achieve and yet has so frequently evaporated my courage.

'In the past five years, as the illness took its relentless hold on my mother, there have been hints of vulnerability and uncertainty and a willingness to talk about what has in the past been utterly taboo, but we have continued to dance around each other. I know I'm not the only woman to have had a difficult relationship with her mother, but our family history and the times in which we live seem to have militated against any possibility of reconciliation. We were two women forever joined by an invisible umbilical cord but torn apart by circumstance, education and a sexual revolution that opened opportunities for me that for her had been unimaginable.

'Some of the things I did to offend or upset her were, even as an adult, carried out in childlike defiance. Others were political acts, rooted in my convictions but at odds with her own, as I rushed

1

with wild enthusiasm through the new gender landscape that stretched before me. Some were designed to please her but never seemed quite to hit the mark; at other times I was paralysed, unable to say or do the things I wanted to do because she sat on my shoulder, critical and displeased, oozing disappointment and disgust.

'Now my mother lies dishevelled and desperate, needing me as she has never appeared to need me before, and I feel a rush of love for her that I have never been able to acknowledge. I tell her I do love her. That I always have, but have often been too angry or too sad to express it. I ask her to forgive me if I have made her feel uncared-for.

'I have a photograph of her aged six, her dark, straight, shiny hair cut into a pudding-basin style. She had the same dead straight, sleek locks I had as a child and a young woman, before either of us discovered the delights of the permanent wave or the highlight. There are other strong physical similarities—shape of face, height, colour of eyes—except that I inherited my father's build, big-boned and powerful, while she, as she has never ceased to remind me, is delicately boned, almost skinny. I can't count the number of times she has sighed and, in what frequently felt like a crowing tone, bemoaned my deficiencies in the feminine delicacy department.

'In the photo, even at that young age, she's wearing black-rimmed, bottle-bottomed spectacles. Now, her poor sight further clouded by cataracts, she asks me to wipe away the sticky gum that accumulates on her left eye and causes her so many problems that she can no longer summon up the energy to read—our one shared pastime.

2

'I look into a mirror image of my own best feature, hers now fuzzy with age. She fights hard to focus and to articulate. "I love you too," she says, "more than anything and I'm sorry too that I haven't always shown it."

'As I leave the lonely little room she's occupying—she's generally alone on the many occasions she has to be admitted as she can be disruptive if there are other patients around her—she looks over to the flowers I brought her.

' "They're beautiful. Thank you," she whispers and makes a supreme effort to smile. "And you're beautiful too."

'It is the first time she has ever paid me an unconditional compliment. I am fifty-six years old. I weep all the way home.'

It was this entry in my diary in the summer of 2006 that made me think seriously of writing this book. How, I wondered often, could two women be so close, so full of love for each other and at the same time so full of hate that they broke each other's heart?

My mother's slow deterioration as Parkinson's disease did its worst and my frequent visits to her and my father—far more than I had ever made in the years since I left home at the age of eighteen—drew me back to a book I had read when I was still at school. *Memoirs of a Dutiful Daughter* was my introduction to the work of the French philosopher Simone de Beauvoir. She wrote of the conventional, bourgeois childhood she had escaped through a determination to educate herself and break away from the constraints of her mother's plan that her daughter would become, like her, a loyal wife and mother.

3

Instead, Simone became one of the great intellectuals of twentieth-century France and wrote one of the most influential of all feminist texts, *The Second Sex*. But it was the *Memoirs*, the first volume of her autobiography, that had stayed most clearly in my mind. Like her, I had no brothers. She had a younger sister while I was an only child, but we were both accorded many of the privileges generally only open to boys. Like me, she adored the father who described her as having a 'man's brain'. Like me, she had a mother who saw her job as conditioning her daughter to become a woman who knew her place—which would be secondary to a man. But she never sought to blame her mother, acknowledging in a later book, *A Very Easy Death*, how Maman de Beauvoir 'lived against herself. She had appetites in plenty; she spent all her strength in repressing them and she underwent this denial in anger . . . she had been taught to pull the laces hard and tight herself.'

It was from De Beauvoir that I learned to understand why my mother behaved towards me as she did. Mum's outlook was shaped by the privations of the Second World War, and she was raised by Edwardians. It was not her fault that she felt it her business to pull my laces hard and tight (a Playtex girdle at the age of fifteen, as I recall— soon abandoned, along with, for a short time, my bra).

Until my middle and her old age, I was a 'not so dutiful daughter'. I had the benefit of the women's movement and the chance to go to university, have a career and a family and I escaped my mother's control, often neglecting her but never free of her influence or the guilt I felt at my selfishness. But

4

again there was solace in De Beauvoir. She too asked herself if her ambition was 'selfish' or simply 'self-possessed'. I often accuse myself of the former, but hope it's been the latter.

After I began this book life took a distinctly downward turn. I had always thought myself lucky. I had work that I loved, a man on whom I could rely, children I adored and who were turning out well. I did, though, frequently wake in the night full of fear that somehow I would be found out as a fraud and everything would fall apart. I often felt that a working-class girl from Barnsley had had ideas above her station and was bound to be brought down.

It was a terror my father always had. Redundancy was what scared him. Me too. What happened was much worse. My mother and my father died within six months of each other, and on the day of my mother's death I was told I would have to have a mastectomy because of breast cancer. So this book became a diary of that terrible year and a memoir of what is a universally complex set of relationships: the eternal triangle made up of an only daughter, her mother and her father.

July 2006

This summer has no right to the title. The rain is relentless and perfectly suits the gloom of my mood as I drive across the backbone of England. It's a landscape which used to delight me, but now I barely notice the all-too-familiar hills and valleys. I'm shaken by an enormous lorry which has come far too close for comfort—practically demolishing the driver's side of my vehicle. It's a rude awakening from what can only be described as a driving daze.

I curse angrily through the open window at the driver who's pounding far too fast through the narrow streets of Tideswell, a town in the midst of the Peak District which more or less marks the halfway point between home and my mum and dad. But it's not altogether his fault. I should have been more awake, concentrating on the matter in hand—driving the car. This journey has become so routine, I realize I've noticed none of it since I bypassed Buxton.

It takes one and a half hours there and one and a half hours back and I've been doing it pretty much every weekend for nearly ten years, as we've lurched from one medical disaster to another. First, soon after my mother's seventieth birthday, there was the diagnosis of Parkinson's. Bad fall number one and the broken hip. The bodged repair. The second broken hip. The fractured wrist. The inability to travel to see us. The shaking. The flat blank face that was once so animated. All the classic symptoms of the condition. And now she's in hospital as they try to help her become mobile again. The physiotherapists and medical

9

staff are beginning to acknowledge that their battle is all but lost and Dad's getting ill and exhausted from the strain of it all.

Nor am I immune from the strain, hence the doziness of my driving. I'm really only aware this is Tideswell because I'm hungry. This is where I stop to buy the best cheese and onion sandwiches in Derbyshire to eat en route. I've obviously joked too many times about my car knowing its own way to Barnsley to visit my parents. If I don't apply more concentration, it'll be the end of me.

Finally, towards the end of their lives, I've learned how to be my parents' dutiful daughter. But it's a terrible chore. I'm more than a little ashamed that I dread the trips so much, but, even as an adult, the pleasure of visiting the folks was all about relaxing back into childhood: being ticked off for minor misdemeanours, getting a cuddle when things are going wrong, being reassured that everything will be all right and being spoiled with delicious home-cooked comfort food. Now Mum's in hospital, I hardly go to the house. Dad spends every second he's allowed at her bedside—the nurses have to throw him out at the end of the day—so this is where we meet.

The most crippling fatigue overtakes me before I even arrive. I know that when I get to the hospital the room will be hot and I'll just want to curl up in the arms of one of my parents and fall into an untroubled sleep, but I am the grown-up now, responsible for comforting them, sorting out their affairs and guiding them through the awesome bureaucracy that passes for care of the elderly and infirm. I'm disgusted with myself because I find it such an awful burden. Will my two sons one day

10

feel this about me? For now, they and their father are doing everything they can to support me, but the bottom line is still me. I am my parents' only child. The sense of duty and the umbilical bond that bind us are mine and mine alone.

I park the car outside the hospital, gather up the flowers, jelly babies and liquorice allsorts—always my mother's favourites—and make my way towards her room. The hospital is dedicated to the elderly and infirm—a place she'd dreaded all her life—but she's completely isolated from those around her. She has to be in a room by herself because the drugs she takes for the Parkinson's can bring about angry, noisy, disruptive behaviour and the most frightening hallucinations. She pictures malevolent strangers invading her private space. Sometimes she offers sweets to imaginary children. She once told the boys on one of their visits to watch out for the rabbit that frequently ran past her room.

'But Grandma,' they giggled, 'we're in a hospital. There's no rabbits here.'

A rare flash of comedy during these sad times.

Today, I push open the door, throw out a cheery greeting and am confronted with an atmosphere of desperate tension. My father, the kindest, gentlest, most faithful of men, is huddled in a chair in the corner, his white face etched with pain.

'Dad,' I ask, 'whatever's the matter?'

He says nothing. He can't formulate the words.

'Don't speak to that man,' my mother bellows. It's astonishing that such powerful venom can emerge from someone so thin and frail. She's tucked up in her sterile hospital bed, unable to move her wasted, useless legs and supported by a

11

pile of pillows.

'Mum,' I gasp, 'what are you talking about? It's Dad. He's here, looking after you, like always.'

'Looking after me?' Her voice loses none of its truly evil tone. 'Don't make me laugh. Do not speak to that man. He's a faithless vagabond.' Her facility with wounding words is clearly undiminished.

Dad sobs quietly in the background. I tell her not to be so silly and not to hurt his feelings—to no avail. She beckons me over to her bedside and explains in conspiratorial tones that one of the nurses is blonde and very pretty and she and Dad are having an affair.

'Mum, the nurse is probably still in her teens. Dad is nudging eighty and barely leaves your bedside. You're being ridiculous.' But, of course, I am not dealing with an entirely sound mind. Not today anyway. Tomorrow it may be completely different and she'll be her old loving self again with never a bad word to say about him. But today there is nothing to be done.

I spend a couple of hours flitting between the two of them, listening to my mother's rant and desperately trying to explain to Dad that it's the drugs that are making her behave this way. That maybe they've removed any inhibition or rationale she had and she is now able to express her greatest lifelong, albeit entirely unjustified, fear: that somehow she wasn't good enough for this handsome, charming, lovely man and she would lose him to someone else. She once confided it to me when I was a teenager, when Dad was working abroad and we were at home together, but generally it was one of those issues that remain

12

unspoken within a family. She had certainly never shared her concerns with him until now. My poor father is inconsolable.

Eventually I have to leave them for the long drive back across the Pennines. Through tears of frustration and tiredness I hold in my mind an image of the photograph which my father brought to my mother's hospital room. He explained that he wanted the staff always to be reminded that the elderly husk whose most intimate needs they are there to service was once like them. She was young, full of fun and unquestionably beautiful.

The year is 1944. My father, Alvin, was seventeen and my mother, christened Winifred, known as Winnie but preferring Win, was eighteen, although he lied about his age and added an extra year. They are walking arm in arm along the Prom at Blackpool on their first holiday together. They were heavily chaperoned—Grandma and Grandpa were lurking somewhere in the background— occupied separate rooms at the boarding house and were clearly, grinningly, hopelessly in love, a state from which they seem never to have wavered in more than sixty years.

They had met when my mother was playing what she always described as 'a fallen woman' in a play at the local amateur dramatic society. Dad has been only too aware of her lifelong condemnation of what she called 'the selfishness or simple immorality' of the 'unmarried mother', and he told me some time ago, with more than a hint of irony, that she was performing just such a role with sympathy and gusto. Perhaps her view on this, so forcibly expressed over many years, was merely intended as a warning to a potentially wayward

13

daughter? There's so much that I don't know of what my mother really thought.

My father, a trainee electrician, was there to do the lights and had opened the door to the women's changing room by mistake. He'd caught the merest glimpse of her in a state of partial undress and decided on the basis of those few seconds that this was the woman with whom he would spend the rest of his life.

He asked her out. She played hard to get for a little while, which, she assured me, one should always do. It wasn't right to let men think you were keen or easy, as they wouldn't respect you. Eventually she relented and allowed him to take her to the pictures. He was earning next to nothing as an apprentice while she, a junior civil servant, was salaried and relatively well off.

'Did you go Dutch then?' I remember asking her. It seemed obvious to me, even during my teenage years, that being paid for was somehow demeaning and positively wicked, especially if you were the one with the most cash.

'Good grief,' she replied, 'the very idea! You should never let a man think you don't depend on him. It makes him feel inferior.' We were, you see, worlds apart from the start.

As my father walked her home from one of their early dates, she asked him why, if he too was eighteen, he hadn't yet been called up for National Service. He confessed to having told a fib, because he'd suspected she wouldn't consider him if he was so young. She sent him packing at the kitchen door. My grandfather, who had recognized a good man when he saw one, chased after him along the road.

14

'She didn't mean it! Come back, lad,' he called. 'She's in the sitting room, sobbing her heart out.'

My father went back. My mother relented, but made him promise never to reveal their age gap. Her birthday was February and his was April. She was ready to acknowledge being older by a month or so, but not a whole year; it simply wasn't done for a woman to marry a younger man.

He kept his vow for years, only letting the cat out of the bag during a solo visit to me at university after I had plied him with more beer than he was used to in the Union Bar. My mother still has no idea I know their secret, and no one in the family has ever asked why we don't celebrate big, milestone birthdays. At the turn of every decade, Dad has always said that growing older is no cause for any kind of jubilation, a policy with which my mother readily agrees, although I would have loved to mark her eightieth earlier this year.

Dad was called up eventually, luckily too late to suffer any action or witness any of the real horrors of war my mother's older suitors might have seen. Nevertheless, they were separated for the best part of two years. Yet their closeness seems always to have stretched across continents. There's a story my mother told me when I was a child which she believed demonstrated the tie that bound them. She was at work at the Food Office in the village of Worsborough where she lived. It was her job to manage rationing and ensure that women with young babies received their allocation of orange juice and cod liver oil tablets. She suddenly felt a searing pain across the right side of her face. She told me how she'd squealed and spoken Dad's name—a tale which is corroborated by her friend Eleanor, who sat opposite her and who was later to become my godmother.

After work Mum crossed town to visit my father's mother. By now her cheek was red and stung like a severe burn. My grandmother had heard nothing—unsurprisingly as Dad was in Egypt and any news would have taken an eternity to reach Barnsley. But she later confirmed, when I demanded to know if the story was true, that my mother had indeed arrived at her home in a state of great anxiety and physical pain. Some weeks later my mother received a letter in Dad's familiar, spidery handwriting, composed on the date of her 'face incident'.

Earlier that day—at around the time she had been in the office with Eleanor—my father had been sitting in the NAAFI when a fellow soldier had tripped and spilt a mug of boiling hot tea down the right side of his face. His first thought, he wrote, was that he would be scarred for life and she wouldn't fancy him any more. I've always been rather sceptical about such matters as extrasensory perception, having never experienced it myself, but the evidence my mother gave, backed up by all the witnesses, has always seemed compelling.

It was a story that delighted me as a child. To have such confirmation of the absolute adoration your parents have for each other at a time when you appear to be the centre of their small universe is profoundly comforting and reassuring. And my earliest years were entirely untroubled. Dad went off every morning 'to earn pennies for Jennifer', Mum stayed at home cooking, baking and cleaning and my grandparents, with whom we lived until I was three, were just around the corner after we moved to our own house.

In the early 1950s no one thought of child abduction or abuse and my mother would watch from her kitchen window as I trotted happily across the road and rolled head first through the hole in the hedge which gave me access to my grandfather's garden. His carefully tended plot was a hymn to wartime making do and boasted the tastiest sprouts and cabbages in the neighbourhood, the most blight-free potatoes, and beds of strawberries and canes of raspberries which were regularly raided by me and my small gang of pals.

Only the gooseberry bush was to be the source of a lifelong loathing. After one particularly enthusiastic raid, I was sicker than I ever remember before or since. When presented with gooseberry tart during a recent cookery broadcast I found myself turning up my nose at beautifully cooked food for the first time in living memory.

So I had constant access to the comforts of two homes where the women made wonderful food and spent hours of every day keeping everything startlingly clean. My grandmother often boasted

17

that you could eat your dinner from her toilet seat. It's one of the few household obsessions I inherited. In the days when she was able, my mother would often visit my home and run her finger along my mantelpiece or banister rail with a disapproving 'tut!' at the dust she picked up. But my toilet was always immaculate and still is. Raising two boys through the thoughtless and sloppy-aim stage was purgatory.

The men of our little family went out to work— my grandfather as a winder at the local pit and my father as an electrician—and looked after the garden. The allocation of tasks by gender was never questioned and when we were together there seemed to be harmony and, for spoiled little me, a never-ending stream of treats.

I can't remember what age I was when I began to wonder whether I was not quite all my mother had wanted, but I know I was around seven years old when I told the dinner ladies at my primary school that my mother would not be turning up to the beetle drive organized by the PTA that night. She was in St Helen's Maternity Hospital, I said, and had already had the baby. They seemed surprised, but I assured them that she had had a little boy, that he was lovely, and his name was David Robert.

This story was not merely the product of a vivid imagination. At some point in my early childhood my mother had told me how surprised she had been when she gave birth to me to find that I was a girl. All through her pregnancy, she said, she had longed for a little boy, and right until the moment the midwives had placed me in her arms she had called the baby that she carried David Robert.

18

The midwives, she told me often, had greeted my arrival with the awful words, 'Ah, look, you have a sweet little girl' (I'm quite sure I determined right then not to fulfil their infuriating prediction—sweet I was never going to be).

She hadn't been able to think of a name for me, so Grandma had come up with Jennifer, after a popular movie star of the time, Jennifer Jones, and Dad chose Susan as my middle name. Mum had been prepared to go along with whatever they suggested. I heard the wistful disappointment in her voice every time she told the story.

Maybe if I couldn't be quite what she wanted I could conjure up a baby brother simply by saying he existed? My mother found out, of course, when she did attend the beetle drive and the dinner ladies expressed their surprise at seeing her. How come she'd got out of hospital so quickly and how had she managed to conceal her pregnancy? She was furious with me and never seemed to consider what might have induced me to make up such a story. Child psychology in Barnsley must have been in its infancy.

My mother did, though, tell me very early on what an awful time she had had giving birth to me. I sometimes think it's strange that some mothers tell their daughters nothing of what happened to them in the delivery room, perhaps because they want to protect them from fear of an experience that they will one day be expected to endure.

My mother was not one of them.

I would not describe her as a religious woman— she always called herself loosely C of E, and never attended church except for occasions of hatch, match or dispatch, but she appeared to have absorbed with unquestioning faith God's diktat in Genesis chapter 3 to the wayward Eve. As punishment for failing to resist the temptation to eat the fruit of the tree of knowledge, 'Unto the woman he said, I will greatly multiply thy sorrow and thy conception; in sorrow thou shalt bring forth children; and thy desire shall be to thy husband, and he shall rule over thee.'

When Dad was working away from home she and I would snuggle up in bed together and I would ask her about the day I was born. I must have been a sucker for punishment because she pulled no punches as she regaled me with the horror story of her long labour and near demise. She should, of course, have been benefiting, as so many women of the period were assured they would, from the new National Health Service which was formed two years before my birth in 1950.

Until then confinement for most women had been a domestic affair. In such books as *Doctor at Large* Richard Gordon relates the experiences of a young GP who arrives at a house where a woman is in labour. The husband is in the kitchen boiling endless kettles of hot water for sterilization and the woman is in the bedroom, walking around or sitting on the bed, attended with bustling efficiency by the local midwife. The imprint of the *Daily Express* on her bottom is no surprise as newsprint is the only sterile material to hand. In the later stages of labour she will crouch on the bed and deliver.

The NHS brought the hierarchy of the hospital to the experience of birth, no doubt with the best of intentions. Maternal and infant mortality rates were still high in the 1940s and it was assumed that

20

the sterile environment of the hospital would be safer for mother and baby. It's now accepted that reductions in mortality have been achieved by high-tech interventions in high-risk pregnancies and by general improvements in diet, cleanliness and antenatal care for those who can expect a normal delivery. Whether the birth takes place at home or in hospital is now considered irrelevant to safe delivery as long as there are no anticipated complications and the woman is attended by a proficient and experienced midwife. But for my mother it was assumed that going into hospital had to be the best option and she is of the generation that never thought to challenge the authority of the trained professional.

It must have been terrifying. She was twenty-four years old and married for only a year. I doubt my grandmother, also the mother of an only daughter, ever divulged her own experience of birth. Certainly she never mentioned it to me and it was, I suspect, a taboo subject in her respectable household. So for my mother labour was a journey into the unknown. Hospital protocol demanded that a woman in the early stages of labour be shaved and given an enema. She was made to lie down on a hospital bed, legs akimbo with her ankles held in stirrups. Never was there a more unnatural way for a woman to labour; it was a position designed to facilitate easy access for the midwives and doctor, but which limited any help gravity might offer.

Deprived of my father, who was not allowed near her, my mother was left alone for most of her twenty-four hours in labour. She remembers terrible pain and a sense that she had left her own

21

body and was floating close to the ceiling, watching herself slowly fading away. We were, evidently, both at a critical stage when the consultant, a Dr Bhattacharya, came to see her and immediately ordered a forceps delivery. We made it, but, according to Mum, only just and she was so damaged internally as a result that she had to return to hospital some weeks later for surgical repair.

The long-term consequences of this life-threatening bloodbath were profound: there would be no more children. I don't even want to imagine the impact on passion in the days long before reliable contraception. For me, there were headaches. Always, when I have been anxious or stressed, studying for exams or reading small print late into the night, a sickening thud would begin at the base of my skull and wend its way towards my right eye and my temple. I dreaded it, but could do nothing to avoid it and only the most powerful painkillers—the marketing of Ibuprofen was a boon—could touch it.

Then, in the mid-nineties, after a nasty contretemps with an impossible office chair which would suddenly sink, entirely of its own volition, I developed a crippling back pain and was recommended to see an osteopath. Before beginning treatment, she took a thorough history and I told her about the headaches I'd suffered for as long as I could remember.

'I don't know if you've heard of cranial osteopathy,' she offered, 'but I'm qualified to do it, if you'd like me to have a go.'

I hadn't heard of it, but could see no harm in giving anything a try. So, after manipulation and

22

massage of my lower back, she began to range her hands over my head. It was the most peculiar sensation. I'm convinced she never actually touched me, but it felt as though separate parts of my skull were shifting around of their own accord. When she finished I rose from the treatment couch and sat by her desk.

'Mmmm,' she said. 'Not surprised about the headaches. Very nasty forceps delivery.'

'How did you know?' I asked, truly astonished.

'I could feel the indentations and the impact the forceps had had on the shape of your skull. But don't worry; I've manipulated everything back into place. I don't think you'll have any more problems.' I walked out of her consulting room convinced that my £30 would not have been well spent.

I was wrong. I've never had one of those headaches since.

My feelings about the graphic manner in which my mother described what happened have veered between extreme fury that a young woman, full of hope, should have been so inhumanely treated, terrible sadness that her subsequent fears deprived me of a brother or sister, and anger that she should have made me conscious of her resentment of the harm I had, albeit unwittingly, caused.

It's rarely acknowledged that, even in the most apparently loving and affectionate mother/ daughter relationships, there is frequently a deep well of jealousy that exists in the mother, who inevitably compares her no longer perfect physique with that of the fresh, unspoiled, hopeful girl she has brought into the world, and in whom she sees her old self reflected. The most enlightened and honest psychologists—and I'm thinking particularly of Dorothy Rowe, with whom I've had a number of conversations on the subject— encourage us to acknowledge and understand that such envy can cause terrible emotional damage if we fail as daughters to recognize and forgive it. It's taken me a long time to get there.

It struck me forcibly when, some twenty-five years ago, as a presenter and reporter on the news and current affairs programme *Newsnight*, it came to my attention through contacts with schoolteachers in the East End of London and in Cardiff that small girls of six and seven were being taken back to their family villages in Somalia— both cities have significant Somali communities because of their seafaring traditions—for the most radical form of female genital mutilation.

I talked to African activists who were trying to stop the practice in both cities and they insisted I should talk to the mothers to begin to understand why, even though their daughters were born in the UK and the practice was illegal here, they were prepared to take them home for such a cruel operation, carried out by village practitioners in the most crude and unhygienic manner.

'You have to understand the mothers if you're to comprehend why it continues,' explained one such worker.

I met a large group of warm and welcoming women in a community centre in the East End and questioned them closely about why they insisted that their girls should make such a long journey for such a damaging practice. 'It's our culture,' they told me. 'Without it, no one will ever want to marry our daughters.'

One could almost understand the cultural pressures they were under, but there was more.

'It was done to me,' a number of them said, 'and yes, it was terrible. The pain was dreadful and, of course, there is no pleasure in sex and it's dangerous—some die—and they have to cut you open when you are married and more when you have a baby, but then they sew you up again. But it's what we women have to bear to please our husbands. They did it to me. Why should it be different for my daughter?'

I don't blame them for it, though it offends every principle I've ever held dear and I can only condemn a practice which mutilates millions of women around the world. But it's a strong, courageous and supremely confident mother who would struggle to overturn centuries of cultural pressure, and an extraordinary one who could entirely set aside her sense of outrage at the harm done to her by the birth of her perfect daughter.

There can have been no reassurance for my

mother in the atmosphere in which she was expected to deliver me. The building in which I was born—St Helen's Hospital—was grey, cold and forbidding, a Dickensian structure which had been converted in the forties from a workhouse to a maternity unit. That I was 'born in the workhouse' was a family joke of which I was constantly reminded throughout my childhood and it was only as I grew up that I fully understood why the word 'workhouse' held such resonance.

My maternal grandmother, Edna, came from Yorkshire farming and pub-owning stock around Huddersfield and Holmfirth and was the youngest of twelve children. She had met my grandfather, Walter, while on holiday in Southport with her family and fallen for his smart dress, silver-topped cane, dashing looks and easy charm. His background was less secure and comfortable than hers. His family were miners in North Wales who had migrated to Yorkshire when the North Welsh industry began to fail.

Most had managed to find jobs—my grandfather ending up above rather than below ground, winding the men and the coal up and down in the cage at the pithead. But a sense of insecurity haunted him all his life. My father too, the youngest of six, had a dad who was a miner and who died in his fifties—when I was three years old—from the suffocating effects of silicosis, the miner's lung disease. The shadow of redundancy and unemployment and the memory of the disgrace of the old workhouses, despite the arrival of the welfare state, were never far from my parents' thoughts.

It seems unthinkable now—in an era where a

father who refuses to be present in the delivery room is considered to be greatly behind the times—that dads then were kept so far away from the end stage of the business of reproduction. It was also common at the time of my birth for new mothers and babies to spend a couple of weeks in the hospital before returning home. Dad still talks about his longing, during that long and lonely period, to hold me, or even just touch my cheek. But visiting hours were strictly regulated and babies totally inaccessible.

'I was always first in the queue,' he boasts even now, his memory as clear as if it were yesterday. 'The maternity ward was on the first floor and we dads had to wait at the bottom of the stone staircase behind a thick red rope that was strung across the steps. The matron, a right old battleaxe in a starched apron and cap, would stand by the rope with her watch in her hand. On the dot of six in the evening—there was no visiting in the afternoon because we were all supposed to be at work—she would lift the barrier and I ran as fast as I could so as to be the first on the ward.

'I'd see your mum and take her some flowers or grapes or something and then, as we were leaving, we were allowed to pass the nursery. All the babies lay in row after row of cots and they let us see you through a big glass window. I was lucky because I managed to sweet-talk one of the nurses and she brought you right up to the glass. She put your hand on it and I put mine up on the other side. I was so proud. It was the closest I got to touching you until you came home. I was a bit frightened then—you seemed so small and delicate and my hands were so big and rough. I was terrified I might hurt you or drop you and break you.'

He needn't have worried. His hands were indeed big and rough from the manual work he did every day, but for me they have always been comforting and reassuring. Nothing in my childhood gave me greater pleasure than to see his imposing, powerful physique in the doorway, his soft brown eyes sparkling with pleasure as he lifted me high in the air, grinned and planted one of his 'big sloppy kisses' on my cheek.

I'm sure that instinctively both my parents would have approached the care of their child with warmth and affection. Dr Benjamin Spock was an American paediatrician whose book *Baby and Child Care*, published in 1946, is one of the biggest bestsellers of all time. It preached a revolutionary message. The first paediatrician to study psycho-analysis in order to understand how families worked best and what children needed from their parents, Spock told mothers that they knew more than they thought they knew. He encouraged them to follow their instincts and to be flexible and affectionate towards their children so as to allow their individual traits to develop.

Unfortunately for my parents—and in turn for me—this more relaxed attitude had not reached Barnsley in 1950. Instead of Spock's humane assertion that parents should respond instinctively to their individual baby's needs and avoid applying a one-size-fits-all philosophy to child-rearing, it was the techniques of Sir Frederick Truby King that held sway in the Barnsley maternity ward, and it was his regimented approach that the young, inexperienced mothers were taught during their two weeks' recuperation from the trauma of birth.

Truby King was born in New Zealand in 1858, but travelled to Scotland to study medicine at Edinburgh University and began practising in Glasgow as a surgeon. At the turn of the nineteenth century he became interested in the application of scientific principles to the nutrition of babies. He also, rightly, worked out that domestic hygiene and the education of mothers were vital for the rearing of healthy children. Regrettably, his formula for the raising of a first-rate specimen has proved to be a psychological disaster. His first book, *Feeding and Care of Baby*, laid down the principles that my mother was ordered to follow.

Children, he believed, must be trained in discipline from the moment they emerged from the womb. They should be made to feed on a strict four-hourly rotation, sleep whenever they were put down and must be encouraged to have regular bowel movements. They should not be cuddled when they cried, but left to sob themselves to sleep. So impressed were the British authorities by

29

this mechanistic approach to the rearing of disciplined children, he was invited to help set up the UK's first Child Public Health Service. The consequent damage to the emotional security of both mothers and children is surely incalculable.

My mother, like all newly delivered, nervous young mums, wanted to do her very best for her baby and never thought to ask to be given time to bond with her. It was the done thing for the baby to be carted off to the nursery immediately 'to give mum time to rest'. I can only imagine the aching void she must have felt when I was taken away and brought back only to be fed, bathed and changed. I hardly know how she could have borne lying in her hospital bed—tucked up tightly in starched and pristine sheets—wondering where her baby was and how she was faring.

When I had my own new babies I hated being parted from them for a second. I spent hours, full of fear and, at the same time, thrilling with excitement, holding them close or simply gazing at them as they snuffled and slept. I touched their fingers and their toes and clutched them to my breast at the slightest whimper. I would have wanted to kill anyone who suggested they be taken elsewhere. But the idea of questioning authority would have been unthinkable for my parents—it still is. The doctors have always known best and commanded respect and absolute obedience. The patients did as they were told. I suppose the one consolation is that, at least in the hospital, hidden in the nursery behind that glass wall, neither my mother nor my father would have heard me screaming for attention.

That was not the case, of course, when I went

home and a much-repeated family story illustrates only too well how utterly unnatural and potentially dangerous the Truby King method was. Every Saturday afternoon, when she'd recovered sufficiently from the trauma of the delivery, my mother and grandmother would do themselves up in their smartest clothes and catch the two o'clock bus into Barnsley.

The town boasted the finest open-air market in the north and for these two thrifty women it was a weekly delight to wander around, looking at soft furnishings and joining the crowd watching Joe, the bone china man, putting on the most amazing show. His patter would have matched the finest music-hall comedian and his magical way with crockery would put Paul Daniels to shame. He displayed his china—a whole dinner or tea set—in wicker baskets, the kind used to carry the laundry out to the line for drying and back into the kitchen ready for ironing.

He and his helpers would toss the heavy baskets to each other and Joe would throw the entire service up in the air, catching the items as they fell and never so much as cracking a cup. You could stand there for hours, fascinated, and not even buy anything, despite his continuous exhortations to purchase his wares. 'Come on, missus—finest bone china—and I'm not asking five pound, I'm not asking two pound, I'm offering you this wonderful service—fit for the table of the gentry—for the unbelievable price of only two shillings and sixpence.' It was a free afternoon's entertainment and a bargain hunter's paradise. (I know this because he was still doing his tricks when I was considered old enough to join the women on their

31

weekly trips.)

At the end of the afternoon, just before the fish, butcher and fruit and veg stalls shut up shop for the day, my grandmother would begin making her purchases. A crab or mussels for tea, a joint for Sunday and apples, oranges, bananas and whatever vegetables were not available from the garden would be bought for next to nothing. She knew all the stallholders by name and they knew she would drive the hardest of bargains. 'Nay, lad,' she would say, 'you'd best let me 'ave it cheaper than that or you'll end up chucking it away.' She'd operated for a long time on the principle that there'd be giveaway prices at the end of the day, because it was preferable to make a little money rather than let the produce rot and be wasted.

Anyway, there was I at home on this particular Saturday afternoon. I'd been out in the pram all morning—as much fresh air as possible was part of the Truby King regime whether it be rain, snow or shine. I'd been given the two o'clock feed a little early, so Mum and Gran could be sure of catching the right bus, and been put down in the cot for the afternoon. And the men were issued with strict instructions. They were not, under any circumstances, to go upstairs and see me. I must be left to sleep until Mum got back ready for the next feed at six o'clock.

Dad still shudders when he tells me what happened next. They were listening to the sport on the wireless—Grandpa was not a big gambler, but he liked to have a couple of bob on the horses and he did the pools religiously every week. The fire was blazing—free coal was one of the perks of working at the pit—and they might have shared a brown ale between them as they sucked on untipped Park Drives. Their contentment was shattered when they heard the most heart-rending screams from upstairs.

'Alvin, lad,' said Grandpa, 'that doesn't sound right to me. I think we should go and check she's all right.'

'Best not, Dad. Winnie said we shouldn't go up no matter what. You haven't to spoil them.' So they sat it out—these two affectionate men whose natural instinct was to work their socks off for no other purpose than to spoil their beloved offspring.

They lasted a further half-hour until my grandfather said, 'Bugger the book. That baby's in trouble. Come on, lad.'

They rushed upstairs and into the bedroom to find me with my head stuck between the bars of the cot, red-faced, whimpering and, according to them both, not breathing terribly well.

Dad was dispatched across the road to fetch Nurse Manley while my grandfather did his best to manoeuvre me out, but failed. Luckily the district nurse was in and directed operations as they sawed away one of the bars and released me. She declared me relatively unharmed, but recommended that the book should be ignored.

'A screaming baby,' she said, 'really should be attended to straight away—just in case.'

August

Will this wretched rain never stop? It's been a rush to get here in time for a two o'clock meeting and the roads were awash. At least it improved my concentration. I had to squint to see through the murk and the danger of aquaplaning over some impressive puddles was ever-present. I find a parking space and see Dad's car is already here. It's not in a disabled spot—they're all full of cars with no disabled sticker. He'll be outraged—again.

I rush to Mum's bedside, remind him we're due at the meeting and he makes his way slowly along the ward corridor to the dayroom. The chintz-covered wing chairs have been ranged around the room, it's stuffy, the rain pounds against the windows and the various professionals sit officiously with an 'and what time do you call this?' look on their faces. We're a mere five minutes late. We sit in the two vacant chairs as I offer insincere apologies.

It's a bit like facing a McCarthyite investigations committee. You know you've done nothing wrong and your intentions are of the very best, but your motives for wanting to take your nearest and dearest home are the subject of close scrutiny by a dreadfully intimidating bank of nurses, physiotherapists, doctors and social workers. My suspicion is they're just looking for the easiest way out. Get her out of hospital and into a home. So we've been required to attend what they call a multi-disciplinary meeting to decide the fate of one querulous, ill old woman. My mother. My father's beloved wife.

Dad and I are overwhelmed by their number

37

and the seeming hostility of their attitude and their questions. For so-called professionals in care of the elderly, not one seems to have registered the fact, of which I constantly remind them, that Dad's hearing leaves a great deal to be desired. They witter and mutter, immersed in their own professional jargon. Dad looks lost and confused— his face pale with stress; every line a chasm; his eyes full of fear that he is losing control of his and her future.

I find myself having to repeat every harsh word the sister utters for his benefit as he asks, 'What does she say, love?'

'She says there's nothing more to be done for Mum, Dad. They've tried everything. The physiotherapists can't improve her mobility. She'll never walk again. Sister says she has to be discharged from the hospital as soon as possible because she's taking up bed space. She'll need to be cared for twenty-four hours a day.'

Dad's eyes harden and his chin sets in the way I've seen so many times in the past when he's made a decision from which he will not be deflected.

'She is not going into a home,' he states defiantly. 'She's coming back with me.'

The muttering begins again and I translate the questions. Who'll be at home to look after her? How will Dad manage on his own both night and day? What contribution will the daughter be able to make when she lives so far away, has a job and a family of her own? I'm shot through with guilt. I can't say I'll take them both home and care for them. I've got one kid at university and one still at school and I'm the family's main wage-earner. And, anyway, I recall a long-ago discussion about

38

what we'd do in these kind of circumstances when Mum said, 'The last thing on earth I would want is to be cared for by you.' She never did have much confidence in my potential qualities as a Florence Nightingale.

Even when I was very little and expressed an interest in becoming a nurse—one of only two jobs, alongside teaching, considered suitable for a woman in those days—I remember her choking with laughter and shrieking, 'Pity the poor patient who had to depend on *you*.'

I am at least able to talk to the professionals on their level and feel some pride in my ability to arm myself with the correct information. I know from extensive research carried out through Age Concern that my mother has a right to what's known as a 'Care Package' specially designed for her needs. I explain to Dad that I'm requesting that the woman from social services goes away and prepares such a package for twenty-four-hour care. Because my mother needs nursing as well as social care—jargon for washing, dressing, feeding, etc.—I would expect the nursing care to be provided free on the NHS, although I'm aware that we will have to pay for the social care.

Proud and prudent man that he is, he pronounces to the assembled company, 'Money is no object. Whatever she needs, we can pay for.'

It's clear the social worker doesn't hold out much hope of being able to provide good-quality round-the-clock care at home. Neither in my heart of hearts do I. We've had carers—for whom Dad has paid handsomely—during earlier periods of crisis when she's come home from hospital after a fall. Some have been lovely. Others have turned up when they felt like it and done as little as they could get away with. Mum found it distressing to have the strangers she didn't like coming into her home and dealing with her most intimate needs.

We pop into Mum's room to explain what we've decided and leave her full of hope that she'll soon be back in her own house with a chance to see Dad's lovely garden in its finest bloom. We kiss her goodbye and I take Dad home. He's quiet and sad and I am rigid with fury. My parents are of the generation that never put a foot wrong. They lived through the Second World War without complaint. They worked hard to improve themselves, obeyed the law, kept a respectable house, paid their taxes and raised a child who I think became useful and equally law-abiding. They might have expected, at this time of need towards the end of their lives, that the society to which they had made such a loyal contribution would pay them back. I have no confidence at all in the current system's willingness to do what should be its duty.

Back at home Dad slumps in his usual chair in the kitchen, head resting exhausted on the Formica-topped table, the news blaring out from the little black-and-white TV that sits on the work surface. He has colour in the sitting room but has kept this old one going for what seems like centuries, claiming to prefer black and white, and of course the sound level is deafening to anyone but him. I have a fleeting dash of concern about how he'll react when TV goes digital and I have to get rid of his old favourite (ever hopeful that he will last for ever). Then I get on with cooking the food I've brought.

He had learned, when Mum became too ill to

manage the household tasks for which she'd always taken full responsibility, to do more than the proverbial boiling of an egg, but I know that when he is alone he takes little care of his own needs. The freezer is full of pre-prepared foods from M&S—lasagne seems to be a favourite—which he simply pops into the microwave. The fridge is always amply supplied with his favourite bilberry pie from White's the bakers in the village, but he sniffs like a Bisto kid as I busy myself with steak, potatoes, fresh green veg, sponge pudding and custard. He eats like a man newly released from the culinary horrors of an institution whenever I cook for him.

'Ah,' he sighs with satisfaction, 'home cooking. Your mother taught you well.' She did indeed and the love of food she and my grandmother instilled in me has been a source of pleasure to those around me—and the bane of my life.

A friend of mine who had a small son of six or seven at the height of the famine in Ethiopia tells me a story which fills me with admiration, and envy that I couldn't have been equally assertive as a kid.

The scenario is a familiar one. The family sits round the dinner table and the child is pushing his food around the plate aimlessly, obviously not hungry at all.

'Eat your food, stop playing with it,' says his dad, as parents do.

'Why?' asks the child. 'Why do I have to eat if I'm not hungry?'

'Because you're very lucky to have food on your plate,' comes the stock response. 'Think of all those poor children in Ethiopia who have nothing at all to eat. They would be so grateful to have

41

what you have.'

'Name one,' demands the boy, 'and I'll parcel this up and send it.' Brave lad and clever parents to let the matter rest without forcing the issue. I was neither so quick-witted nor so lucky.

It comes as no surprise to me that I have what Susie Orbach, the author of *Fat Is a Feminist Issue*, would describe as 'an unhealthy relationship with food'. Neither is there any doubt that early food deprivation is a contributory factor. Having breastfed two babies on demand—as was happily the fashion when I came to breed—and experienced both the frequency with which hunger strikes a tiny baby and the pleasure a relaxed attitude affords both mother and child, I seethe with anger at the diktat that forced my mother and me to treat feeding times as a military operation.

It all goes back to the infamous Truby King, of course, and his regimen of four-hourly feeds, ten minutes on either side, regular as clockwork.

My parents often joked, as the films they'd watched during their early married life began to appear as classics on television, that now at last they could find out how the movie ended. When I was young, the cinema was the only form of entertainment, apart from the wireless, available to them and once a week Grandma and Grandpa would babysit while they went to the Ritz or the Princess. But they always had to leave before the end in order to be back for the ten o'clock feed, which had to be delivered on time whether I was awake or not.

I'm certain that those few months before weaning contributed to a lifetime's habit of needing to occupy my mouth with something. I sucked my thumb, to my mother's despair, until my early teens. In my thirties, taking advantage of free treatment on the NHS for pregnant and nursing mothers, I asked my dentist, Norma, for a full overhaul.

'These front teeth at the top,' she observed as she poked and prodded about, 'they really need attention—they're wearing down and probably need crowns. I'll take an impression and send them off to the specialist at the hospital. See what he thinks would be the right treatment.'

When the results came back she read me the letter with a wry smile. ' "Definitely need to be dealt with now. In another ten years there won't be enough tooth left to crown. Persistent pipe smoker?"

'I know you don't smoke a pipe,' she continued, 'so what is causing the erosion?' She finally demanded to see inside my bag. As a good journalist I'm never without several pens and a note pad. They were the first things she found.

'This might, I think, be the culprit.' She waved a handful of plastic Bics at me, all with the little plug at the end removed (chewed away) and with evidence of teeth marks on what remained of the clear plastic. 'I'll crown these teeth and, as the specialist says they need treatment urgently, it can be done on the NHS, but I never want to see you chewing the end of a pen again.' She's a friend, so has no compunction about being bossy.

I threw the lot out and went to buy two metal pens which even the hungriest writer could never bring herself to nibble. I have them still and the crowns are just fine.

If only the smoking problem could have been so

easily resolved. I ask myself at least twenty times a day why an intelligent woman in her fifties with extensive knowledge of the health risks can bring herself to suck so needily on something that is without doubt contributing to an early demise. I can only assume it's the adult version of the thumb-sucking and assuages to some degree a hungry emptiness that's both physical and emotional.

It's also associated with some of the most comforting times I remember. It's Saturday afternoon and the women have gone out to town. I'm anything from three to seven years old. Dad is probably out working, trying to earn extra cash, and Grandpa sits in his armchair watching the racing on TV. His packet of untipped Park Drive and box of Swan Vesta matches are on a small table at his side. The fire glows in the grate, piled high with the free coal he gets from the pit as part of his wages. I'm curled up on the floor between his knees.

We pick our horses for each race and the runner from the local betting shop comes round to pick up our two-bob bets (10p in today's money, but worth a lot more then). As the horses gather at the start, Grandpa lights up and we cheer on our jockey excitedly. At the finish we've won more often than not—as an ex-household-cavalry soldier, he's a fine judge of horseflesh and he's made a careful study of the form. He flicks the fag end into the fire and we relax back into reliving every moment of the race. I hold and stroke his hand and sniff his yellow, nicotine-stained fingers. The smell is sweet and slightly pungent. I love it.

When the women return, laden with enough

44

food to feed the entire neighbourhood, there's hell to pay. 'Dad, Jen says she's doubled her pocket money on the horses and this room stinks of cigarettes. What are you thinking about, setting such a bad example?'

Shamefacedly, Grandpa would apologize and vow never to be so badly behaved again, treating me to a conspiratorial wink that suggested his contrition was anything but. I never saw him as a bad example. To me he was full of fun and stories, a naughty renegade. And what we did seemed so much more thrilling than trotting off to Barnsley market every week just to buy stuff which would then require hours of slog in the kitchen. Give me the going out to work, bringing home the bacon and then relaxing into purely pleasurable pursuits any day.

That, though, was really only acceptable for the men in the house. A woman's work, I was to discover, was never done and my mother had embarked upon a lifelong battle with herself. It was her duty, she felt, to make of me the kind of woman she felt I should be. Pretty, elegant, well spoken and domestically adept. At the same time I was the focus of all her ambition, her own having been thwarted in part willingly—she adored my dad and wanted to be the best wife and mother it was possible to be—but any thoughts of career progression on her own behalf had been forcibly laid aside.

Today's young women have so many opportunities for a life at home and in the workplace. But for women of my mother's generation there was really no such choice. Until 1944 it was illegal for a married woman to teach. It

45

was not until 1946 that the Civil Service, my mother's employer, lifted a similar marriage bar. Even though my mother didn't marry until '49 and produce me until '50, the pressure to quit paid work and become a full-time housewife was pretty irresistible.

I can only imagine how she weighed her principles in an ever-shifting balance. She struggled to teach me to be conventionally ladylike, but, at the same time, as the only child in whom she might invest her ambitions, she wanted to give me a chance to succeed in the outside world as well. I couldn't help thinking that, if David Robert had ever become a reality and there'd been a brother in the house, the relative ease with which I managed to pass from the pursuits of one sex to the other would have been greatly reduced.

There are many disadvantages to being an only child—I still expect if there's one sweet left it will be mine, and when I want to be alone I demand that my wish be respected, which makes for difficulties in friendships and relationships. But the one great advantage for a girl being raised in the fifties, when gender-related choices were prescribed from birth, was that I was the centre of everyone's attention, both male and female, and was given access to both those worlds despite my mother's constant attempts—and failure—to ensure the feminine overrode the masculine influence.

The women in my family were far from being doormats. The blood of a long line of tough-minded Yorkshire matriarchs running through our veins has us pre-programmed to rule the domestic roost. The men went out to work, but brought back their pay packets unopened. The women counted the cash, made sure it tallied with the payslip and handed out pocket money for beer, cigarettes and, when my father was finally able to buy an Austin A35 van, travelling expenses. The rest was managed by the women, who paid rent or mortgages, bought insurance, provided for all household needs and chose the clothes. I don't think my father ever saw the inside of a clothes shop as a working man. My mother knew his size and dressed him according to her taste.

Dad wasn't a great one for going out. He worked such long hours that he was pleased to be home whenever he could be, but my grandfather had always been more of a social animal and liked his pint at the end of the day with his mates from work. He never came home late, though, or drunk. Family legend has it that early in their marriage he went once to the working men's club for the evening and rolled home late and considerably the worse for wear. My grandmother was waiting for him behind the kitchen door with the poker, with which he claimed she whacked him on the back.

'Start as you mean to go along' was her watchword when it came to handling men. 'Give them an inch and they'll take a mile.' He seemed to love her none the less for it.

Both of these women who were so influential as I grew up had suffered as civilians the fear, privation and dangers of world wars and embraced with seemingly grateful thanks the domestic ethos of the fifties. They were also lucky in that their men were just too young to have seen action. My grandfather was called up in 1918, completed his training in London with the Household Cavalry and served his entire term in the capital. Years later I would take him on a trip to the Isle of Wight and he called it 'the first and last time I ever went abroad!' My father had been involved in the clean-up operation in 1945, but again had seen none of the killing fields. We were lucky that they both came back with their humanity intact.

When the men had returned from military service and taken what jobs were available, it was for the women to go back to the kitchen and re-embrace their traditional role as homemakers. My mother and my grandmother both ran their households with ruthless efficiency, cleaning, polishing, scrubbing and cooking from morning till night; their only real fault stemmed from an overpowering pride in a job well done which could, at times, spill into irritation at the natural messiness generated by human occupation. You came into the house and generally met a tirade of barked orders.

'Take off those dirty shoes, I've just washed the floor.' 'Hang up your coat, I don't want it littering the kitchen.' 'Don't sit there, I've just plumped those cushions.' 'Straighten the covers on the back of that chair, will you.'

It's a difficult early training to throw off and I'm sure my own children, reading this, will hear echoes of my voice in the words of their grandmother and great-grandmother. I, like them, keep a sitting room for best—only to be used when guests come over, and out of bounds to children, animals and TV dinners. I have, though, learned to accept a much lower standard of tidiness than they would ever have tolerated.

Men, I've found, perform domestic tasks only

occasionally and will plump a cushion only when it's about to be sat on rather than for show, and the wiping of kitchen surfaces other than immediately before use is anathema to them. When I became the breadwinner in my own family I realized the only way to retain my sanity was to ignore the crumbs and general chaos: an extreme case of if you can't beat 'em join 'em.

The only time I ever insisted on a major clean and tidy was when I knew my mother was to visit. Then it was 'all hands on deck', but even when we thought it was shipshape for her arrival there would still be that difficult moment when she would do her dust check, look sternly at her hand, rub the fingers together with distaste and sniff, 'I do think you should make more of an effort, love. It can't be healthy for two small boys to live in such a tip.' A friend gave me a plaque which read 'Boring women have immaculate houses'. I placed it in a prominent position in my kitchen. She blithely ignored it.

The women's magazines my mother bought advertised shiny new kitchen appliances which we slowly acquired over the years and for which she did her best to fill me with enthusiasm. When we lived with my grandmother—which was for the first three years of my life, until Dad's wage was enough to pay the rent on a council house—washday, Monday, was quite thrilling for a small child. My grandmother had a huge metal tub, barrel-shaped, into which she would pour hot water, boiled over the coal fire. In went the whites first of all with the detergent and I was told to stay away.

'Too hot,' my mother would warn. Hot was a word I understood from early on, having tripped in my grandmother's kitchen when I was learning to walk and broken my fall by putting my hand on the hearth. I bear the scars still. I would stand by and watch them take turns agitating the steaming laundry with a tool known as a posser. It was a broomstick with a copper gadget attached where the broom would normally be, and which resembled a kitchen colander, the shape of a military helmet and full of holes. The work was hard and physical and I was only allowed to have a go with the posser when the rinsing with cold water was in process. For me the whole business—wash, rinse, mangle, hang out to dry and iron—was vastly entertaining. For them it was an entire day of hard slog which invariably led to spectacular rows.

It must have been tough for my mother, trying to build her own family life under the constant critical supervision of my grandmother. The power relationship shifted subtly when we moved into 14 Allandale, and the first electrically driven washing machine arrived. Grandma resisted my mother's encouragement to buy her own machine and insisted on walking up the hill with a suitcase full of her week's washing so that they could continue the tradition of working together.

It was, I think, partly her need to stay in close touch with us both, partly her naturally parsimonious nature—'Why waste all that money on two machines when we can manage perfectly well with one?'—and partly a deep resistance among the women of my family to anything that smacks of technological progress. I insisted on writing on a typewriter for years after everyone else took to the computer and even now, having accepted the inevitable, have to call for support at

50

the slightest hitch.

My mother was content to embrace any labour-saving device—hardly surprising after all those years of the tub, posser and mangle and cooking on an open fire and in a coal-fired oven, which my grandmother did till the day she died—but wouldn't have anything so newfangled as a telephone ('I wouldn't want it to ring and bring bad news'). Even the radio and TV were viewed as a constant fire hazard and had to be unplugged every night and each time we went out.

Many's the time we've walked to the bus stop to go to town together only for her to say, 'Oh, crikey, did I switch off the electric?' I'd be sent rushing back home to check she had indeed turned the electricity off at the mains, with 'And make sure you don't forget to lock the door' ringing in my ears.

It's a neurosis which remains with me and while I do have a phone and a computer—and it would be impossible now to switch the mains electricity off without ruining clocks on everything from the video recorder to the microwave—I still have a slight anxiety that I'll come home to find everything burned to the ground. And I have been known to turn back from quite an advanced stage of a trip to make sure the door is locked. Which it invariably is.

Our new washing machine was the yellowing cream colour you see now on retro fridges and absolutely enormous. It was not much further advanced than the old tub and mangle arrangement. The huge new tub had to be filled from the tap with a hose that stretched across the kitchen (with which I one morning in helpful mode managed to flood most of the bottom floor of the house) and emptied via the same hose into the sink.

The new mangle was two rubber-coated rollers which worked at the flick of a switch and it became one of my jobs to feed the soaking sheets and clothes through it, ready for folding and hanging out on the line. I was relieved of my duties at about four and a half after I forgot to let go of whatever I was feeding through and ended up in hospital with a severely squashed hand and lower arm. I recall most vividly the sensation of being gripped by a force more powerful than myself and being too small to reach the off switch.

My grandmother's silent reproach of my mother—'I told you so'—led to one of their most memorable bust-ups. It was, for me, a useful lesson in studied incompetence. I discovered early that if you couldn't do things properly and safely on the domestic front you'd generally be excused. On rainy days, a huge clothes horse would be placed around the fire and the laundry left to steam itself dry. I would position myself in the hearth, between the clothes and the fire, and indulge my favourite passion, reading a book, well away from the arguments and mayhem of washing day in the kitchen. I'd lose myself in *Shadow the Sheep Dog* or the antics of my favourite character, George from the Famous Five, with their distant banter forming the soundtrack to the day. I can still feel the warm dampness and smell the sweet and slightly sickly aroma of hot, wet, fresh washing.

On fine days I'd be sent out to play with the little gang of kids who roamed the street. They were mostly boys, my favourite being the foul-mouthed John Lewis from next door, whose father ran a strange combination of small businesses—a brick-making company and an ice cream factory. From being tiny he'd gone out with the guys who drove the brick lorries or the ice cream vans. Sometimes I went too and we'd be given our favourite, a vanilla cone with raspberry vinegar—one of life's greatest treats. But we'd only get what we wanted as a reward. 'Say bugger, John,' the burly workmen would giggle, 'and I'll give thee a tanner.' Sixpence was the price of a couple of cornets so John would curse, make them laugh and we got what our hearts desired.

My mother, happily, found him cute and liked his mother, otherwise I doubt I would have been allowed to don dungarees or my Annie Oakley cowboy outfit and six guns and go off climbing trees, falling in the duck pond and generally running riot. She did, though, make it her mission to improve John's language. His worst offence came during one of my birthday parties. It was the first—I must have been five—to which schoolfriends were invited. My mother, who boasted proudly that I could read before I could walk, was determined that I should go to a posh school, where, aided by weekly elocution lessons, I would grow up a cut above the young ruffians in the neighbourhood.

I was indeed a passionate reader and keen to start school early. My grandparents agreed to pay for me to go to the only school that would take a four-year-old and not make too much fuss about her lack of religious conviction. The Catholic convent school in the centre of town was known for its high academic achievement and strict discipline,

53

so the other kids who came to my birthday party sat nicely round the table for the birthday tea. My mother, an absolute genius with food, had made sandwiches of every possible appeal to small children, an exquisite cake and her speciality for such occasions, a lily pond. This consisted of a green jelly decorated with tinned pears and cream for the lilies and sticks of angelica for the reeds. It would be the star turn of many a school 'do' throughout my life.

Only John was shuffling uncomfortably at my side and not eating. He clearly detested all the other stuck-up kids. 'Come on, John,' said my mother, never happy if someone turned their nose up at her carefully prepared feasts. 'What kind of sandwich would you like, love? There's egg, potted meat, cheese and if you'd like something else tell me and if I've got it I'll make it for you.'

John paused for a beat and with perfect timing delivered the fatal line, 'Mrs Bailey, do you know what I'd really like . . . a shit sandwich.' All the other children knew exactly what he meant and in the stunned, shocked silence he disappeared under the table and refused to emerge. He was eventually dragged out by my mother and packed off home in disgrace for 'spoiling the party with your disgusting behaviour'. It didn't stop several repeat performances.

She had a little more success on the expletive front with me. No one ever swore in her household, at least not in front of the child, so my foul mouth was no doubt picked up from the street. In one of my rare bouts of domestic enthusiasm I was sitting on the ground outside an open kitchen window, scrubbing at the grate, not

54

realizing she was at the sink and could hear every word. (Steps, paths and grates all had to be as immaculate as the indoors.)

'I can't get this bloody grate clean,' I moaned as I rubbed away.

My mother angry was a terrifying sight. She towered over me, glowering, took hold of my arm and dragged me into the kitchen. Pants were pulled down, buttocks smacked, tears flowed and I was sent to sit on the bottom step.

'You can sit there thinking about how unladylike it is to have such a filthy mouth and how cross I am with you until I say it's all right for you to leave those stairs.' The punishment was harsh and could last a couple of hours. I was allowed no book to read, no toy to play with and not even the comfort of my own bed to lie on. Generally I sobbed for a while, mustered a little anger and defiance at the injustice of it all and then became quiet and conciliatory; at which point I would be allowed to rejoin her.

On this occasion—it must have been a Tuesday, doing upstairs day—she passed me on the stairs, Hoover, polish and duster in hand, acting as if I were not there. I could hear her running the vacuum cleaner around my parents' bedroom. I was firm in my conviction that saying 'bloody' wasn't all that terrible; I had, after all, overheard Dad, only the previous weekend, looking out of the back window on his prize dahlias and laughing about the guy next door's pathetic attempts at emulating his green fingers. 'Look at that bloody idiot, he's digging so deep he'll get to Australia!' He, of course, had no idea I was earwigging behind the door.

I went through the tears phase and on the wave of anger and defiance that followed I crept quietly up the stairs and, through the half-open bedroom door, but, as I thought, completely out of sight as she had her back to me, pulled the most horrible face I could manage. Eyes crossed, tongue out, thumbs on temples, fingers sticking out and vigorously waggling around.

She stormed out of the room to where I was grinning on the landing. 'What do you think you are doing?' she shrieked.

I trembled. 'Nothing' . . . quick thinking . . . 'just going to the toilet.'

'Number one,' her voice was now at its most quiet and lethal, 'I do not recall giving you permission to move from those stairs. Number two. Do not imagine for one moment that you can do things behind my back that I don't see. I saw you pulling that revolting face, you rude girl. Don't you know that mummies can see every little thing their children do whether they're with them or not?' Another smack and back to the bottom of the stairs to ponder my misdemeanour.

How had she known what I was doing? Was it true that she could observe everything I did? Stupidly, it took me years to figure out that she had seen my reflection in her dressing-table mirror and I lived for a very long time with the entirely erroneous supposition that she really did know what I was up to all the time. It's a chilling thought I've never quite been able to shake off!

It seems astonishing to me now that so much time could have been spent on keeping up appearances and trying to figure out how to feminize such a natural tomboy to fit the requirements of the 1950s female ideal. Mercifully for my mother it was not an entirely thankless task. From a very young age I was intrigued by beautiful clothes and make-up and took great delight in dressing as a fairy for the coronation street party in 1953—complete with wings, wand and coronet— and even managed to stay clean for most of the day.

Mum, of course, was tremendously pleased with me, and with the day in general. Dad's job at the time was as an electrical repairman in the local radio and television shop. We were the only people in the street to have a TV—one of his perks—and everyone gathered round to watch the ceremony in Westminster Abbey being played out within the confines of our own immaculate front room. From that day on, for all of us in those small provincial northern towns, thanks to the development of television, the sophisticated world of kings and queens, lords and ladies and high society in general became just a little less remote. The streets of London were obviously not paved with gold, but being there became the goal of all my wildest fantasies.

I have no idea who made my fairy costume, but I know it was not my mother. She must have spent a little more of Dad's hard-earned cash than was usual on a professional dressmaker because, while she shone in all other domestic arts, sewing was a mystery to her. Not so knitting. Some years ago I came across an archive copy of a *Woman's Weekly* of 1953 and there, on the front cover, was the swimming costume I had so badgered her to make.

The straps which went over my shoulders and crossed at the back were yellow and the body was a dusty blue. On the centre of the chest was an animal of indeterminate species, knitted in the same yellow as the straps. It was a complex pattern, even for someone with her expertise, and a number of late nights were invested to get it ready for our week's summer holiday in Scarborough. I was three and determined to learn to swim and this costume, I reckoned, would be the very thing to keep me afloat.

Seaside holidays were the highlight of every year. The five of us—Grandma, Grandpa, Mum, Dad and I—would set off by coach or, as our prosperity progressed, in a van or much later a car, and head for Blackpool, Rhyl, Filey or Scarborough. Scarborough, with its combination of craggy hills, golden sands and a castle, was the favourite. We stayed in boarding houses with fierce landladies who laid on a good spread, but expected you to be out from under their feet from breakfast till lunch, and then lunch till tea time, regardless of the weather.

Mum, Dad and I would share a room and

Grandma and Grandpa had their own. First thing in the morning I would shake my father awake.

'Come on, Daddy, time to get up and get the paper.'

'Shh, let Mummy have a lie-in. It'll be just you and me.'

Those times with him were precious. He worked so hard all year round, I rarely saw him. He was gone before I woke and returned long after my bedtime. On those early mornings we would watch the sun rising over the east coast, walk hand in hand along the Prom, call at the paper shop to buy the *Daily Mail* and pop into a coffee bar. Glass of milk for me, cup of tea for him and chitter-chatter about whatever was in the news. Then back to the boarding house for a proper breakfast before the walk to the beach.

Only Dad and I were interested in the water. The other three would flop down in their deckchairs, Grandpa's only concession to the holiday mood being a pair of sandals with his socks. 'I'm not going out without a jacket and tie, it's not decent' was a constant refrain as we tried to encourage him to be more relaxed in his garb, but to no avail.

Dad and I would hide behind huge beach towels to change into our swimming costumes. My new knitted one fitted perfectly.

Swimming lessons involved paddling in the shallows while I watched Dad execute a powerful crawl in the deeper water and then he would come and carry me just out of my depth. He would put his hand under my tummy, I would let my legs float to the surface and he would hold me safe while I did the strokes. Gradually he would let go

for longer and longer periods. I trusted him completely. All seemed to be going well, I was gaining confidence and skill—until this day with the new cossie. None of us had accounted for the weight of wet wool.

'Blimey, love, I don't think this is working,' said Dad. 'You won't float in this thing.'

He carried me to shallower water. Stood me down. And the thing sank to my knees, yellow straps stretched almost to breaking. Children, grandparents, other families on the beach hooted with laughter. I think I have never been more humiliated. Mum came quickly to the rescue. She rubbed me down vigorously and hid me again in that big towel.

'Don't worry, love, I've got your dry one here. Silly of us not to think it would stretch when it got wet. Wear your normal costume for swimming and we'll dry this one off and you can wear it just for playing in. Like those posh women in their fancy costumes that never get wet!' She did her best to mollify me and make me feel less uncomfortable and embarrassed.

I was grateful for her sensitivity. Some mothers

60

might have simply joined in the gaiety of the moment, but I never wore the wretched garment again and developed an enduring dislike of anything home- or hand-knitted. This meant a miserable future in many a school sweater as both my mother and grandmother insisted it was a waste of money to buy ready-made knits.

My mother could be the kindest and most thoughtful of women and, seconds later, the most difficult, demanding and strait-laced. The inevitable tensions, which grew ever more stressful as I got older, were developing in my earliest years during the long hours we spent together when my father was at work. But much of the time I recall as happy and contented: we shared many a pleasurable moment, just the two of us, during those short periods between the end of housework and the start of cooking the evening meal—always prepared so that the two of us could eat well in advance of my bedtime and a second sitting would be ready for Dad's return from the job. We read stories and dressed up from her old stuff box. I

loved to float around the house in her wedding dress and veil, long before it came anywhere near fitting me and years in advance of the development of my antipathy towards the symbolism of the virgin bride.

I don't know how much it confused my mother that there seemed to be two warring factions in my childish personality. On the one hand there was the action girl in dungarees with scabs on her knees, and on the other the preening princess who would sit for hours in front of the mirror, dressed in faded, feminine best, pursing her lips to smear on the permitted ends of almost used-up carmine lipstick.

To me there seemed to be no contest, no battle. The two aspects of me sat easily alongside each other, but the dungarees felt freer and I was never so constrained when wearing them. In a skirt it was always, 'Sit down nicely. Don't cross your legs. It's not polite to sit with your knees apart. Only boys and bad girls would sit like that. Put your legs to one side when you sit and it's all right if you want to cross your ankles. That's quite dainty.'

Somehow dainty was never a description that could easily fit my strong, athletic physique. It could, though, be applied to Mum, who had wrists so slender even the tiniest watches slid over her hand and ankles that were perfect in court shoes with stiletto heels. She was elegant, slim and dressed immaculately with not a hair out of place, nor a smudged lip. A fashion plate, even for a short trip to the shops.

I knew I would never be able to compete. From time to time she would bemoan the lottery of genetic inheritance. 'Such a pity you seem to take after your dad and not me when it comes to bone structure.' And that meant hefty wrists, ankles, shoulders, feet and my chubby chops rather than her cheekbones to die for. I'm sure she never meant to be mean and genuinely tried to advise me how to make the best of what I had, but I was always conscious it was not quite good enough.

I remember seeing Chekhov's *Uncle Vanya* on a school trip as a teenager and hearing the Helena character say to Sonia, who's saying how ugly she feels, 'You have lovely hair.' To which Sonia replies, 'Don't say that. When a woman is ugly they always say she has beautiful hair or eyes.' My mother always told me I had nice hair and nice eyes. I could have written Sonia's line.

The kitchen, though, was another territory altogether. Here we shared the delights of creating wonderful food. Until I was tall enough to stand at the blue Formica work surface, I was perched on a high stool, hair held back in plaits, apron tied and sleeves rolled up. This was where I was to learn to wave the wand my grandfather said hovered over the Yorkshire puddings, pastry and scones produced by the two women, my mother and grandmother, who put the food on our tables. They made magic of raw ingredients and invested all their love in tempting appetites and titillating taste buds.

I learned to chop and slice, rub in and stir, roast, bake and stew. When my mother made apple pie, I would be given what was left of the pastry to make jam tarts for tea. We would eat one each and the rest were saved for Dad's return from work (the women were never expected to eat quite as much as the men!). They were at times a little grubby

63

from too much handling by lazily washed hands, but when I got up in the morning they were all gone and I swelled with pride when told he had pronounced them 'delicious'. It was how I learned my mother's mantra, 'the way to a man's heart is through his stomach'. To feed someone artfully and with pleasure was to express how much you loved the person you nourished.

Consequently, at the table, I felt adored and rarely had cause to refuse a dish or leave so much as a mouthful on the plate. Eating everything up was how you showed your love in return. Except on washing day. When we three females were together on a Monday it had to be an 'easy-peasy' lunch. On Sunday we would have had roast lamb, beef or pork with all the trimmings followed by bilberry tart (so much more pungent than modern blueberries) or treacle or ginger sponge with custard—light as a feather. The butcher would have been generous with his portions. Our family were good customers. Food was never skimped no matter how paltry the income.

But on Monday there was meat left over. My mother would fry an onion in dripping, throw in the meat, cut into cubes, and, when it was thoroughly and safely cooked through for the second time, add gravy. She served it with mashed potato and frozen peas and it was the most disgusting thing I've ever tasted. Week after week we'd have the same battle. I would push the food around. She would tell me, irritated, to eat up; there was the washing to hang out and so much else to be done.

'But I'm not hungry,' I would whine.

'Stop being so fussy and get on with it.' She was

relentless. I was not to leave a scrap, and if I didn't eat it now it would be there for tea and supper and breakfast if necessary. And she would trot out the line about children in other parts of the world who would be so grateful to have what I was turning my nose up at. I never did have the wit to suggest sending it off to a starving child, but held my nose and, like the obedient girl I was expected to be, ate what was there, gobbling down even things I disliked, looking forward to the pudding that would inevitably follow. Something sweet to take away any nasty taste.

And still, as I anticipate a break from sitting at the computer, it's the cup of tea and a biscuit, a bar of chocolate or a nice glass of wine that will satisfy the ever-present hunger.

September

September already, a whole month after the meeting which was supposed to settle Mum's care and make it possible to bring her home, but she's still in hospital, the difficult ward sister continues to mutter darkly about bed-blocking and imminent discharge and I am more frustrated than I have ever been in my life. Phone call after phone call. Discussion after discussion. Argument after argument.

It is now generally agreed by those who have power over Mum's future that she would be better off at home to spend what it seems are going to be her last few months in her comfortable, familiar surroundings. It would also be best for Dad. That too appears to be universally approved, as the professionals surrounding him see his determination to take her home and the terrible stress he's suffering as we try to sort things out.

I have a private meeting with the young and dedicated geriatrician who's been responsible for Mum's care in the hospital. I insist on describing her as a geriatrician—thanks, Mum, for supporting me through the benefits of a classical education— despite being told off during one of my frequent spats with the domineering nursing sister, who has the gall to pick me up on the use of such language.

'We prefer to call it care of the elderly,' she says. I can't resist reminding her of the etymology of the word—from the Greek *geras* meaning old age— and suggest we concentrate on the care of my mother rather than indulging in pointless discourse on the question of linguistics. She obviously writes me off as a stuck-up bitch and avoids me whenever possible. Which is fine by me, except, of course, I worry that she'll take out her dislike of me on Mum.

The geriatrician herself could not have been more helpful, explaining to me, away from Dad's presence, some of the really hard things I needed to know. Mum, she says, will not last for very much longer. The Parkinson's disease has progressed so far it has arrested all her movement. She can't move her legs unaided, her hands are too weak to hold a cup or a spoon so she needs to be fed and helped with drinking (she already has one of those cups we used to use for the boys when they were babies) and the end will come, in perhaps two or three months' time, when her ability to swallow ceases.

She will, it seems, simply starve to death. I am horrified. I mention my and my mother's belief in assisted suicide, carefully pointing out that I know it's illegal but asking, as subtly as I can, what help Mum will be given to ease her pain and distress when the end comes near. The doctor is too frightened even to discuss it. I'm full of dread at what Mum's going to have to endure—and afraid for my father. How on earth will he cope with watching his beloved wife disappear before his eyes? Nevertheless, the doctor is backing our desire for this terrible ending to take place at home.

But all my lobbying, investigating and pressure is proving fruitless. The woman from social services calls to tell me that she would be able to provide care, both nursing and social, during the day, but can't find anyone to cover the nights. I make my own series of calls to 'care providers',

70

assuring them that there is a bedroom that could be used for a night-time nurse and that we are prepared to pay for it, but no one is available. I even ask friends and neighbours if they know any nurses who're retired or who have young children who would appreciate a short-term, night-time job, but draw a blank. Meanwhile the hospital is continuing its pressure to have her discharged.

I explain it all to Dad, sparing him the ghastly details of what's to come, and he sadly concedes that we will have to find a nursing home. We begin our heavy-hearted trudge around the ones that are near enough to home to make it possible for Dad to spend as much time as he can with her without having to drive too far.

The smell is the first thing to hit us at each of the homes we visit. The stale aroma of incontinence. The décor in each is faded and tired and the open doors to most of the rooms reveal husk after husk tucked up in cots from which they can't fall—dozens of people facing their final days virtually alone. In the communal rooms old men and women sit around the walls gazing aimlessly into space—the ever-present television playing lowest common denominator programmes at full volume. Mum would hate every one of the homes we've surveyed, but we have no choice but to pick one.

We choose the one which seems cleanest and where the staff seem to be warm and friendly. We arrange for Mum to be admitted on the Friday and brace ourselves to go to the hospital and tell her about our plans. Dad delegates the task to me. His clothing is crumpled, his hair overlong and dishevelled and he could have done with a shave.

71

He's unable to pay attention to anything but the awful task of explaining what's going to happen. We reach her room, already exhausted, bearing flowers and treats. She smiles with delight at seeing us both. Dad sits in the armchair at the end of her bed and I pull a seat up to her side and take her hand.

'Mum,' I say, and already the tone of my voice alarms her.

'What,' she asks, 'what's happened?'

'Mum, the hospital says you can't stay here any longer.'

'Good,' she sighs, relieved, 'so take me home right now.'

'It's not quite that simple, Mum.'

Again her face contorts with anxiety. She knows exactly what's coming. I explain how hard we've tried to find good people who could help look after her at home, but it's proved impossible and the doctors and nurses say the only solution is for her to go into a nursing home. Her face hardens in a way I've seen so many times before when she's made it clear that she feels I don't come up to scratch. Her eyes turn to me, full of anger and disdain, and she spits out, in that cold, hard tone I know so well expresses her total displeasure, 'So, you've decided to dump me.'

So, yet again, I've done my best and it is not good enough. She refuses to listen to Dad's explanations, as he tells her how hard I've tried to find a way to take her home, but she is inconsolable and orders us to leave her alone. We leave, feeling wretched, and Dad, ever the one to jolly me along, says, 'Why don't we just spirit her away? We could discharge her ourselves and take

72

her home. We can pop her in the car, it's only just around the corner.'

For one mad moment it seems almost feasible, but the sensible part of us knows it's really not an option. There is no way we can take on the responsibility of someone who is so sick. We go our separate ways and I agree to pick him up on the Friday when we will accompany her to the home.

Bright and early on the Friday morning we fill my car with everything we can think of to make her more comfortable. Clothes, in the fond hope that she may have days when she's fit enough to get up and be wheeled to the dining room. Her own TV and radio. Books and magazines, flowers and photos. Lots of photos. Her and Dad courting. Her and Dad getting married. Me as a baby. The grandchildren. Me and Prince Charles making a film together. Me and the Queen on OBE day. Me and the last three prime ministers. Plenty to remind the staff of her life as a young woman and of her family. A few things to show off about. She may be hypercritical of me, but not a hint of it will be communicated to the staff when she shares the pictures which seem to indicate my successes.

She's already arrived by ambulance when we get there and is tucked up in her cot looking more miserable than I've ever seen her. She's in a lot of pain. The move has distressed her and she gazes around the unfamiliar room in utter despair. There's an unspoken awareness for all of us that these will be the last four walls she'll ever see. We spend all day arranging things to make it more familiar for her, holding her hand as she dozes, helping her eat lunch and supper—her appetite is tiny—and eventually kissing her goodbye as we have to leave.

As I come close she begins to whisper, 'I want to die, Jen, help me. I don't want to live like this.'

I hold her tight, tell her I love her, that we'll see her tomorrow, that I'll bring the boys over . . . anything to give her something to look forward to. Other than that, there is nothing I can do to help her.

Dad is beyond sad. He says he can't get past the feeling that he has let her down. He promised to care for her and to be always at her side till death did them part, but he has been forced to relinquish the responsibility to others. I can't console him.

I'm glad to be driving him home tonight. He's been quite scatty for some time now and I worry about him being behind the wheel of a car, although his GP assures me he has no signs of dementia. She had persuaded him to go and visit her after I prompted her to invite him to the surgery on some pretext or other—his care of himself is the least of his priorities—and he scored very well on the cognitive tests.

My father has always considered himself the intellectual inferior of the women in his family—unjustifiably so, although he never had the educational opportunities my mother and, to an even greater extent, I enjoyed. He left school at fourteen and became an apprentice electrician without too much hope of advancement. A problem with his hearing was unacknowledged throughout his childhood and, indeed, neither diagnosed nor treated until his fifties when a chance meeting with an ear, nose and throat specialist on a plane to Belfast led to his taking part in trials of a new operation to remove the

74

stirrup bone, damaged since infancy, and replace it with a prosthetic. There followed many months of having to go around wearing ear plugs because life was simply too noisy.

He was the youngest child of a family of five and began life, as the son of a miner, in a back-to-back, two-up two-down near the centre of Barnsley. His father died at the age of fifty-six when I was only three, his lungs destroyed by the silicosis brought on by a lifetime of inhaling coal dust. They had progressed to a slightly bigger house in the suburbs by the time Dad met my mother, but his humble background in Keir Street was something to which she banned any reference. She was forever at pains to point out that her father, even though he worked at the pit, was a winder who worked above ground, and consequently a cut above those who toiled below.

Her stories of her own schooldays in the pit-village infant and primary school of Worsborough Dale used to fill me with sadness, as did the photograph displayed across the table at my great-aunt Polly's house which I used to visit regularly for tea with her sister, my grandmother. I would be forced to sit up straight at the Victorian mahogany table on a faded, velvet-covered dining chair stuffed with horsehair. The hairs scratched my legs as I shuffled and, not wanting to appear 'soft in the head', I passed this off as the reason for the tears which poured down my cheeks on every visit.

The child in the picture—Polly's daughter, who would have been my aunt—wore a long dress and coverall apron, her hair in beautiful, flowing, golden ringlets. She was exquisite and had died soon after the picture was taken, aged eight, from diphtheria. I'd had the jabs—my mother made sure I was protected by every medical advance available—so I knew I wouldn't share her fate. The discomfort of the horsehair on the bare legs exposed by my fashionably short skirts (acceptable to Mum for an eight- to ten-year-old, but not, by the time they were really stylish in the mid-sixties, for a fourteen- or fifteen-year-old) seemed a small price to pay for the prospect of survival beyond childhood.

My mother's memories of her schooldays were equally heartbreaking tales of unimaginable poverty. Her generation benefited from the 1918 Education Act which provided free basic education for every child up to the age of fourteen, although she would be the only one in the entire school whose parents could afford the fees that, until 1944, would have to be found if a child passed for grammar school. She, born in 1926, had also been the only child in the village to go to her classes wearing shoes. The other families could not provide such luxuries.

A couple of the children in her class would come to school with egg yolk dabbed into a corner of their mouths. Their father, apparently, would eat the only egg available for his own breakfast and smear a dab on each child with instructions to say they too had had a nourishing start to the day. When my mother took an apple to eat at playtime, there was a queue every day begging her, 'Let me 'ave yer coke, Win.' She would donate the apple core to the thinnest and most needy. It's hardly surprising that she grew up with an acute sense of the need to better herself so as never to fall into the poverty with which she was only too familiar.

It was to her mother's relatives that she looked for a suitably respectable heritage. They were farmers, publicans and landowners and the implication hung constantly in the air that both she and my grandmother had married for love and chosen handsome, charming, gentle and generous men, who were, nevertheless, somewhat beneath them and must be dragged up by their boot strings. Both men were, on the whole, content to comply.

My mother was scathing about my paternal grandmother's lack of drive, her husband's fecklessness—he had liked a drink apparently—and their lack of interest in the aspirations of their youngest son. But my father needn't have worried. My mother made up for it in spades. It was she who pressed him to go to night school and study electrical engineering, which he did without complaint, working long hours in his job to pay the bills and struggling with his studies late into the night.

A Protestant work ethic prevailed and pleasure in leisure was considered somewhat decadent. Only my grandfather consistently broke the mould. He did his shifts, fetched and carried for my gran at home, took responsibility for fires and clean shoes, but made sure his right to a couple of hours at the working men's club, a pint or two and a game of bingo was unassailable.

He was constantly teased for it, accused of wasting time 'titivating himself' in front of the mirror—he would always ask, 'Is my hair sticking up at the back?' and never leave the house less than immaculately turned out—but stuck admirably, I always thought, to his need for 'relaxation'. My grandmother never accompanied him until his retirement in the late sixties, by which time it wasn't quite 'decent' for a woman to go to the club but didn't represent the social suicide it would have in earlier years.

Slowly Dad's job prospects improved and, despite his constant terror of redundancy or overreaching himself and being unable to perform whatever tasks were required of him, he eventually landed a position as a foreman electrician with a Stockport firm—J. R. Williams. For him it was the beginning of years and years of travelling across the Pennines to head office and around the country to whatever site installation he was supervising. He was often away for weeks on end and we missed him terribly.

I recall with absolute clarity the night he came home with momentous news and can summon still the sensation of my stomach sinking as I realized my life was about to change profoundly. My resistance to major changes has haunted me ever since to a ridiculous degree. I can't bear to come home and find so much as a stick of furniture out of its usual place.

Mum and I were sitting by the fire watching television and he rushed in, quite breathless.

'I've been offered a new job,' were the first words he spoke. 'Simon-Carves is a big engineering firm and they want to poach me from Williams and employ me as an engineer. Only one problem. The work's in Madras.'

I knew immediately that it spelled the end of my lying awake, waiting for him to come home to kiss me good night. There'd be no more weekends with him at home, no little walks together to fetch the paper and, most worryingly, no one to mediate in

78

the increasingly edgy relationship with my mother. I was eleven going on twenty-one and her intention, or so it seemed, was to hold me at a steady ten.

She was livid when I took myself off to have the plaits she had brushed and cherished daily chopped off in favour of a pudding-basin cut. On reflection, she was quite right. It didn't suit me, but for me it was a sign of growing up that I was making my own decisions about my appearance. (Dad hated it too. He drove past me in the street and said he thought he'd passed a boy!) Nor was she too happy with my blossoming relationship with Auntie Mary.

Mary Youel was one of her best friends, so not a genuine aunt at all, and for me she was a manifestation of one of the most puzzling aspects of my mother's character. Mary and Mum had gone to school together and, still unmarried, Mary ran her father's grocery store. She was what the French would call a *jolie laide*. Her features were unremarkable and, as I thought, squishy, but she wore Wallis suits in the days when the brand was the height of elegance and her hair and make-up were immaculate. It was one of my greatest pleasures as a growing girl to eavesdrop on Mary and Mum's conversations. They never spoke openly in front of me, but it's a foolish parent who believes children live in ignorance of the mysteries of the adult world that surrounds them.

When Mary came to tea I would always be asked to 'find something to do and leave them to chat in private', which generally meant hiding behind the door or sitting on the stairs, ears flapping at the intimacy of their exchanges. Their conversations were my window on the real world of women and their 'troubles'. They whispered about a friend who had died of breast cancer—never referred to by name but even I knew what 'C' meant—after being hit in the chest by a violent husband. There's no evidence, as far as I now know, that breast cancer can be caused in such a way, but for years I was terrified of ever being thumped in the chest area—a constant hazard for a reluctant hockey player.

I've thought of Mary whenever I've had occasion to visit a gynaecologist. My mother's questions on that day were about Mary's fibroids, which they'd discussed darkly during several previous meetings. 'Big as an orange, one of them, according to the doctor,' Mary had confided. 'He's going to send me to the specialist.' Her descriptions were so vivid I had no doubts about which bits of herself she was detailing.

'Win, I absolutely hated him poking about . . . and I shall have to have an operation, which Gerry isn't going to like. The worst bit, though, was sitting in the waiting room. I got there early and the place was full of the most disgusting-looking females. Some were really overweight and, frankly, not too savoury. I was the last appointment of the morning and I honestly felt quite sorry for him. It's difficult to know what would make a man want to poke about all morning in women's privates—there's got to be something a bit strange about him and have you noticed how they're all a bit on the short and arrogant side—but I did wonder how on earth he could face his lunch!'

The Gerry of the conversation was Mary's lover. She was unmarried because he, the dapper Jacob's biscuits rep who came regularly to her father's store, was already wed to someone else. And my mother, my oh so respectable, upstanding matriarch—believer in no sex before marriage and complete fidelity thereafter—appeared to condone what was going on. She acted as poste restante for Gerry's letters, which Mary would collect weekly. They even had the occasional assignation (only tea and talk, my mother wasn't that liberal about it all) chez nous. Like Mary, he was neat, dressed in made-to-measure dark pinstripe suits and wire glasses. He may have only been a biscuit salesman but he affected the airs of the Prince of Wales. And we were never short of free Cream Crackers—then his bestselling line.

For me, Mary's finest hour came around my eleventh birthday. Some of the girls at school had been given a new type of bra, the cups of which were made of a stretch material into which a budding chest could grow. Some of my classmates, even at that age, were beginning to develop an impressive 'bust', as we called it. I was not. Indeed, for most of my early teens I had to endure the nickname Peanut on account of retarded development in that area, but I, like the others, was longing for the accoutrements of the adult woman—bra, suspender belt, stockings and Cuban-heeled shoes.

Mary bought them all for me and my mother was too polite to complain, although I was never allowed to wear them to go out, except in her company. She'd read *Lolita*, I think, and made sure if I was out alone I was in big pants, vest and Liberty bodice. I dressed in my new things secretly in my bedroom and thought Mary racy, worldly-

81

wise and magnificent. Everything my mother appeared not to be. Mum's only contribution in the lingerie department would come much later when she advised a control girdle to keep my stomach in and a strong support bra. Her aim, as ever, was the suppression of seduction. I naturally didn't want to be seen dead in either of them.

Dad's posting to India was for six months, so there was no question of either of us joining him, but it was too good an opportunity to turn down. The money was good and the promotion exactly what the two of them had been hoping for. He left; my mother was heartbroken, clung to me for support and waited hungrily for his letters. It could take weeks to hear from him as we had no phone and email hadn't even been dreamed of. It was the start of many years of separation which would have a more profound effect than I ever thought possible.

During his absence, I took my 11-plus and passed for the high school. It had been my mother's dearest wish that I should attend the school for which she had also been accepted a generation before. As my father's star had risen, we'd bought the first house we ever owned within the catchment area of Barnsley Girls' High. It was a huge step up from the council accommodation in which we'd spent my early childhood. It was a semi-detached, late Edwardian building with three sizeable bedrooms—mine decorated in pinks and blues with pictures of ballet dancers on the wall (Mum's choice) and later Paul McCartney and Elvis Presley. Among my friends, you were either Paul and Elvis or John and Cliff, never both. I guess we all went for a combination of the sweet and the dangerous.

There was a large kitchen, a dining/sitting/everyday room and a front room for best, in which I was to have a bureau at which I could do my homework without being disturbed. We hadn't realized there was Mrs Goodall next door who taught singing and piano. Pupils doing scales drove me practically insane. She did offer at one point to give me lessons, despite my having demonstrated neither talent nor interest in learning to play a musical instrument. I lasted a week after being rapped over the knuckles for 'wasting time' trying to pick out the tune of 'Little Donkey' when I should have been practising the hated scales. Apart from later forays into the Wheatsheaf Folk Club on a Saturday night, posing as a Joan Baez look-and soundalike, I lost any musical curiosity I might have had.

We had unquestionably come up in the world as far as the 'class' of the neighbourhood was concerned, but there was a dearth of local children to play with. My mother was hugely relieved at removing me from the influence of the rougher elements. I was lonelier than ever, but comforted myself with the knowledge that, as long as I got through the exam, I would be sure of pleasing her by getting into the best girls' school in town.

All seemed settled. Dad would be back after his six-month stint. He would be there to see me don my grey blazer, beret and sweet-smelling leather satchel and all, I hoped, would go back to normal. Not so. I remember the telegram arriving and my mother going into a flat spin of excitement. My father told me only recently, during one of our long periods of reminiscence since my mother's illness, how it was from his end.

'I got a call from head office to say there were problems in Calcutta, just as I was due to finish in Madras. The electrical engineer there had flipped his lid—I think the gin might have had something to do with it—and had been admitted to a mental facility. As I was in the country, would I be prepared to go up and finish the contract? It would be for about two years. I was flattered; it meant I'd done well in Madras. I said I'd do it on one condition: they were to send a telegram to your mum and ask her if she'd be prepared to come out and join me. I knew I couldn't survive another six months without her. She said yes straight away.'

Mum couldn't wait to be on the first plane. It's lovely to have parents who adore each other and can't bear to be parted, but it's also a recipe for maniacal jealousy. Even now, when Dad doesn't mention me in his recital of these events, I'm ashamed to confess that I can't quite believe it was only her he wanted—I, the so-called apple of his eye, was to come as an afterthought. She appeared to feel the same way.

'Yes,' she responded joyously and began booking jabs at the doctor and planning shopping trips for summer frocks.

'But what about me?' I asked.

'Oh, don't worry.' She brushed my concerns aside. 'I'll take you with me, if you like.' She was only thirty-four years old and here was a chance to travel halfway across the world to rejoin the love of her life. I can't blame her for what seemed such a cavalier attitude to my anxiety, although I was deeply resentful of her decision to up sticks and follow my dad.

My joining them turned out not to be quite as simple as she had assumed. The company would not ship me back and forth for holidays. It would be too expensive and could only be done if the employee was to work within Europe. Their policy with children during a long-haul contract was to send them to school in the relevant country. There was an excellent girls' school in Darjeeling at the foot of the Himalayas, so I would go there as a boarder.

'There you are,' said Mum, 'problem solved. You can come with me and go to this school, which is apparently very good, and be with us for the holidays.'

Even now I am astonished that she could so easily be persuaded to abandon her oft-stated principles about boarding schools—'I can't see the point of having children if you're just going to send them away'—or willingly cast aside the fulfilment of our educational ambition.

My mother was shocked by the immediacy and vehemence of my response.

'I'm not going,' I told her. 'I'm going to stay here and go to the high school.'

'But you can't stay here by yourself, love. There'll be no one to look after you. And you're much too young to be on your own.'

Then she did the usual and, rather belatedly and for once ineffectually, turned on the taps. 'And Daddy and I will miss you terribly.'

'You'd miss me just as much if I was stuck in a boarding school. I'm not going and that's that.'

Grandma, of course, came up with the solution. 'She can stay with us. We'd be thrilled to look after her.'

I'd packed my bag in a heartbeat and prepared to spend the long summer holiday with her before starting the new school. I'd be near my old and undesirable pals and in what I knew instinctively would be a considerably less regimented household than the one I was used to. I never thought at the time that I would have regrets at my decision, although, of course, I did as I grew older wonder if I'd made a terrible mistake depriving myself of the opportunity to experience a culture so different from the one I was used to.

The doubts lingered until I read a novel by my friend Yvonne Roberts, called *A History of Insects*. She draws for her story on her own experience of living with her parents in an expatriate community in Pakistan and being sent to the school that was intended for me. She hated it. It was cold, spartan and populated by the kind of spoilt upper-class girls with no interests apart from finding themselves a rich and well-appointed husband. I would have despised them and hated the cursory education on offer.

My decision was not to be without its sadness and pitfalls, but, bearing in mind the thorough academic teaching for which the high school was rightly famous and the prospect of making friends who would interest and excite me during a decade that offered unprecedented opportunities for bright girls who were prepared to work hard, it was undoubtedly the right one.

And so, at the age of eleven, I accompanied my mother to Manchester airport to wave her off. On the way there I simply wanted to be rid of her. No more fussing about what I was wearing; no more lectures on the dangers of boys; no pressure about

86

whether I spoke nicely or not; no hassle about my hair; no more whingeing about 'that revolting Elvis Presley on your wall' (he was dressed in leather and sitting provocatively astride a motorcycle—the devil incarnate to any anxious mother); no complaints about 'always having your nose stuck in a book when you should be here helping me'. Grandma and Grandpa were guaranteed to run around and do everything for me and find me totally adorable no matter what. The 'me, me, me' little voice in the head that's dominant in the personality of every child was running on top-grade fuel.

I had not anticipated the horror of watching my mother walk across the tarmac—her presence slipping away with every footfall towards the steps of the plane. She, of course, had needed a boxful of tissues before she let go of me as her flight was called. When she sobbed and clung and told me over and over how much she loved me I found it embarrassing. Now, though, as she turned back one last time and waved and I felt the first hollow pangs of separation, I truly thought my heart was breaking. She had meant it. She was really going. She was abandoning me. I cried and cried, clinging to my grandmother's hand like a baby.

And then, as Gran and I walked towards the bus stop for the long trip home across the Pennines, a strangely cold feeling overcame me. In that moment I knew what love was and realized I did love my mother passionately and would long for her physical closeness, even though there seemed to be little on which we could agree. I was far too young to deal rationally with it being taken away. This is silly, I thought. I don't want to feel sad like this. If this is loving someone, perhaps it's best not to bother. It hurts too much when they go. Then and there I made a conscious effort not to miss my mother and to try not to feel anything that might make me miserable. I pretty much succeeded.

I can't count the number of relationships with men and with friends that I've blown because I need to attract attention and be reassured how wonderful I am—I lost my mum's somewhat critical attention at a formative time and revelled in my grandparents' unconditional adoration. It's probably why I threw myself with such gusto into the public eye, searching for the approval of an audience. But I also have the ability when I'm not satisfied to simply switch off and walk away. It took the birth of my children for anyone to really get under my skin again.

Five or six years ago there was a reunion at the high school, then part of Barnsley College and due to be sold off to speculators for housing development. My mother and I, both old girls, were invited and spent the day furious that such an

institution, struggled for by enlightened women in the early 1900s to give chances to girls who would otherwise be denied access to learning, was to be simply thrown away.

We walked around the familiar classrooms and remembered being taught Latin in the corner here, maths at the end of the corridor, art on the top floor, domestic science in the basement—I recalled gutting and pickling a herring, one of few dishes I can't stomach to this day. My mother laughed at her memories of being taught how to scrub a deal table—the academic teaching was first-rate, but the domestic crafts were never neglected. Even in my day it was assumed the best one could hope for was a short career in teaching, marriage, children and then perhaps returning part-time. The brightest and best might make it to medical school and would then be expected to remain child-free and devote themselves to their career.

We were both struck on that day by how tiny the school seemed now. The wall bars in the gym, which had once seemed huge and insurmountable, were absolutely insignificant. The school hall—scene of some of my most pleasurable moments, performing in the annual play—had appeared to be a vast auditorium, holding hundreds of girls sitting cross-legged on the floor as the head and the teaching staff sat on the platform for daily assembly in caps and gowns. Now it was just a rather scruffy, small school hall.

The boards with the records of sporting triumphs, educational attainment and head girls were still there—my name was not among them— and it was easy to picture oneself back under the beady eye of the elegant and cultured

Miss Baldwin—head for my first year—and then the alarming squint of the less appealing Miss Dawson who took over when Miss Baldwin retired.

While our academic education was second to none, our sex education left a great deal to be desired. Gory details were never on the curriculum at home either from my mother or grandmother and the only information we ever gleaned officially at school came during a series of religious education lessons on the Ten Commandments. Margaret, one of the older girls in the class, was the chief purveyor of hair-raising knowledge behind the bike sheds and, when we came to 'Thou shalt not commit adultery', Margaret, predictably, put up her hand and asked what it meant. The flustered teacher tried her best to bat away the meaning of extramarital relations, but Margaret pleaded total ignorance of what she was talking about and demanded more detailed explanations.

Of course, Margaret knew perfectly well what would happen when the teacher suggested we should write down our questions on the topic of S.E.X. We could be completely anonymous and she would do her best to answer at the next lesson. Margaret claimed to have 'done it' (I doubt it as we were only eleven or twelve but she certainly knew what 'it' was all about). Her questions were specific and to the point and I have never forgotten the drawing on the board of an erect penis and this poor, unmarried, devout woman trying to describe the intricacies of sexual intimacy.

'You will notice, girls, that the penis when excited changes shape and rises to resemble—well, shall we say it looks rather like an ice cream cone.' God knows what impact she had on our later attitudes to oral sex. My best friend, Linda Mead, with whom I'm still in regular contact, reminded me recently of a gossip session after class in the corner of the hockey field when Valerie, another of our more worldly-wise classmates, told us that in her experience it was 'more like a carrot'. It would be some time before Linda and I found out for ourselves.

On the whole, school, apart from Aveyard's Graveyard, was terrific. The maths mistress was called Mrs Aveyard and I seemed to be her least favourite pupil. I have no doubt my complete lack of ability in the numbers department can be traced back to my mother, who told me from when I was tiny that she had been 'hopeless at sums' but really good at English, history and languages. Maybe it's genetic, maybe she unwittingly gave me permission to fail, but I was so rubbish at the subject I was later dropped from the GCE course and advised to take biology as my science for university entrance.

I couldn't wait to give up maths. Not only were equations and calculus utterly unfathomable, I considered Mrs Aveyard a philistine. Her favourite put-down when I was, inevitably, unable to answer her questions was 'So, Jennifer Bailey, I suppose you've been wasting your time in the school play or learning poetry again.' How could anyone who thought poetry and drama insignificant possibly command my respect?

There was, though, one major drawback to following my mother's footsteps into school. A significant number of the teachers had been there for so long they had taught her too. I heard how talented she had been at Latin, how brilliant her essays had been, what an attentive girl she had

91

been in music and how disappointed the staff were when she had decided to leave school at the age of sixteen.

'Your mother was definitely university material,' said Miss Bridges, deputy head in my day. 'She was a pupil who really stands out in my mind. Such a waste of talent. I do hope you won't let us down as she did.'

It was a heavy burden to live up to and a source of constant irritation to be called frequently by her name. Our names—Winifred and Jennifer—do come from the same root, Guinevere, and we do, I suppose, have features in common—dark, naturally straight hair and big brown eyes—but every time a teacher asked, 'And Winifred, what do you think?' or 'Winifred, would you like to read for us now?' I would mutter, 'It's Jennifer, miss,' and wonder if I had any memorable traits of my own at all.

From time to time I had asked my mother why she had left school at sixteen and joined the Civil Service, living at home with her parents throughout her late teens and early twenties, even after she was married. I couldn't imagine anything worse than remaining under the control of your parents for such a long time. Her answer always was 'Ah well, it was the war and most of my boyfriends had been called up and gone off to fight. So many were killed and I wanted to do my bit. I did want to join the women's branch of the air force and get to see a bit of the world, but it wasn't to be.'

When I pressed her and asked why she was evasive, 'Well, it just didn't happen,' she said. 'The Food Office seemed like a good job—useful, but safer.'

It was only when I was left alone with my grandmother and my mother was, for the first time, far away that I began to understand why she may have felt compelled to remain at home.

For the first month of my stay with my grandparents everything seemed fine. Grandma was her usual jolly self, the life and soul of the party. She played the piano, sang and read the romantic novels she consumed hungrily—three a week for her from the library and three cowboy books for Grandpa. They woke me for school in the morning with everything laid out clean, pressed and ready to be put on—polished shoes waiting by the back door. Breakfast was sizzling on the open fire as I came down. Bacon, eggs and fried bread have never tasted better than the way she cooked them. I'd be packed off to the bus, to return at the end of the school day to freshly baked bread and scones for tea and a delicious corned beef hash with Yorkshire puddings, stew or meat and potato pie for supper. Life was measured out from one culinary delight to another.

Then, little by little, I began to notice she was becoming quieter and Grandpa was often left to do some of the cooking and work around the house while she 'just had a lie-down'. The full extent of her malaise became apparent one afternoon when we were alone in the house and Grandpa was on shift at the pit. She stood in the bay window of the sitting room, still wearing the housework overall which she normally took off in the afternoon. I was in an armchair reading.

Unmoving, she gazed out, and I could hear her muttering under her breath, 'I'm going funny, I'm

93

going funny.' Over and over again.

Suddenly, she turned and headed for the back door, still muttering and saying, 'I'll end it, I'll finish it.'

I ran after her. She was making for the lane opposite the house which led to the railway line and the canal where we'd spent so many happy hours when I was little fishing for tadpoles and sticklebacks. I recognized straight away that something was seriously wrong, caught up with her and begged her to come home. Eventually she did, and when we got inside she seemed to come to her senses, begging me not to tell my grandfather and not to mention it in letters to my mother. I promised her my silence.

But it got worse. I had no idea what was going on, but soon learned to dread the zombie-like demeanour which would seem to surround her all of a sudden, the repeat performances as she muttered at the window and the sudden quitting of the house with me running after her to bring her back.

Eventually I did tell Grandpa that I thought she

wasn't well. He agreed and said she'd probably got a bit down and he would take her to the doctor. I remember her taking pills and spending a little time in hospital where I was not allowed to visit. She came back with strange marks on the side of her head, a vacant look and difficulty remembering things.

When my mother came home, I asked her what had happened. I'd never seen Grandma like this before. She brushed it aside and said, 'Don't worry about it. It's her nerves. They just bother her sometimes. She'll be fine.'

I knew I was being lied to, but no one talked about depression, antidepressants or electro-convulsive therapy in those days. While my mother was with me—she divided her time between Dad and me during the foreign contracts that went on throughout my teenage years—Grandma was well. When Mum went away she began to slide back. After a while, I started to suspect this might have been the reason for my mother's decision to forgo her opportunity to join the WAAF and stay at home. Was it my grandmother's fear of abandonment that triggered her 'nervous breakdowns'?

In my mid-teens, again during one of my mother's periods at home, we received the terrible news that my grandmother's eldest sister, Sarah, had died. I'd always been fond of her. She was a tall, imposing woman, who, like my grandmother, presented a bright, funny and cheery front. As the eldest of a family of twelve surviving children she had virtually brought up my grandmother, who was the youngest, and they had been very close. No one told me how she had died. As usual I had to find out through earwigging on adult conversations while hiding behind the sitting-room door. She had killed herself. She'd lain down in front of the oven and turned on the gas.

My childish thoughts immediately went to Grandma and to our lonely journeys to the canal with me leading her back. 'Thank goodness she cooks our food in a coal-fired oven,' I said to myself.

These incidents have preyed on my mind constantly throughout my life. My mother, it always seemed, was central to my emotional well-being and that of my grandmother. Grandma's fear of losing her daughter—her only child—seemed to precipitate what I now understand may well have been manic depression. The symptoms were classic. One minute she was 'up' to an almost overwhelming degree of cheerfulness, the next she could be rock bottom and suicidal. And, of course, after Aunt Sarah's death I worried it might run in families. So far, so good. Both my mother and I have had periods of being down, but never to that awful degree.

I have, though, always shared that terror of being abandoned, but dealt with it quite differently. My strategy, learned at the time of kissing my mother goodbye at Manchester airport, was to shut down any emotion that might prove painful. My mother, I suspect, had a similar response to mine as she would often appear to push me away into activities—guide camp, holidays with friends, school trips—without so much as a flicker of emotion.

I tried, often, to ask her about it all, but she would dismiss my enquiries, denying that Grandma

96

ever had any problems with depression and telling me I wasted my time reading too much into things. I began to wonder if I'd made it all up—could it be that Grandma's dramas with depression and my feeling that Mum didn't care much for me had all been the product of an overactive teenage imagination and sense of the melodramatic?

It was only in her eightieth year and my fifty-sixth, just before she went into hospital for the final time, that Mum brought up the subject herself. She was having one of her better days and was tucked into the armchair in the sitting room of my parents' bungalow.

'Jen,' she said, hesitantly, 'you know when I seemed not to care very much when you were going off to do something or when you were leaving home? It's true, I did give that impression, but it wasn't what I was really feeling. It broke my heart every time you went away. But I never wanted to tie you to my apron strings like Grandma did with me. And I know I've never acknowledged how ill Grandma could be with her depression. But it is true. I had a very difficult childhood at times when she went downhill and I had to deal with it. I think I never wanted to admit it to you because I felt ashamed. I was split in two between you and Dad and leaving you with Grandma was the only solution, even though I guessed what would happen when I left. I am sorry.'

If only she'd explained all that years earlier, she might have bridged so much of the distance between us. Thank goodness she found the courage to say it before it was too late.

October

Mum's condition is deteriorating with relentless rapidity and the combination of work, home, worrying, travelling up and down to London and back and forth to Barnsley is beginning to take its toll. I'm tired and not really concentrating on anything very well. I've even developed an unpleasant habit of spilling food on my chest when I'm eating. The boys have noticed I have black rings under my eyes and can't help but giggle as I 'eat like a baby'.

'Keep your mind on what you're doing, Mum,' is a constant refrain from the pair of them and David looks at this unusually distracted me with astonishment and slight disdain.

I have a premonition of disaster at the start of a cold, rainy October day when *Woman's Hour*, the radio programme I've presented for the best part of twenty years, is to celebrate its sixtieth birthday with a big party in the Council Chamber at Broadcasting House. It's on a Thursday, which is not the best day for me. I spend the early part of the week in London but Thursday is the day we do an edition from Manchester, so it means getting up at home at five thirty, starting work as usual around seven, finishing at midday, catching the lunchtime train to London and getting ready for the party, which is due to start at six thirty.

I arrive at my flat in Camden around four and it's bucketing down. My two homes couldn't be more different. The family home in the Peak District is known as Wuthering Heights and is surrounded by green and very pleasant hills. The London pied-à-terre, a somewhat dingy basement, is Wuthering Depths. It has its own entrance down a rather treacherous wooden staircase. I am not concentrating on the matter in hand—or in this case, foot—as I rush towards the steps, carrying bags over both shoulders and books and mobile phone—all of which means I'm not hanging on to the hand rail as I usually do.

Whoosh. There are wet leaves on the top step and I tumble the entire length, landing with a loud bump at the bottom with my left foot awkwardly twisted underneath me. The pain is awful. I sit there in a puddle for several minutes, tears coursing down my cheeks. There's no alternative but to force myself upright and assess the damage. The ankle is swelling already, but I manage to put my weight on it and hobble indoors. I get ready for the party, hop, literally, into the taxi and arrive on time to find the Council Chamber already abuzz with the great and the good.

I loathe parties. I've never learned how to circulate and engage relative strangers in idle chit-chat and generally prefer to install myself on a seat in a corner in the hope that someone I know well will come over and sit next to me, thus absolving me of the responsibility of having to 'work the room'.

I now have the perfect excuse for sitting down and people do come over, express their concern and offer advice on what I should be doing about the ankle. I'm sure it can't be broken as I've been able to sort of walk on it—others, many of them medically qualified, are not so sure. I promise some of the country's leading obstetricians, gynaecologists and breast surgeons—regular contributors to the programme, but not an orthopaedic specialist among them—that I will heed their concerns and go to casualty the following day when I get home.

Getting my shoe on the next morning is a bit of a job and the ankle is painful. I've promised to spend the day judging the young woman engineer of the year and, not one to let anyone down, I take a taxi to the venue next to the Savoy Hotel, do the job, and drag myself back to Euston station to get a late afternoon train. By now I'm beginning to get seriously worried about the ankle. The pain is excruciating and I call David to pick me up and take me straight to the hospital.

'You are such an idiot' is not quite the loving, sympathetic greeting he might have offered, but I can't deny I should have had it looked at sooner.

The medical staff at the hospital are obviously in full agreement with his assessment, declare the fibula well and truly smashed and put me in plaster. It's to stay on for six weeks. I am not to bear weight on it for four of them, so I'll be hopping on crutches. And under no circumstances am I to try and drive. How on earth am I going to manage Mum and Dad?

Happily there are three willing volunteers to run a taxi service. David, Ed and Charlie agree to take turns—a solution which delights my mother as it means she gets to see her beloved grandsons more often. And so we arrive, visit after visit, the boys turning up their noses at the sour smell of the elderly as we enter the home and averting their eyes from the sad sight of old and lonely people living out their last days in states of awful decrepitude. I wish I didn't have to expose them to such horrors, but they bear it with kindness and gentleness and I'm proud of what fine young men Ed and Charlie are becoming.

They also inject a much-needed sense of humour into the proceedings when we arrive in Mum's little room, their youthful enthusiasm for everything deflecting the worried misery that generally infects the atmosphere. They even seem to distract Mum from her constant pain and entreaties for me to help her on her way to her death. She won't even whisper such things in their presence.

They help her with her drinks and the favourite food the care assistants make for her—baked potato, the only nourishing thing for which she seems to have the stomach nowadays—and keep her supplied with a constant stream of jelly babies. They tease Dad about his stick—his arthritic knee is giving him trouble—and, once I'm off the crutches and managing with a rather elegant, floral cane, warn him not to get mixed up and take mine by mistake.

'You wouldn't want people to see you out with something so girly, Grandpa.' It's a delight to see him laugh again. They chat to him about rugby and football, subjects with which I've never managed to engage, and Charlie, the rugby player, always makes sure at some point that he's standing next to his grandpa. My father, once a sturdy six-footer, has shrunk with age and Charlie, six foot two and rising, towers over him. Charlie knows he'll get the same response every time, but it seems to give them both great pleasure.

'Eee, lad,' says Dad, looking up into Charlie's eyes, 'yer a grand 'un. Do you know what I'd do if I had the ball and you were running up to tackle

104

me?'

'No, what, Grandpa?' asks Charlie, knowing perfectly well what the answer will be.

'I'd give you the bloody ball, lad, that's what I'd do. I wouldn't want you flattening me.' They giggle like children. Strange how all these boys together can lighten the most leaden mood. Ironic too for an ardent feminist, raised in such a matriarchal atmosphere, to find them so delightful. Is it nature or nurture, I wonder? Do boys and men have a naturally jocular attitude to life or did I just raise them with fewer doubts and pressures than my mother and grandmother laid on to me?

The subject of my broken ankle is also a source of great hilarity for everyone but me, even raising a laugh from my mother as I drag the plaster from one side of her bed to the other as I cater for her needs—a taste of lemonade here, a lift of the pillows there or a massage for her tiny feet and skinny calves.

'You always were careless, you know,' she reminds me, her long-term memory obviously unimpaired. 'How many Christmases running was it that you had your arm in plaster when you'd fallen over in the snow? And you always seemed to have cracked shins whenever they managed to get you to play hockey. Or was that just pretending to get yourself out of games? It always seemed funny to me that such a big-boned girl should break so easily.'

There you go, Mum, no matter how sick you are you can never resist an opportunity to remind me how unfortunate I was to inherit Dad's hefty bone structure and not your delicate, feminine one. Again I find myself leaving her presence feeling

105

hurt and angry—and guilty that I can be cross with someone who's in such dire straits.

But I can't deny she has a point. I was and am a big girl and she's right about the avoidance tactics when it came to games. I even learned to forge her handwriting and signature and wrote my own notes for the games mistress, claiming numerous obscure illnesses that would keep me from the hockey pitch or netball court and give me an extra hour in the warm with a book. Even as an adult, I've joined gyms galore at New Year and never lasted beyond February.

Back in the early sixties, there were many advantages to an all-girls school but having to play hockey was not one of them. Neither was there access to boys at a time when I so desperately wanted to find out more about the opposite sex. Here I was, an early teenager, in the midst of a sexual revolution with Dusty Springfield, Joan Baez and Cathy McGowan as role models. Dusty had her beehive and panda eyes, Cathy was presenting the unbelievably cool *Ready Steady Go* and, like Joan, had her long straight hair hanging loosely around her face.

I promptly grew my hair and vowed never to wash my eye make-up off from Friday night to Sunday. But, as Mum was home on one of her six-monthly stays with me, the eye make-up was far from an option and the hair had to be 'put up and kept off your face. I won't have you going around with your hair in those ridiculous curtains.'

And those boys? Forget it. Mum's idea of a good night out was for me to go to a Girl Guide meeting, come home at a reasonable time and have a cup of cocoa and a chat with her before bedtime. There

106

were times in those early teenage years when Dad was away and she and I spent cosy evenings together, but we never spoke about sex, periods or real intimacies. Her attitude was to deal with the onset of menstruation, at the grand old age of fifteen, briskly by giving me a belt and a pack of sanitary towels and a warning that I could now 'get into trouble' if I were not 'very careful'. Had it not been for the Ten Commandments lessons, discussions behind the bike sheds and a widely read copy of *Lady Chatterley's Lover*, covered in brown paper and passed around the class under the guise of a mathematics textbook, *Calculus for Beginners*, I would have had no idea what she was talking about. She merely insisted that on the rare occasions I was allowed out in the evening I must be home no later than the ten o'clock bus and must always sit with my knees demurely together.

It never occurred to me to utilize the relatively new form of sanitary protection—Lil-lets—until, on a rare holiday in Scarborough when both Mum and Dad were home, I met up with a bunch of friends from school who were planning to go swimming. I explained that I couldn't and they said, 'You need to try these things. Come on, we'll show you.'

Off we went to the public loos. I was handed a tampon and the instruction leaflet while my friends stood on the other side of the door whispering encouragement. It worked. Later I asked Mum if she would buy me some. Her response? 'No, love, you can't use those until you're married.' I explained that I already had and felt the chill as she wondered how I'd managed.

'Oh, it's all right, Mum, don't worry. The girls

107

from school said it's because of riding. All of us who go to the stables are OK with them.' She seemed satisfied with the explanation.

I did try to make her more of a liberal with regard to the mood of the times and her daughter's freedoms than was her natural inclination, but no amount of begging—'But Celia Booth's mum lets her wear eye make-up and her hair down and short skirts and high heels and she can go out to a disco on a Saturday night'—had the slightest effect.

'If Celia Booth's mother wants her to get a reputation for being cheap that's entirely up to her. No daughter of mine is going to behave like that. And that is final.'

I couldn't wait to be at Manchester airport again and seeing her off back to India.

Life in her absence was a much more thrilling affair. I became quite used to Grandma's depressive episodes and, with the callousness of a child, dealt with the practical necessities and got on with being a self-obsessed teenager. I learned to separate home and the rest of the outside world, putting all my energy into belonging to the coolest gang of clever, switched-on, stylish girls and making my way as an independent thinker whose only real aim was to get out of Barnsley and the suffocating atmosphere of a small town where everybody seemed to know your business and your mother.

It even got back to my mother that I'd been observed, underage, going to the Odeon cinema to watch *Dr No*, the first of Sean Connery's James Bond films and the one in which the divine Ursula Andress emerged, Venus-like, from the waves.

'Did you know your Jennifer was seen going to

the pictures to see that James Bond?' enquired our nosy neighbour, Mrs Goodall—the one who so failed to teach me to play the piano. 'They say it's quite disgusting and an A, so she shouldn't have been there at her age.'

My mother, not wishing to be made a fool of in public, claimed prior knowledge and said she couldn't see what the problem was; it was just a film. That was not her attitude when she related the encounter to me and gave me a stern warning about 'watching dirty movies that might lead you to think certain practices are all right—which they are not'.

We loved the movie and she really needn't have worried about any temptation that might have been put in our way. There were long debates about whether we wanted to be beautiful, like Andress, and 'have sexual intercourse' (the correct terminology made us giggle and the 'f' word would then never have passed even our modern misses' lips) with the gorgeous Sean Connery or whether we'd prefer to be Bond himself. I wanted to be Bond, as being licensed to kill and in control seemed infinitely more interesting than being bedded and unceremoniously dumped when James moved on to the next seductress.

I became quite a pain for some years ordering vodka martinis, shaken not stirred, at the Wheatsheaf Folk Club at the Town End. Dry vermouth hadn't hit Barnsley yet, so I had to settle for vodka and lime instead. The advantage of vodka as a surreptitious tipple was the fact that we believed it wouldn't be smelt on the breath when we got home.

I saved up my pocket money to buy black

eyeliner, mascara and the palest of lipsticks and acquired the regulation uniform of the Mary Quant sixties cheaply from Barnsley market. I had a pop art frock in black and white, a couple of polo-neck sweaters and two skirts that were indecently short. I never quite managed to afford the white Courrèges boots I craved and never had the money to take a train to London and go to Biba.

There were all-night parties at the homes of more liberal parents, late dances and discos jiggling to the Beatles and the Rolling Stones, and we all lied for each other about which friends we would be spending the night with. Hardly anyone had a phone, so checking up on our activities was nigh on impossible. We fell in and out of love with alarming regularity and indulged in lots of thrilling foreplay, but were far too afraid for anything full blown.

Grandma and Grandpa worried and warned that Mum would not be pleased if she knew how I was dressing, making up and going out, but they were indulgent and made no real effort to hold me back as long as homework got done and results were good.

To come home and have to tell your parents you were pregnant was the ultimate disgrace, but one of our number did it. Mary was one of the prettiest and cleverest girls in the class. Her father was English and her mother Austrian and she spoke English, French and German fluently. Her parents were even stricter than mine and she was never allowed out on our evening forays.

But, as we all knew but our parents seemed to have forgotten, you don't have to be out at night to

get yourself into trouble. In town on a shopping trip she met a guy who was twenty—she was just sixteen. He was a miner, rather dull and no great shakes in the looks department, but she was crazy about him. He had his own little terraced house and she took to spending her afternoons with him when the rest of us were shopping. When she announced she was having a baby she was thrown out of school and home and moved in with him.

We, her close friends, trooped round to see her after her daughter was born, fascinated that one of us should be so grown-up as to have broken free from the control of her parents and set up her own domestic arrangements. It struck us quite quickly that she had not acquired freedom. The guy expected her to run around after him and controlled her every move.

The baby, which seemed like an adorable little doll on first sight, cried and dirtied its nappy. Mary tried to give the impression she was having a wonderful time, but it was clear to us she was bored and anxious. When we left her behind, a bunch of giddy girls off to have a good time, her

111

face was a picture of misery. It was the last time I remember seeing her. I heard that some years later she left the guy, brought up her child alone and went back to education. Whether or not her parents came round, I have no idea. Her experience was probably the best lesson in sex education the rest of us had and we vowed it would never happen to us.

Inevitably I was caught out in my waywardness. I had been to one of the youth clubs in town for a perfectly innocent pre-Christmas dance which didn't end until midnight—way past the time laid down by my mother to my grandparents: 'If she wants to go out on some special occasion, make sure she is back on the ten o'clock bus at the very latest and then only on a weekend. In the week, when it's school the next day, she must be in bed by nine.'

I hopped off the last bus with all the verve of a youngster who's had a jolly good night and ran to where my grandfather was waiting. He always came to meet me, even though the late bus was not the one that passed virtually in front of his house, but stopped a good twenty minutes' walk away. I sensed at once that something was very wrong. It was the moment I discovered where the expression 'my heart sank' came from.

'Jen, love,' his voice shook with anxiety, 'we're in a bit of bother. It's your mother. She decided to come back a week early to give her more time to get ready for Christmas. Here, I've brought a hanky and I've wetted it. Wipe that muck off your face and pull your skirt down a bit—at least then she'll only be mad about the time.'

We rubbed and scrubbed at my eyes and lips and

did our best with the extended belt I was wearing, but it didn't have much effect. As we walked into the sitting room I caught a glimpse of myself in the mirror. It was not a pretty sight. Neither was my mother. She was standing with her back to the fire, looking thunderous.

'What time do you call this? And what do you think you look like? Your hair looks as if you've been dragged through a hedge backwards and your face wouldn't look out of place on a slut—or maybe a miner who's just come up from the pit. I don't know what you think you're playing at, but you've taken advantage of Grandma and Grandpa and you're running around town like a cheap little tart, disgracing the whole family. Now get yourself to bed and I'll come up and talk to you when you've cleaned yourself up. I can't stand to look at you like that.'

Half an hour later, I lay quaking in my bed ready for a further onslaught. When it came I did my best to defend myself with the usual excuses. 'I wasn't up to no good. I just went to a dance with my schoolfriends. No, I haven't been acting silly with any lads. But everybody else wears the latest fashions and everybody goes home when it finishes. Why do I have to be the only one not allowed to go or, if I can go, I have to get home earlier than anybody else? It's not fair.'

'Whoever told you life was fair?' was Mum's familiar retort, one that I'm ashamed to say I've heard myself using with my own children. Every plea fell on deaf ears and her fury refused to subside. In my bedroom, the tirade of insults continued until we were both exhausted. She vowed to ground me completely and stay home

113

longer than had been planned. Dad was to come home for Christmas at the end of his last India contract and would be working in this country for a while. In a few months he'd be going to work in Poland and she would stay with me until she was certain I was straightened out. Then I would come to them for every holiday and she would keep an eye on my 'carryings-on'.

I dreaded getting up in the morning and facing the Gorgon again over the breakfast table, but my mother had a most extraordinary talent for wiping from her mind anything that caused her serious annoyance. We got up, had a genial breakfast with my grandparents—there is nothing more delicious than bacon, eggs and fried bread cooked over an open fire glowing red—and set off for our own house. There was no more mention of the previous night or of my 'whorish' appearance. While I was at school she binned the offending garments, mascara and eyeliner and when pocket-money day came round she calmly told me there would be no more for at least a month, by which time she hoped to be able to trust me again.

It was time to learn how to play her game.

I stayed home with her and affected the behaviour of the perfect daughter, giving a hand with the cooking and cleaning, getting on with homework without needing to be reminded and never asking to go out except to elocution lessons, Guides and the occasional 'educational' trip to Sheffield Playhouse. I also encouraged her to take a job. Auntie Mary had opened a beauty salon in town and together they made up the women of Barnsley for weddings and evenings out.

I used to go and meet her at the salon after

school. I loved being there, watching them cleanse and moisturize and seeing women leave feeling so much better about themselves after all the attention. The make-up style was not what I would have wanted as it was rather stuck in the 1950s— indeed, I don't think I've ever seen my mother go out of the house without foundation, rouge, powder and bright red lips and drenched in a pungent scent called Shocking de Schiaparelli— but I was glad to see her occupied and distracted from me.

Her decision to work had not been taken without much agonizing over how it would be viewed and what Dad's reaction might be. Her concern was that he would be ashamed that people might think he couldn't afford to keep her. I managed to persuade her that times had changed. It was around then that I had the only real dust-up I ever remember with my father. He tended to leave all discipline issues for my mother to deal with—a fairly typical response, I suspect, from any father who was largely absent because of his work and who wanted his home to run on entirely comfortable and peaceful lines.

He would come home from work around eight. My mother and I would have scuttled around doing the tidying up and lighting the fire and already eaten our meal. She would cook again in readiness for his return, and as he walked through the door his slippers would be warm and his dinner would immediately be placed on the table. She would sit with him as he ate and they'd chat about their day. Sometimes I would be included, but more often I'd be doing homework in the front room.

I generally finished my work as he cleaned his plate. He would go at once from the table to an armchair and open up his newspaper. My mother would start to clear the table and ask for my help with the washing-up.

'Dad, why do you just sit down? Why don't you clear up and do the pots when Mum's been at work all day, as well as shopping and cooking?'

I know he was shocked at the very notion of a man taking any part in 'woman's work', but, to his credit, he said he didn't mind giving a hand.

'Why do men always think they needn't do anything around the house, or, if they do, it's just helping out?' I demanded. 'Why can't you see that, if everybody in a household eats and needs clean clothes and a tidy environment, it should be up to everybody to pull their weight?'

They were both furious with me and my 'stupid, newfangled ideas' and I had no effect at all. I realize now it was the first time a feminist light bulb switched itself on inside my head.

*   *   *

Mum moved on from Mary's salon to become a receptionist for a local architect and began to brush up her old clerical skills, but wherever she was employed it was always with the proviso that she could leave whenever she needed to follow her husband. She was such a good and reliable worker that she was welcomed back even after her frequent six-monthly absences.

It was only when she was at home that I adopted the art of subterfuge. When the pocket money started coming in again, I saved up and replaced the make-up and the fashionable gear. But I left it all with friends. We'd meet in the toilets at the Barnsley bus station and I would change and make up, hiding the clothes of which Mum approved and the make-up bag in the toilets, hidden behind a cistern. I still had to leave whatever entertainment we'd attended before my friends and change back into her approved style of twinset and pearls, remove the make-up, put the Alice band on to hold back the hair and leave the stuff in the hiding place for Linda, Joy or Celia to pick up on their way home at a later hour.

I can still see her now, as I dutifully alighted from the ten o'clock bus, standing in the bay window of our house, arms folded, nodding approvingly at my compliance with her rules. I spent most of my time feeling angry and resentful at her strictness. She seemed to want to deny me such simple pleasures. I like to think she did it because she cared, because she was genuinely anxious for my safety, but I still live with the terrible suspicion that she took pleasure in holding me down, clipping my wings and exercising her power over me.

There is ample evidence that the green-eyed monster is frequently a mother whose jealousy is directed at her daughter. The psychoanalyst Melanie Klein writes of the destructiveness that can be casually meted out by a mother to a daughter. She explains that it results from a desire on the part of the mother for omnipotence which is fired by her feelings of hatred and denial as her daughter's sexuality begins to mature and the child starts to grow away from the mother who gave up so much to nurture her.

117

Klein was herself subjected to a painful public denunciation by her own daughter, Melitta Schideberg, who was also a psychoanalyst. Klein, it seems, could never accept that her daughter might have overtaken her professionally. Their rift was so acute, Schideberg did not even attend her mother's funeral.

Similarly, in an essay called 'Hate in the Countertransference', another psychoanalyst, Donald Woods Winnicott, states, 'the mother hates the infant from the word go.' He goes on to explain that the mother suffers a psychic and physical threat from the tyrannical baby, who brings about a drastic interference to the mother's private life while at the same time demanding her unconditional love. It was Winnicott who invented the concept of the 'good enough mother', who was able to withdraw herself at various stages in her child's life to enable the child to develop independence. Mine, I think, could never accept being 'good enough'. She wanted to be the 'perfect mother', feeling it was her job to keep tight control, lest I let her down after all she'd invested in me.

I didn't bring many boyfriends home. On the rare occasions I did, Mum was charming and flirtatious and they thought she was lovely. She would offer tea and biscuits on arrival, which they would consume politely at the table. She would then graciously give permission for us to go into the sitting room—always kept for best or homework—with a simpering 'I suppose you'd like to spend some time alone' to the boy and a fierce look in my direction that said, 'I'll be in to check on you in half an hour and woe betide you if I

118

catch you up to anything you shouldn't.'

There'd be snogging and a bit of feeling up. It was full of promise for exciting things to come, but we never dared to remove a garment or even let hands wander to any bits of naked flesh. All had to be intact on the off chance that she would suddenly barge in. Kissing good night in the kitchen and pressing up close to something upright and stiff inside the boy's trousers could induce an orgasm on both sides, but only rarely. There was generally a 'Charles, Lyndsay, Philip . . . isn't it time you were getting off?' in her piercing tones from another part of the house, as we gasped in the dark kitchen by the back door.

All passion spent or more often killed, the boys would leave for home and my mother would snarl disapprovingly at my reddened chin. Then she would pick them apart. Charles was 'clever, but plain and smells of toothpaste'. Lyndsay was 'like a galloping hairgrip and I don't know how you could bear to kiss him with all those spots' and Philip, the best-looking and most overtly sensuous of them all, was 'not a grammar school boy and not from the best of families. He's going nowhere. I'd drop him if I were you.'

The character assassination was generally followed by a hymn to my father's good looks, charm and ambition and a wistful 'You'll be a lucky girl if you ever manage to find someone as wonderful as Daddy.' The obvious implication was that no one of real quality would fancy someone as smart-mouthed, difficult and 'unfeminine' as me. Or maybe she meant that no one would ever be good enough for me, at least not in her besotted eyes, because, as she saw it, my father had no

119

equal.

I had to agree with her. I adored him too and, while I berated him for his inadequacies in the domestic chores department, I found him handsome, clever, witty, kind, hard-working and loyal to a fault. Two women and one spectacular man—bound to end in tears!

*　　　*　　　*

By now Dad was in Poland and the firm agreed to pay for me to travel back and forth for the holidays. Dad had established himself in a small, newly built, first-floor flat in an anonymous block in the small village of Blachovnia in the centre of what had been, before the war, the German territory of Silesia. It was the beginning of a holiday when everything was ready for my mother to join him, so we flew out together to Warsaw and he came to meet us, planning a few days in the capital before travelling south to settle Mum into her new home.

Dad was excited at the airport. 'I've booked us into the best hotel in Warsaw and I've got a special treat for you, Jen. I've got you your own room.' It was the first time we'd been in a strange place together and not shared a family room. I lay in my lonely little bed that night, listening to the sounds of a strange city and feeling furious. I could not convince myself he'd been doing me a favour by treating me as an adult entitled to her own room.

I felt I'd been excluded so that they could spend time together alone—which, to an adult, seems a perfectly reasonable thing to do and my reaction as a fifteen-year-old appears alarmingly infantile. But

120

we'd always shared a room to save money and, as I thought, to be close to each other. Suddenly, sex reared its head and I told myself over and over, bitterly, 'I know what they're up to!'

As a teenager who worshipped her now rather distant father and was developing a serious antipathy towards her mother, it was devastating. Again, it was that double-edged sword suffered by the only child. You seem to be the absolute centre of your parents' world until they want to be alone. Then you're discarded, with no siblings with whom to play and talk. It's the ultimate eternal triangle.

So now I was jealous of her. Freud wouldn't quite have got it, as he appeared never to get his head around the possibility that women and girls might have rampant sexual desires. He formulated the Oedipus Complex to account for the boy who falls in love with his mother and wishes his father away. For girls he invented penis envy. He thought the girl blames the mother for having taken her penis away and so the daughter looks to the father as a substitute for what she sees as her loss and is driven to desire sexual union with him.

I can honestly say I have never envied anyone their penis, but that I was in love for a time with my dad is indisputable. My mother knew it too. For some years she had warned that my sitting on his lap for a cuddle was 'inappropriate', innocent though it always was. It was Jung who would call an all-too-common girlhood obsession with the most important man in her life 'the Electra Complex'. I had it in spades.

It was, though, a tremendous privilege to be taken to a Communist country at the height of the Cold War, not just as a holidaymaker but as part of the working population, with a chance to get close to the way people had to live. The very air seemed intimidating and the people lurched from nervous silence—politics and religion were never discussed as you never knew who you could trust—to uproarious celebration. We had some of the jolliest parties I've ever attended in that atmosphere of repression and deprivation.

On my second visit for the Christmas holidays, Dad decided he would take a break and we would spend some time touring. We stayed in a grand suite of rooms in Crakow, in a hotel that had been used as the German High Command during the war, and had a wonderful dinner on Christmas Eve. We went to candlelit Midnight Mass in the city's great cathedral, which was more packed than any church I've ever seen before or since, and got up on Christmas Day ready for a good breakfast and more sightseeing. We hadn't realized that Poland shut down completely on Christmas Day and we were left to scour the kitchens for food. We found nothing but bread and jam.

We went to Zakopane in the Tatra mountains and toured the exquisite church carved from salt at the mines in Wieliczka, and then Dad announced we must go to Auschwitz. My mother said no and they had the first and only serious disagreement I've ever witnessed, and it was the only time my father insisted on doing something to which my mother objected. My mother refused to come with us, so Dad and I drove through a barren, snow-covered landscape as he explained what had happened to Poland's Jewish population and the horrors of the Final Solution.

We were the only visitors. We walked hand in hand through the gate with its terrible slogan—*Arbeit Macht Frei*, Work Makes You Free—and made our own way around the huts with their bare wooden beds, the shelves on which thousands of people had lived and often died. We saw the gas chambers, the ovens, the photographs which lined the walls of thin, pinched faces with shaved scalps and terror in their eyes. There was the beginning of an attempt to turn such a dreadful place into a tourist attraction with one building devoted to displays of piles of human hair, clothing, children's toys, abandoned suitcases and the meticulous records kept by the Germans of every individual who had been at the death camp.

I was nearly sixteen years old and could not have imagined that such cruelty and inhumanity were possible. We left, white-faced and silent, and looked back on that evil place as we arrived at our car. My father sighed, looked at me and said, 'There but for the grace of God.' I asked him what

123

he meant. 'If we had been in Europe then we might have ended up here. We were very lucky.' He told me, 'There is Jewish in our family, but I don't really want to talk about it.'

It was the first I had heard of it. He refused to elaborate. It did, however, come up again when I was pregnant with my first child, and my mother, during a discussion on possible names for the baby, said to David, 'I don't suppose you'll be wanting Moses, Aaron, Reuben or Alvin, will you? You know, Dave, there is a bit of Jewish in our family.' Quite why it was a source of such fear and shame I can only imagine. I suspect my father was no stranger to anti-semitism as a child and had simply decided to wipe his heritage from his mind. At Auschwitz he had felt compelled to share with me the fate he had been lucky enough to evade. I asked him often to explain where the connection lay, but he remained stubbornly silent. Nor, he made it clear, was I to ask other members of the family. It remains a secret I feel I should honour.

A spell in Turkey followed the Polish contract and I had my first encounter with a Middle Eastern country in the summer holiday before I was due to go to university. Sixth form at school had been two years of sheer delight. My subjects were English, French and history and I had given in to my mother's opposition to an application for drama school and instead applied to study French and Drama at one of only four universities that offered drama as an academic subject. They were Bristol, Manchester, Birmingham and Hull and I opted for Hull as the newest and freshest course on offer. I needed two As and a B to get in.

I was still waiting for news of my results as I flew

124

alone to Turkey. My arrival in the small town of Adana on the Mediterranean coast was a revelation. The semi-tropical heat that met me as I emerged from the plane was overwhelming, the noise of the crickets deafening and as I walked across the tarmac towards the waiting crowds I saw my mother flanked by a tall, elegant blonde woman and a young man of such physical charm my tired eyes almost popped out of my head.

Dad was ill in bed, suffering a recurrence of the dysentery he'd first contracted in India, so Joan and her son, Muhtar, had kindly agreed to come and meet me. I was offered the option of travelling in Joan's car with my mother or with Muhtar in his battered, blue VW Beetle. No contest. It was the start of my first real, grown-up, passionately romantic affair.

Joan was an English woman who had met her Turkish husband at Oxford and spent her entire married life with him in Turkey. He had died some ten years previously, but she stayed with her two boys. Muhtar was twenty-eight and a curious mix

of English good manners—he was educated in England—and Turkish passion. I was eighteen and head over heels at first sight. Their farm was a few miles outside the town. They grew cotton and avocados in the days before the avocado pear arrived on a British menu. They had no electricity, so the nights were lit by oil lamps and the house was furnished with the most exquisite antique furniture and carpeted in priceless Persian silk.

The first time I was invited there for dinner it was served by two ancient retainers and, as the lamplight flickered, I could hear the sound of wolves howling in the orchard. Muhtar had raised two she-wolves almost from birth, having come across them mewling on the farm. The mother had been shot by hunters. It was all the stuff of a romantic, gothic novel and I was hooked.

We would spend our days on the beach which was part of the farm, swimming and sunbathing. I learned to shoot. Muhtar always carried a gun in the glove compartment of the car in case of bandits—God, it was thrilling. Eventually, he borrowed the flat of a friend of his and—wait for the cliché—we made well-protected love to the strains of José Feliciano's 'Light My Fire'. I've always been grateful that I finally lost my virginity to a practised lover and not to one of the inept spotty oiks who'd preceded him.

My friend Joy Wilson and I had always referred jokingly to our virgin state as the 'tin can', saying we felt rather like cats with a tin can tied to our tails—we wanted to get rid of it, but didn't really know how. I wrote to her, 'Tin can gone, loads of times.' She wrote back wanting to know every small detail and I hid her letter in my underwear drawer, confident my mother would never find it and, even if she did, would not be so crass as to actually read it.

For some time that summer things went swimmingly. My 'A' level results arrived and I had the grades that were required. My mother was sort of satisfied, although she couldn't help enquiring why I hadn't achieved straight As. I was never quite sure whether the message was 'You could have done better if you'd tried harder' or 'There, see, you're not so smart as you think you are.' It was the latter, I suspect, as we were both acutely conscious that I had passed beyond her in my educational achievements and would be the first in my family to attend university. She was proud, but she wouldn't have been human if she hadn't felt a pang of jealousy.

Not long before I was due to leave for England and my new life as a student, I came home from one of my delicious days with Muhtar to find my mother pacing the floor of the flat in a fury. She had been suspicious, had obviously been rooting around my drawers and had succumbed to the temptation to read Joy's correspondence. Didn't I know that Muhtar's reputation for going with wives on the American base was legendary? What kind of little slut had I turned out to be? I was not to see him again. God only knew what sort of dirty behaviour I'd be up to when I was on my own at university if I could behave like this under parental supervision.

I didn't feel the slightest bit ashamed, just angry. I hadn't put my future at stake by indulging in sex without adequate protection—although I didn't go into details with her—and couldn't wait to get away from the stifling atmosphere of being at home in such disgrace. Once again I was in big trouble, but this time there was nothing she could do about it. You can't ground an eighteen-year-old and even she would never withdraw her financial support for my education.

The next day she and my father drove me to the airport in silence. My father kissed me goodbye and wished me luck. My mother didn't even speak to me. I suspect her behaviour hurt her more than it did me. I was off to pastures new and she, I'm sure, rued her furious dismissal of me, although she never wrote to me during that first term and she never picked up the phone either to discuss the row in a cooler atmosphere or apologize for her intrusion into my privacy.

When I came back for the Christmas holidays Mum was all smiles and warm welcome at the airport, full of questions about my new life. As soon as I arrived at the flat, the phone rang. It was Muhtar, inviting me to dinner at the only decent restaurant in town. This time I didn't ask, I just told my parents I was going out.

When Muhtar arrived to pick me up he was welcomed by Mum in her usual flirtatious manner and it quickly became clear she had done it again. Swept it under the carpet. Pretended it hadn't happened. 'Have a lovely time, you two,' she said. 'And Muhtar, make sure you have her back here by ten o'clock.'

Our love-hate relationship was sealed.

November

At last I can drive again. The plaster is off and I'm going twice a week to a terrific physiotherapist—he's treated some of Charlie's rugby injuries and runs his own private practice. I was a bit miffed to discover the NHS these days takes off the plaster, asks you to put the bare, withered limb to the floor and walk across the room, then declares you discharged with no offer of physio, nor advice as to where you might find it. Which is fine if you're resourceful enough to find a practitioner yourself and pay for it. Not at all fine if you can't.

I set off across the Peaks under a heavy, brooding sky with some trepidation. I've known all my life how fast a blizzard can blow up on the higher ground in the winter months and have not, for once, taken my father's advice about adequate preparation for the journey. He became a master at crossing the Pennines in all weathers during his periods of commuting to his office in Stockport and never set out between October and April without a shovel, salt, warm blankets, a torch and a couple of flasks of hot drinks. He'll tick me off for being too distracted to make proper preparations.

I encounter nothing more than a cursory flurry of snow which mercifully doesn't settle, but even with the heating blowing a storm I feel chilled. I am horrified when I arrive in Mum's room to find Dad huddled in his chair at her bedside wearing his coat, scarf and gloves and Mum muffled up in so many bedclothes she can barely breathe. The radiator in her room has packed up and the embarrassed staff tell me they've tried to get the plumber in, but to no avail. I persuade them to find a fan heater to take some of the chill off the room and insist they get on with the repair job. The sister in charge looks none too hopeful. I take the number of the owners of the home in London and vow to blast them at the earliest opportunity.

Several phone calls later, when I've left messages for the owners to call me, I have made no progress. Dad is paying more than a thousand pounds a month for the privilege of having my mother practically freeze to death. What's more galling still, they have finally managed to employ two new care workers, bringing the complement of staff up to its full and still inadequate level, but they are two Polish girls who speak virtually no English. How on earth is an old and infirm man or woman to be expected to communicate their needs through such a language barrier?

I don't blame the staff for the inadequate care my parents are receiving. They are kind and committed women who work ludicrously long hours to try and give the attention their charges need, but their task is too great. I blame a system that has reneged on its promise to provide free health care at the point of need from the cradle to the grave. Successive governments have allowed the private sector to profit from the old and needy with, in my experience, a minimal degree of accountability. Distant owners, 200 miles away in London in my case, seemed to be employing the minimum number of staff they could get away with and paying them paltry wages. It's a scandal.

Plumbers of any description, Polish or otherwise, are clearly thin on the ground in Barnsley, so we have no alternative but to have my mother moved from the room to which she's now become accustomed to another one further down the corridor. It's a double room and she's anxious that someone else will be coming into the adjoining bed. I reassure her that Dad and I will make sure that her privacy is not disturbed, but she's unsettled by the move and begs me again to help her die.

I fervently wish I could be of some use to her, but she's lucid enough to understand my explaining, yet again, that what she's asking is illegal and, anyway, I wouldn't know where to begin. I resolve, again, to campaign for a change in the law which would enable doctors to assist in suicide. Now would be the right time. Mum is in her right mind, knows what she wants and is still able to swallow, although she's finding it increasingly difficult and is becoming alarmingly thin.

At least this room is warmer. Mum drifts off into a fitful sleep and Dad turns on the TV. It's *Strictly Come Dancing* and Dad wanders back into memories of their honeymoon in Blackpool and dancing together in the Tower Ballroom. Mum wakes and asks for a drink. I pour lemonade into her safety cup and hold it to her lips, carrying on my conversation with Dad.

I'm telling him about another of these competitive 'celebrity' shows—*The Two of Us*—which is to be shown after Christmas. It pairs professional singers with people like me and I've agreed to take part. He's laughing at the thought of me singing on TV when there's a choking sound from Mum's bed. I take the cup away, grab tissues and lift her head as she splutters. From somewhere she summons the strength to express her fury.

'For God's sake, Jennifer' (always Jennifer when she's angry), 'can't you concentrate for one second? It's always been the same—all you can ever think about is yourself and showing off about the bloody BBC.'

I apologize, tearfully, truly ashamed that I had indeed been concentrating on bigging myself up in front of Dad and had not, for those few seconds, paid her the attention she was due. But I also had one of those reprehensible moments of suspicion that she'd done it on purpose. Another example of her jealousy of what seemed to her to be my thrilling life and another time when she had to come between me and my dad. It was ever thus. She was a little sulky when I kissed her goodbye and didn't seem to have the strength left to articulate anything. I was not to know that night that those angry words would be the last she ever spoke to me.

Dad would always regale any captive audience with his proud boasts of my achievements, especially when I fulfilled his dream that I would go on to higher education.

'Of course, Jen, my daughter, is going to university,' he would tell anyone who'd listen. 'She's the first one in our family, you know. Very bright girl.'

This would be followed by a familiar echo from Mum, 'Well, I should have gone. My teachers always used to tell Jen how disappointed they were that I left school at sixteen. We went to the same high school, you see. But, of course, it was the war and I wanted to do my bit.'

'My plan was to join the WAAF, but my mother was afraid of losing me,' Mum would continue. 'We

134

knew so many people who had gone and hadn't come back. I stayed and helped her with our evacuee. She was a rough little miss from London and a handful, but we did our best. I had to sit the Civil Service exam, which was tough, and I passed. I was in the Food Office, you know, issuing coupons and orange juice and milk for children. So I did my bit in a way.'

It always infuriated me that she seemed unable to bask in her daughter's glory, although now I can understand how, as she saw me race ahead of her in education and sophistication, she would need to convince others and, indeed, herself that she too, given less troubled times and a more accommodating parent, had the intelligence for a glittering future. The war, my grandmother's need to have her within easy reach, her passion for my father and the fact that, back then, she had done what was expected of a young, respectable woman had all combined to make her turn her back on other opportunities.

I'm sure she was bursting with pride at my academic success. She never ceased in private to support and encourage me to aim as high as was possible and she certainly urged me to make the right decisions. Nevertheless, I doubt that she would have been quite so supportive had David Robert arrived first, as had been hoped. While tuition was free in those days for higher education, the earning levels for means-tested maintenance grants were set pretty low and my parents had to make a substantial contribution towards my living costs. Had there been two kids to support, one male, I'm not convinced my parents could have afforded such a commitment and, as happened in so many families, it would have been the boy who had the backing.

It's a question that's now raising its head again. The National Union of Students worries that, as higher education becomes prohibitively expensive, parents of limited means are again considering whether they can afford to send all their children to university. Their evidence is, thus far, anecdotal, but there are concerns that girls are again beginning to lose out.

The concept of equality of opportunity would never have occurred to my parents, nor any of their contemporaries. It was generally accepted that boys would need to be pushed as hard as possible into good jobs which would secure their roles as reliable breadwinners. Accountants, doctors and solicitors were particularly prized. A girl who showed promise might have been encouraged to go to teacher training college before marrying one of these paragons. I remember my mother mentioning it on a number of occasions. To her, teaching seemed the ideal profession for a girl. 'You can get some experience before you get married and then give up when you want to have children. Then, if you insist on going to work outside the home, you can always go back to it part-time when they're older. You could fit the hours around the children and you'd have the same long holidays.'

I was keen, after my many 'triumphs' on the school stage and success in Guildhall Speech and Drama exams, to go to drama school and become an actor—this despite a nagging doubt about my real talent, after my elocution teacher, Miss Florence D. Firth, took her pet pupils to see

136

Vanessa Redgrave play Rosalind in *As You Like It*. It was obvious from the moment she appeared on stage that there was something transporting and incandescent about a true performer and it was clear to me I didn't have it.

I did put up a fight in spite of my mother's wise counselling:

'No, you have a chance to go to university. I'm not saying don't act, if you really think it's what you want, but get a degree first, then you'll always have something to fall back on.' (I've recently heard myself repeating precisely those words to my younger son, who's passionately keen on playing rugby professionally. 'One injury away from the dole queue' must have come from somewhere— both my parents, I think.)

A compromise was agreed and I had been accepted to study French and Drama at Hull. My mother, helped along by Vanessa, undoubtedly saved me from a lifetime of erratic employment.

I never showed her any gratitude or sympathy, taking every cruel opportunity to expose her arrested intellectual development. When she talked Pearl S. Buck, I waxed lyrical on Zola or Flaubert—read, naturally, in the original. If she'd seen *My Fair Lady* I was derisive about the musical and sang the praises of the 'serious' theatre of Osborne or Wesker or Ionesco. When she danced around the sitting room to one of Dad's favourite Strauss waltzes, the pair of them laughing at his appalling sense of rhythm and his tendency to count every 'one, two, three', I would disappear to my bedroom, where I had my own Dansette record player, and claim a liking for Schoenberg or Stravinsky.

I was an insufferable intellectual snob and a liar. I could consume popular fiction with the best, knew 'The Street Where You Live' by heart, had listened surreptitiously to Radio Luxembourg under the covers at night, developing a passion for the Beatles, the Rolling Stones and the Dave Clark Five, and would have much preferred to be jigging with Dad to a melodious Strauss than grappling with the atonality of modern music. I'm even confident enough now to confess publicly how much I'd rather a Tchaikovsky or Beethoven Prom to anything 'plinky plonky'. Perhaps it was the only way I could find to pay her back for her consistent slights on my behaviour and appearance and draw myself away from the control she exercised over me whether she was with me or not. Or maybe I was just a difficult, spoilt little madam.

We had grown apart during her long absences from home. My experience was that of a teenager immersed in a culture that was changing its fashions, styles and morality at an unprecedented pace. Hers was that of a part-time expatriate, shifting her focus between Britons abroad and small-town northern England. She was firmly rooted in the fifties and shielded from the dramatic movements in acceptable mores. It was my grandmother who took me to see Cliff Richard in the film *Expresso Bongo*—a movie which marked the start of the pop revolution and teen power as the fifties turned into the sixties. Mum missed it all as she ferried herself back and forth between me and my dad.

The space between us was never more marked than in my early teenage years when she returned from one of her trips to India with what remain

138

two of my most prized possessions: the autograph of the Russian cosmonaut and first woman in space Valentina Tereshkova, and that of Paul McCartney.

They'd met Tereshkova, whose orbit of the earth took place in 1963, at a reception in Calcutta and, even though I doubt Mum had heard the word feminist, she seemed to know instinctively that Valentina would be one of her wayward daughter's weird heroines and plucked up the courage to approach her for her autograph. (As a mother myself, I know now that I would never have been far from her thoughts and her desire, frequently thwarted by my stubborn lack of co-operation, was only to please me.) Mum's presentation of the prize on her return home was attended by the comment, 'Typical of the Russians to send a woman into space. They have no respect for femininity, you know. They even have women driving lorries and sweeping the streets in Russia. That's communism for you. Disgusting.'

Then she pulled out the precious piece of paper that would give me unimaginable street cred at school.

I hadn't gone to Manchester airport with her on her 1964 trip back to join Dad for her six-month stint in India. After the shock of that first parting which left me so upset I decided it was better to say goodbye at home, so she'd gone off by herself. I could have kicked myself when she told me what happened.

'The airport was heaving with young girls when I got there and as we walked across the tarmac they were behaving appallingly, screaming their heads off. Anyway, I got on to the plane and sat down.

Then these four scruffy-looking lads got on and one of them sat next to me. He said hello and I asked him whatever did he think was going on out there. He looked at me a bit oddly and said, "I think it's us, missus." Then he told me they were the Beatles and they were on their way to America to be on the *Ed Sullivan Show*. I said to him that, now I thought about it, I did recognize his face because I thought my daughter had his picture up on her bedroom wall alongside Elvis. He said it was nice to be ranked with Elvis and I said he'd better give me his autograph then. He seemed like a nice lad, but he did look scruffy. I don't like that long hair.'

It seemed astonishing that she could have been so divorced from popular culture that she didn't immediately recognize the source of the screeching furore at the airport. The Beatles, in just a couple of years, had become the biggest thing ever, but had clearly pretty well passed my mother by. And despite her assessment of McCartney as a nice enough lad, she sent strict instructions to my grandparents that I was not to be given the money to go to the '64 concert the Beatles gave in Sheffield, to which all my friends had tickets. I have the letter still which states, 'No daughter of mine is going to make a fool of herself screaming and fainting like those silly girls I saw in Manchester.'

Regardless of the physical, emotional and intellectual distance between us, she remained the authoritarian figure who appeared to watch over my every move, whether present or not, so powerful was her influence. I knew throughout my teens and into my twenties that my code of

140

morality differed from hers, but I feared her disapproval and was frequently consumed with guilt at my lack of respect and my inability to find common ground between us.

She must have wanted to slap me most of the time, frequently did and, on one occasion, so did my father. It was Christmas time during one of Dad's periods at home. In order to earn extra money I had been delivering the post and had fallen over in the snow and ice, unbalanced by the heavy bag, put my hand down to save myself and broken the wrist. I was in plaster and we were watching some inconsequential but enjoyable variety show on BBC1 or ITV. BBC2 had launched in 1964 and was known for its avant-garde plays and high culture.

There was a ballet on the other side that night, which I didn't particularly want to see but recognized as a major point-scoring opportunity. I pestered and demanded and criticized my mother's choice of viewing. The fire was blazing and the atmosphere grew more and more heated. She and I exchanged rapid-fire insults until she was finally worn down and burst into tears.

My father was sitting in his chair to my left and for the first and only time in my life—he'd never raised so much as a finger in eighteen years—his arm flew out and clocked me one across the face. My nose bled profusely all over the plaster. I don't remember ever being so shocked; neither of us recalls ever being so ashamed and he and I made up with hugs, apologies and cuddles. But Mum was the one I couldn't forgive. In the lunacy of my jealousy of her closeness to him I blamed her for driving him beyond control. He, it seemed, had hit

141

me in defence of her. I hated her for it.

*   *   *

When the time came for me to strike out on my own and go off to Hull to begin my undergraduate student life, they were still in Turkey. It's been instructive as a parent sending kids off to university to compare their experiences with mine. Today family cars are filled with clothes, computers, TV sets, mobile phones—everything required to create a home from home. Siblings come along, excited to see what the future may hold in store, while morose parents contemplate the loneliness of an emptying nest. It's a rite of passage that most families seem keen to share with their offspring.

My grandparents didn't have a car. Neither of them knew how to drive. I packed the biggest suitcase I could carry with a collection of the coolest clothes I had managed to muster—I was particularly proud of a black leather skirt of quite indecent shortness—kissed them both goodbye at the back door and walked to the bus stop. The bus took me into Barnsley. The bus station and railway station were not far apart. I took the small diesel train that shuttled between Sheffield and Leeds—the one we'd always used for shopping trips in either of our two major cities—and headed for Leeds.

There, a little overwhelmed by the bustle and size of a station with which I was familiar but had never before negotiated alone, I found the Hull train and got into a carriage with dozens of other equally bemused and nervous youngsters. After an hour or so, we arrived at the end of the line—any further and you're in the North Sea—and the moment I stepped on to the platform at the gloriously named Hull Paragon Railway Station (I would not be a paragon of virtue during my undergraduate years) I knew I was going to love the place.

There was a light airiness about the high glass-vaulted roof of the station itself and, as you emerge from the platforms, you're immediately aware of the highly decorated nature of those buildings in the city that survived the appalling bombardment of the Second World War and the ravages of the 'modernist' rebuilding under the Abercrombie plan. I assume the influence is from the Dutch, long-established trading partners through Hull and Rotterdam, because there are beautiful coloured tiles everywhere, lending a slightly exotic, European feel to what was then a hard-living working port.

Buses were to take us to our designated accommodation, so a number of us queued outside the station full of equal measures of excitement and fear. I don't recall talking to anyone. We were far too scared to make conversation as most of us were only eighteen, leaving home alone and bracing ourselves to stand on our own two feet for the first time ever. We clutched our bags as the coach took us through the unfamiliar city centre and out to the campus a couple of miles away.

I had opted, mistakenly as it turned out, for a student house. The streets which flanked the campus had row upon row of the kind of bay-windowed, three-bedroomed semis or terraces I always associate with seaside landladies. The coach pulled up at the end of my street—Cranbrook

Avenue—and I remember the long walk with the heavy bags, but can't recall the number. I rang the doorbell and it was answered by a short, plump, smiling but unprepossessing redhead wearing the kind of clothes of which my mother would have approved—twinset and skirt of unfashionably decent length. She immediately pointed out she would be in charge—as a final-year student she was there to keep an eye on us 'freshers'.

I was apparently to share a room, although I'd asked for a single. The prospect was horrific for an only child who'd never been forced to share anything with anyone and had been wise to every subterfuge going to avoid undressing in front of other girls at school—virtually endless periods, colds, verrucas, skin infections, it's a wonder the PE teachers hadn't had me hospitalized.

The door to the double room was on the ground floor—it would have been the front room to the house—so it was near a loo and the kitchen, but other than that it had little to recommend it. Two identical beds of barely habitable narrowness plus two desks, two chairs and everything in beige. As was my roommate. She stood up from the bed where she'd been sitting (and, I suspected, sobbing). For the first time I saw how apt the term 'galloping hairgrip'—one of my mother's favourites—could be. She was tall, with long, blonde, wispy hair, caught up in an Alice band (by choice!), pale and impossibly thin. She was dressed straight out of Country Casuals.

She extended a limp hand and in a little voice said, 'How do you do. My name is Amanda and I'm from Harpenden in Hertfordshire.' She was everything I was not: skinny, obviously loaded and

144

posh. I detested her on sight. 'Hiya,' was my casual response, 'I'm Jenni and I come from Barnsley.' I had decided in advance that I would change my name from the Jen or Jennifer favoured by my mother. Jen when she was pleased with me, Jennifer when she was angry and she'd always hated Jenni. She said, quite unaccountably I thought, it sounded like a name for a cow. It was a small but satisfying strike for some independence.

For the first time in my life I affected a broader Yorkshire accent than came naturally, flopped on to the bed, hitched up my skirt to make it even shorter and began to unroll the poster a friend from school had given me as a parting gift. It was huge, black and white and showed a woman with her head thrown back, her eyes half shut in ecstasy and her mouth wide open. It was called 'The Orgasm'. It was immediately obvious that the deep loathing was mutual.

In the kitchen other members of the household, six in all, were gathering. Hilary, a stunningly attractive English student from London, looked interesting, although her accent too was strictly cut-glass. The others were older, studying theology, and it was made plain from the outset that alcohol and cigarettes were strongly disapproved of. Whoever had thought it a good idea to house us all together must have had a bizarre sense of humour, given my insistence on my application form that I was pretty much a heathen, northern working class and smoked like a chimney. I determined to get out as soon as was feasible.

It took longer than I thought—three whole terms of purgatory in the lodgings and lurching

145

between extreme pain and pleasure on the work side of university life. The leap from the relative comfort and control of school to the free and easy independence of university is a difficult transition to make and, I suspect, a whole generation of us who were the first in their families to get such an opportunity was thrown into an atmosphere for which neither school nor parents had thought adequately to prepare us. No one to care about what we ate, what time we got home, what we wore, how we did our hair, how we motivated ourselves to study alone—it was a liberation of sorts, but it was pretty scary too.

Theories about the development of the brain now suggest that a full command of reasoning power doesn't kick in until the early twenties and young people need rather more support than it used to be assumed. Parents who had gone through the war and been forced to see their friends grow up and be sent to die on the battlefield at eighteen had no truck with any sign of dependency in their offspring. When I'd left my father behind in Turkey at the end of that heady summer of '68 and set off for my new life he'd said, 'That's it now, love. I'll make up whatever's required for your maintenance grant and the firm will pay if you need to come to us for holidays until you're twenty-one. Other than that, you're on your own. Don't come to me asking for money. I had to do it, and now so will you.'

By Christmas I had a substantial overdraft and the bank manager I shared with my parents, breaking all known rules of client confidentiality, let them know what difficulties I was in, thus denying me the fur coat I'd been promised as a

146

present. They were all the rage that winter and I ended up instead with my mother's ancient beaver lamb—not quite the height of style when rabbit was the pelt of choice for the most stylish—and the money destined for the Christmas present went into the bank account instead. They clearly meant business when it came to financial assistance. None was to be forthcoming and I was to learn their talent for managing money—living on as little as possible and saving for a rainy day.

I, though, seemed to have inherited my grandfather's profligacy with any cash that was available. They'd only stayed out of Queer Street thanks to my grandmother's talent for balancing the books every month and giving him only a small personal allowance. My mother inherited her genius and my father had it too. Clearly with me it skipped a generation. I changed banks and lurched from crisis to crisis, taking little jobs here and there when the letters came from bank managers warning me I'd gone too far. I admired their creativity: 'Dear Miss Bailey, I note from our records that your spending has again exceeded your somewhat paltry income. This cavalier attitude to your financial affairs must cease forthwith. I suggest a meeting at this branch to discuss your proposals' was my favourite.

To this day, despite my best efforts, I continue to check every statement with a trepidation which is frequently justified. It's a source of constant worry which, having dogged me for more than thirty years, is unlikely to be remedied. As my mother says, 'What is it with you that every penny burns a hole in your pocket?'

My French course was dull and rather stodgy.

My interest in the subject was the literature of the nineteenth and twentieth centuries and speaking the language. I found myself bogged down in Old French, the *Chanson de Roland* and the *Lays of Marie de France*, the title of which provided the only amusement on the entire curriculum. Drama could be heavy; several volumes of Glynne Wickham's *Early English Stages* had to be ploughed through.

At times it was thrilling beyond imagining; a part in Samuel Beckett's *Play* was the highlight of the performing calendar. Three of us sat in cardboard urns in complete darkness acting out in a monotone a bitter ménage à trois, our faces covered in white greasepaint and a harsh spotlight shining on whichever character was speaking.

But most of the time I found the academic atmosphere quite terrifying. I was no longer one of the brightest and most mature, but one of the youngest and seemingly least well informed. Or maybe I just hadn't yet learned to bullshit. Tutorials were purgatory. My essays were frequently dismissed as naïve and I crumbled under the questioning of one tutor in particular.

My first-year tutor, Harry Thompson, was famed for the flatness of his voice, his waggling finger, florid face and dandified mode of dress. He would sneeringly ask my opinion of a Chekhov play, sniff disdainfully at my hesitant response and then say, 'Right, let's hand it over to one of the boys.' His misogyny was barely concealed. He called the few women in the group 'the girlies' and we rarely got a mark higher than a B while the boys regularly got an A.

In retrospect, I think he did me a favour. I

148

learned that thorough research was essential to having a well-stocked mind and knowledge was power. I also discovered that the well-constructed and informed question can throw the most difficult person off course. I eventually came to tutorials stuffed with information and asked intelligent questions to avoid being questioned myself. Good training for a future interviewer. Even now, I can't stand the rare occasions when I find myself on the other side of the desk. I'm another interviewer's nightmare.

There was plenty of revolutionary politics in which to become involved. It was 1968, a year of student unrest throughout Europe, and Hull was a welcoming target for the big boys who came to the university to incite rebellion. Cohn-Bendit came over from Paris and Tariq Ali from London. Anti-racism was our baby. The university had close links with Barclays Bank and Reckitt and Colman, then both known for their heavy investments in apartheid South Africa.

We occupied the administration block and sat in for a weekend—drifting off home when the toilets were blocked and the booze and food ran out. I'm not sure we had any impact on the university's financial probity, but it did politicize a whole bunch of us who vowed never to visit the country until the black population was granted equal democratic rights. For years we joined anti-apartheid marches and eschewed any products which came from South Africa.

So ingrained was the passionate belief in racial equality which took root that summer, I had a most bizarre conversation in the late nineties with Cheryl Carolus, the first black South African to occupy the position of High Commissioner in London. We were having dinner in Camden Town. I was planning a holiday and couldn't think of anywhere that would please a partner who likes adventure and hates extreme heat, two teenage boys who love surfing and clubs with great music and me—needing simply to relax on a warm enough beach and eat fantastic food.

'Come to South Africa,' she suggested. 'Cape Town has wonderful restaurants, beaches and clubs and then you could go on safari in Kruger Park.'

'Oh no,' I replied. 'I couldn't spend my money in South Africa. I've never so much as bought an Outspan orange.'

She looked at me in bemused amazement. 'Jenni, it's all right now. We're in charge and we need your pounds. Just go.' I felt a complete idiot, but clearly old habits die very hard. We went to South Africa and found a country beyond beauty, but still in shock at the magnitude of the problems left by years of oppression, separation of communities, anger, poverty and Aids. We've been back several times—spending our pounds there, as directed, and finding immeasurable pleasure in the landscape, the food, the music and the people, but suffused with shame that so perfect a place could have been so abused by my compatriots and their like.

*   *   *

The sexual revolution did have an impact—although sharing a room with the virginal Amanda did nothing to improve my chances of becoming the rampant femme fatale I had intended. That would have to come later, when I finally found a room of my own in the halls of residence which were a little further away from the campus and housed all the 'hip' people I intended to make my associates. But every good Girl Guide has the motto 'Be prepared' engraved on her forehead and I was determined that, should the occasion arise, I would not be caught out depending on a guy to carry condoms as I had been in Turkey with the divine Muhtar. This time, I wanted to be 'in control of my own fertility', as the propaganda went. The pill was the Holy Grail.

It was not so easy to obtain. It had been licensed in Britain in 1961 for married women. (My mother would have had no difficulties with that rule.) Word went around that the Brook Advisory Centres—set up by Lady Helen Brook in 1964 to give advice to the unmarried—would give the pill willingly, but of course there was no branch in Hull. The Family Planning Association was said to be less liberal, but would prescribe if you wore an engagement ring and gave them the date of your intended nuptials or wore a wedding ring and simply said you were married.

Woolworth's did a good trade in cheap imitations and we trooped off—alone, never together as it might seem suspicious, and reported back afterwards. We had our first experiences of intimate examinations. Some came away with a cap and spermicide, a method which always struck me as unreliable and disgustingly messy—but those of us who insisted got the pill. We felt we were really women at last and I have no truck with those who say the sexual revolution was harmful to women. It

151

has long been feminist ideology to claim the sexual revolution gave women permission to say yes, but it wasn't until the women's movement that we won the right to say no; the implication being that we were pushed and pressured into sexual intimacies we didn't want. Not so. We generally had a ball.

Only once did I have any difficulties. A big professional theatre came to town and we, the drama students, were asked to act as dressers. I was allocated one of the leading men—a huge and quite intimidating guy with a reputation for picking up by the neck any actress who annoyed him. He was fine with me—much older, in his late forties I guessed—and charming and funny. After the show we star-struck wannabes went along to the pub with the company, tried to act like seasoned grown-ups and had a little more drink than we were used to.

The flat he'd been allocated was just around the corner and a few of us went back for a nightcap. I was flattered by his attention, was the last to get up to leave and when I began my stagger to the door he became violent, threw me, literally, on to the bed and had his wicked way. I had sobered up pretty fast but was not strong enough to resist, and his freedom with his fists convinced me not to bother trying. He rolled over when he'd finished and fell asleep. I got up, showered, dressed and left, furious with myself because I hadn't seen it coming and gone home with the rest.

I didn't tell anybody, blaming the bruise under my eye on my inebriation of the previous evening and giving the classic 'I ran into a door' excuse used by women who've suffered violence at the hands of a man and can see no means of redress.

No one suspected any different and I convinced myself that he'd been just another meaningless dick to add to the notches on the bedpost denoting those who hadn't been asked back.

No one talked about rape in those days, so it didn't occur to me that what he had done was an offence and I have always treated it as one of those things that you put down to experience and make sure never happen again. I learned to look out for the danger signs of anger and a controlling nature that often lie behind the façade of the most charming of men.

Would I have reported it if it had happened today? Yes, certainly, despite everything I know about the talents of defence counsel who would have done their best to make mincemeat of the reputation of a fairly typical young student of her day—enjoying guilt-free sex whenever she wanted it and not averse to the odd spot of inebriation.

The actor was lucky and I kept it to myself, but I wish I could have told him it was not his unimpressive member that was the terrifying weapon, but the force behind the fist that knocked the resistance out of me. He committed a crime and I allowed him to get away with it and perhaps go on to do it again. He's been dead for a long time now. I hope he's rotting in hell.

I don't know whether it was the pill or the mountains of toast and butter I used to consume at the end of a long day studying, rehearsing and having fun, but I began to realize towards the end of the year that my clothes were getting tighter. I spent most of my time in a large black sweater and stretch leggings, convincing myself I was the height of bohemianism, emulating one of my musical heroes, Juliette Gréco.

I had a letter from my parents. They were planning to come home from Turkey and Dad would be working in the UK, maybe for a year or so before starting another contract in Czechoslovakia. They'd bought a car and had decided to travel overland, taking a couple of months over the journey and making the final leg by boat from Rotterdam to Hull, arriving around Easter. They included details of their arrival time at the ferry terminal and asked if I could be there to meet them and show them my room in the house and where I was working before they carried on home to Barnsley.

I hadn't seen them since my last trip to Turkey the previous Christmas and, as always, looked forward immensely to welcoming them home. I bought food, tidied and cleaned the house—anticipating my mother's habit of a lifetime which was to cast her eyes disapprovingly around any room, tut at its untidiness and run her finger along a piece of furniture or mantelpiece, looking at the dust that lodged there and rubbing her fingers together with unconcealed distaste. She would have no cause for complaint. The place was immaculate.

I took the bus to the ferry terminal and walked to the disembarkation point, anxious that they should see me the minute they drove off the ferry. I spotted them in the queue, waved and my father drove straight past me. I called out to them and ran to catch them up. When Dad realized it was me, he pulled up and jumped out of the car. I ran into his arms and we gave each other a huge hug. My mother stood, looking me up and down, not

154

touching me, just with that angry, appalled, disgusted look on her face with which I was so familiar.

'What in God's name has happened to you? You look like ten-ton Tess. How could you come and meet us looking like that with your hair all over your face, those scruffy-looking clothes and what have you been doing to put on so much weight? You look awful.'

I got into the back of the car, stunned at the vehemence of her tirade. And then began the most bruising shouting match we'd ever had. She accused me of being a slovenly slut and I screamed back that if she were any kind of a mother she'd be happy to see me no matter what I looked like and anyway I thought I looked fine; she was the one who was centuries out of date with her permed hair and flashy red lips. It was awful. I demanded to be dropped outside the student house and, despite my father's attempts to calm things down, refused to invite them in. I stormed inside, slammed the door behind me and sat on my bed and sobbed, vowing never to see the wretched woman again.

Later that evening the pay phone rang. It was my mother, almost hysterical, also calling from a pay phone. No apology, just a rant. 'I just thought you'd like to know that thanks to your disgraceful behaviour and the disgusting state we found you in your father was so upset he managed to run into the back of another car on the way home. The car is badly damaged, but we're not hurt—not, I suppose, that that would bother you.' I put the phone down. The memory of it still hurts.

I also vowed that I would lose weight, quickly, so that when I went home for the summer holidays—

and I had no choice but to go home as I had no money and nowhere else to live—she would have no cause for complaint. I went to the University Health Centre and asked the doctor for something to help me get slim again. He weighed me in at eleven stone—not exactly obese for a woman of five foot seven, but considerably more than my usual nine to nine and a half—and gave me a prescription without any advice or information except to take three a day with water. My diet was one I'd read about in a magazine—all that domestic science at school really had been wasted—and consisted of nothing but boiled eggs and tomatoes.

The pounds just dropped off. I hardly ever felt hungry and I was buzzing—full of energy, the life and soul of every wild party. I got on with my work—staying up all night to finish an essay was no hardship—and hardly noticed that occasionally I would burst into tears with no good reason.

Happily my supervisor, John Harris, a tall and kindly man who was the very image of the academic of his day—long floppy fringe, corduroy trousers, tweed jacket with leather patches over the worn elbows—asked me to come and see him in his cosy, book-lined study.

'I'm a little worried about you. You seem to be getting very thin and you get upset a lot, which I don't think is like you. What's going on?'

'Nothing,' I said, 'I think I'm doing fine. My marks are OK, the work's getting done, I'm to be in the production of *Long Day's Journey into Night*. Nothing's the matter.'

He hesitated before asking the question that was at the forefront of his mind, but then came out with it. 'Jenni, what are you on? What drugs are you taking?'

My answer was truthful—there was cannabis around but I hadn't tried it, and the more extreme drugs of choice of the moment, mescaline and LSD, seemed altogether too scary to contemplate. One friend who'd dropped an LSD tablet reported a terrifying night, looking at himself in the mirror and watching himself age and crumble. I think he'd seen the film of H. Rider Haggard's *She*, where the gorgeous Ursula Andress stepped into the flame of eternal youth once too often, became a hag and then crumbled into dust. It was not a pleasant image.

'I'm not taking any drugs at all, apart from the tablets the doctor gave me to help me to lose the weight I put on.'

He asked me to show him what I'd been given and gasped in horror. 'My God, child, those are black bombers—they're amphetamines, speed . . . Yes, they suppress appetite, but they're terribly dangerous. You must stop.'

He took care of me. There were terrible ructions at the health centre and I was taken into the sick bay there, suffering from dreadful pains in my back and needing help to cope with withdrawal from the tablets and starting to eat sensibly again. I had lost nearly four stone and was weak and far too thin for my frame. After a week, my parents were sent for and they came to take me home. I had to give up the part in the Eugene O'Neill play and promise to stay quietly at home for the summer vacation, so as to come back refreshed and well again.

I think my mother realized that her behaviour at

the ferry terminal had been beyond even her usual standards of criticism, but, as so often, we never discussed it. Perhaps she'd been seasick on her long journey—the North Sea is notorious for it—maybe she was just tired, maybe I really did look a sight and she was truly shocked and disappointed. Whatever her excuse, her reaction had been unforgivable and I think she knew it.

She spent the summer taking good care of me, feeding me the kind of wonderful food I'd been raised on, but never too much of it. I think she sensed instinctively that I had been in a very dangerous place emotionally and physically and had been saved by an attentive tutor. She wasn't going to push me back there again.

I vowed never to diet again and never have, although I still have what the psychotherapist and author of *Fat Is a Feminist Issue*, Susie Orbach, would describe as an unhealthy relationship with food. My weight has always yo-yoed and my fatness or thinness has generally been an indication of my mental state. Bouts of unhappiness or anxiety send me straight to the fridge and, unfortunately, as you get older, it's not so easy to get the weight off.

December

It's beginning to feel like Christmas—tree bought, wreath on the door, cards arriving—and I'm in the shower, revelling in the warmth of the bathroom and the hot water before setting off on another cold and frosty trip across the Pennines with snow threatened. It's Saturday morning and I'm getting ready to make another trip to Mum and Dad with an ever-heavier heart. There is no more talk now. Mum lies, unmoving, in her bed. A tiny, thin figure with a continuous dose of morphine dripping into her hand. I can only make comparison with a victim of a concentration camp or a famine. Her face is skull-like, the thin skin stretched tight across her bones. It's a sight no loving relative should ever have to see.

Her breathing is shallow and laboured and the staff seem astonished that she is still alive. Dad says proudly that she's a fighter. Although all the odds are against it, I think he still harbours some little hope that somehow she will rally and survive. He tells me in a soft whisper that he never imagined she would go first. She was always so strong and so well. He can't believe she may be leaving him alone.

The only consolation for both me and my father, who spends every waking hour at her bedside, disconsolately stroking her fingers, her face and her still thick, white hair, is that this coma I assume is drug-induced means she suffers no more pain and has no fear. We can only trust she hears our muttered words of comfort and love.

Just when you think things can't get any worse, in my recent experience, they do. I've examined my

161

breasts once a week for as long as I can remember. It's rather more frequent than the recommended monthly check, but hypochondria is one of the results of living with a mother who had no truck with any complaint, real or imagined. She was so dismissive of any illness—'You don't get a day off school unless you're a stretcher case'—but at the same time made sure I was wearing a clean pair of knickers every day 'in case you need to be taken to hospital'—that it was almost inevitable that I would develop an acute case of self-obsession, if only as part of my constant attempts to get attention.

Working on *Woman's Hour* hasn't helped diminish my neurosis about my well-being. Indeed I've frequently been accused of being obsessed with 'down below'—a charge which I dismiss on account of the usefulness of the information we disseminate. In fact, one of my son's primary teachers once told me she thought that Charlie was too young at six to be given the proper terminology for these matters, seeing as the class had been asked to write a project about the royal family and Charlie had said the Queen was known as Elizabeth Vagina! (I don't agree. I think it's never too soon for children to have the right language. You just have to hope they use it in the correct context.) He was almost there: trying to translate ER into Elizabeth Regina!

Anyway, my work means I have quite a lot of knowledge when it comes to matters of health, but that doesn't make it any less dangerous a thing. I've had imaginary ovarian cancer, emphysema, depression—all kinds of ailments that we've discussed on the programme.

162

On one occasion I fetched up at the GP, sat down and she said, 'Well, where is it?'

'Where's what?' I asked, astonished.

'Your melanoma?'

As she examined the perfectly benign mole on my calf, which, when I thought about it, I'd had all my life, she explained she'd been listening to the programme the day before when we were talking about skin cancer and had guessed I'd be turning up in the none-too-distant future.

At least it meant that when it came to breast cancer—the scourge of modern womanhood, particularly those of us over the age of fifty— 80 per cent of the 44,000 diagnoses each year occur in the post-menopausal—I knew what I was looking for. So, here I am in the shower on a Saturday morning, fumbling around for lumps, thickening or changes to the quality of the skin— and there's nothing to worry about. But then I notice something odd on the right breast. The nipple is a little less prominent than usual and definitely different from the left one. It's a classic symptom.

As calmly as I can, I stroll, dripping, to the bedroom and ask him indoors to cop a feel. He can't feel any lumps either, but agrees the nipple looks a bit strange.

'Don't worry, it'll be nothing, it's just you and one of your turns.' I can see he's trying to reassure me, but he's become very pale and drawn.

I agree, also trying to be reassuring, as there's not much I can do about it until the GP opens again on Monday. But the feeling I have about this is different from all the imaginary illnesses of the past. I know in my guts that this time the news will not be good.

The knowledge that I'm a high-risk candidate has been niggling in my brain for some time now. There's no breast cancer in my family, so any genetic link is unlikely, but I'm fifty-six and age is the strongest risk factor after gender. I'm significantly overweight—the result of spending far too much time huddled over a computer, and my aversion to sport of all kinds doesn't help either. My favourite leisure activity is sitting around a dinner table with good friends and for too long I've treated dry white wine as a non-alcoholic beverage. It's now known that drinking alcohol can significantly increase your chances of getting breast cancer and, of course, unlike my mother, I had not abandoned the HRT when the warnings came out. My anxiety becomes overwhelming, but there's nothing to be done till Monday.

I see Mum and Dad. And say nothing about my worries. Dad has quite enough to concern him. I gaze at my mother, recalling the time she came for Christmas about ten years ago beset by the most appalling menopausal symptoms. She'd taken HRT for nearly twenty years—on my advice, after she had been threatened with a hysterectomy when she began her natural menopause—but she'd given it up only a few weeks before. She'd been to her doctor about her Parkinson's and been told there was some research showing a possible connection between HRT and breast cancer. The doctor suggested a review of her medication.

My mother went straight home and threw the pills away, hence the horrible hot flushes and exhaustion. As she explained to me, she was terrified of breast cancer; of the awful surgery it

164

would mean; how she couldn't bear to lose a breast or die slowly and painfully as it spread around her body. She'd seen it in friends. At least now she was so poorly she would never have to witness it in me.

By now I'm pretty scared too and kicking myself for having missed a routine mammogram for which I'd been called a year earlier. I'd looked at the date, saw it was a day on which I was working and, instead of phoning up right away and making a new appointment, I'd put it on to the unruly pile of papers I laughingly call my filing system and completely forgotten about it. If only I'd gone then, it might have been caught early. But then Mum would have had to know. She didn't need that worry.

I cry as I leave them there together: Mum still comatose in her bed, offering no response as I kiss her cool cheek and tell her how much I love her and that I will see her soon, Dad dozing in his chair alongside her, lulled by the now excessive heat in the old room she's been moved back to after the radiator was finally fixed. He rouses himself drowsily to kiss me goodbye, hug me and tell me not to worry. He'll be fine, he says, but could I come over again as soon as possible. He's finding his lonely vigil hard to bear. I promise I'll be back as quickly as I can, citing work, an excuse with which he always has sympathy, as my reason for it maybe being a few days. Still no mention of the fact that I have medical appointments to attend. I know I can't face the drive back here and the pain of it all again tomorrow. I just want to hibernate and wish it would all go away.

The GP's response is decisive and swift. I'm bundled off at once to the local testing centre. The mammogram is dodgy. I'm sent straight away for ultrasound and a needle biopsy, an unpleasant but not necessarily painful little procedure which I've likened to the Golden Shot. Right a bit, left a bit, fire! The needle shoots into the breast and brings out samples of cells from the lump. I'll know tomorrow whether we're dealing with a malignant tumour or not, but the look on the face of the radiographer says it all. He's seen it all before and offers no hope.

The following day the diagnosis is confirmed and I stand outside the breast care centre, clutching David's hand and screaming, shouting and swearing far more loudly than appears decent. I go through the what-ifs. Suppose I'd been thinner, suppose I hadn't taken HRT, suppose I'd never drunk alcohol, suppose I'd been more sporty? But then there seems no point in beating myself up and blaming myself. I have friends with cancer who're younger than me, who're skinny and abstemious gym fiends who had their children in their twenties and breastfed for months—friends who were statistically low risk. I guess none of us yet knows what causes the disease, but I do know that had I gone for that wretched mammogram when I was supposed to the tumour might have been less advanced and the treatment less vicious.

I'm also desperately worried about the future. I'm not just concerned about my mortality and the possible mutilation of my body, but about the impact it may have on the career I love and the family I adore. I'm a freelance journalist: what will be the consequences for the family finances if I have to take long periods off work? I'm the main breadwinner. Ed still has a way to go at vet school and Charlie is soon to go to university. How will they all manage if the strong mother on whom they've always depended can't hack it any more and it all falls apart? There's only one way to deal with such terror and panic and that's to force yourself to adopt an icy, practical calm. It's the image of the swan gliding across the water, but paddling like crazy underneath.

At home, I do what I know best and hit the phones, telling people at work who need to know and deciding, with the help of the charities with whom we've worked closely over the years, which surgeon I shall ask to take me on.

The kids come home when summoned. Ed, the vet, who has lots of medical knowledge, is calm, practical and reassuring—or maybe he too has perfected the talent I got from my mother for gliding across the water with only his serene bit showing. She might have been furious inside or have flown off the handle at any minor misdemeanour in private, but would always present a calm exterior in front of others. There was never any washing of her dirty linen in public. It's been a useful trick to employ whenever people have approached me with pity in their eyes ready to ask in hushed tones how I'm coping. My response of 'Fine, thank you,' generally stops them in their tracks and avoids any embarrassing fuss.

Charlie, whose emotions are always on his sleeve, is in bits. I take him to the next appointment with the doctor where he hears the discussions about treatment and the news that the prognosis appears to be good. I'm sure that including him and being so open about everything has alleviated his fear that 'cancer' means his mother's imminent demise.

I decide that the person I want to handle my treatment is the professor of surgical oncology at Manchester University, Nigel Bundred (now known fondly as Nige the Knife). He runs a specialist diagnostic clinic called the Nightingale Centre and operates at the Christie Hospital, internationally famous for its expertise in dealing with all forms of cancer. He agrees to take me on and David is driving me to see him when the phone rings.

It's the sister at the nursing home in Barnsley. My mother died at seven o'clock this morning. It's 20 December 2006 and I'm in a frightening world my mother no longer inhabits. I was not with her. Neither was my father. She died alone and I have never wanted her more.

I call my father and tell him we'll be there as soon as possible, but I have to keep an appointment first. What must he think? That something can be more important than his grief? But I can't miss this meeting. It feels as if every wasted second before surgery is another nail in my own coffin. I steel myself and, with David's support, somehow get through the morning.

There are more Golden Shot tests to determine the size and type of cancer we're dealing with. Nigel has the unenviable task of telling me it's a grade two, so not the most benign but not the most rampant of the three grades of breast cancer, but it is much larger than we'd at first thought—six centimetres across—and I shall need not a lumpectomy but a mastectomy, which will involve the removal of the entire breast and investigation of the lymph nodes in the armpit.

168

A new technique known as sentinel node removal will indicate whether or not the cancerous cells are trying to go walkabout to other parts of my body. It's no longer necessary to remove all the lymph nodes as an insurance policy as the sentinel node is the first to carry any rogue cells. If that is clear there'll be no need for radical removal and the attendant future problems with lymphoedema or swelling in the arm. Surgery is booked for the 28th, three days after Christmas. I thank Nigel, tell him I wish I were looking forward to seeing him again and fall into the car for the drive to Barnsley.

The journey seems interminable. The rain drives down, the traffic is terrible and I can still hardly grasp the idea that my mother is dead. Gone. She'll never shout at me or belittle me again. She'll never be there when I need her comfort. I'll never see the wicked grin that flashes across her face when something amuses her or when she's about to do something that will seem utterly out of character, but will make us all laugh.

She'll never again say, when the boys are driving me mad and I complain to her on the phone, 'Ah well, payback time!' There'll be no Christmas cake and mince pies which she made better than anyone. It was to avoid feelings like this that I tried to switch myself off all those years ago when she left me at Manchester airport to be with my father. I tried not to love. But I do.

I am urging David to drive faster. To dodge around the queues of traffic. To find other routes that might be less congested. I must get to Dad. And a shameful feeling of guilt creeps across me because I'm thinking, with an awful, infantile sense of triumph: he's mine now.

It is, of course, a fantasy on my part. He is so lost. I have no idea how to console him. He sits in his chair, silently weeping. I have hardly ever seen my father cry. When he talks it's to look back to when they met, when they married, when they were abroad together. I stay the night and spend the next day dealing with the leaden practicalities. He insists on going to the home to pay what remains of the bill. 'Neither a borrower nor a lender be' is still his mantra. Bills must be paid, even in extremis.

At the Town Hall, where everyone remembers Mum's years as receptionist, we register the death and Dad revels in sharing memories of what a bright, cheery workmate she had been. We meet the vicar and the undertaker and arrange the funeral service for 4 January—there's to be a longer than usual wait because Christmas falls in between. We discuss coffins, cremation and clothing. Dad leaves it to me to choose a smart suit for her to wear, but insists the coffin should not be open, nor be brought into the house.

I feel a little guilty that she will never come home again, but he is adamant that there should be no sentimental wake. He has no desire to see her lifeless body. He simply wants to remember her the way she was when their lives were full of joy and hope. It's his call and I comply with all his wishes. I find Mum's address book and sob over her neat, precise handwriting. I call her many friends and colleagues, giving them details of the arrangements for the funeral. When I leave Dad—he insists he wants me to go home to the family as he prefers to be in the house alone where he feels Mum is close—he thanks me for all I've done.

'I could not,' he whispers, 'have managed

without you.'

No amount of insistence on my part that he come to us for Christmas can persuade him to leave home. It isn't Christmas for him, he says, without her. He doesn't want us to come over on Christmas Day. He's not interested in cards or turkey or even his favourite Christmas pudding. He just wants to be on his own with the spirit of his wife.

I'm angry and jealous, thinking she will never cease, even in death, to be my rival for his attentions and ashamed that I'm being so selfish at such a sad time. It's as if I've hardly grown up. The boys on the other hand are terrific, behaving in a manner far beyond their years, taking turns to visit their grandfather and spending the days with him.

I know at some point I am going to have to tell him about my problem. On Boxing Day we all pile into the car, taking what's left of the turkey, a fresh Christmas pudding and rum for the white sauce. The boys listen to the stories about their grandparents that they've heard so many times before. He eats heartily, clearly glad that we are there, and at the end of the day we are sitting together in the kitchen and I broach the subject.

'Dad, I have to tell you something that I wish I could keep secret from you, but I can't. I've been diagnosed with breast cancer and in two days' time I have to go into hospital to have a mastectomy.'

For a moment his grey, grieving face falls in horror, but then the strong father I've always known and depended upon rises to the surface.

'Don't worry, love. I'm sure it'll be all right. The doctors can do marvellous things these days and I can manage on my own. You're not to worry about

171

me. You have enough on your plate.'

'I'll be there, Dad, I will be there for the funeral, no matter what.'

*　　　*　　　*

Between Mum's death and Christmas I pre-record a *Woman's Hour* programme for the New Year, knowing work is the only thing that will keep me sane and reassured by David and the boys that they will take care of my father. I decide to go public about the cancer. I've had an intimate relationship with the people who listen to *Woman's Hour* for nearly twenty years and I'm old enough to remember the days when cancer was so feared it was barely breathed about and only ever referred to as the C-word.

I even recall, some fifteen years ago, a trip to Dorchester to help with a fundraiser for the Breakthrough breast cancer charity when the women were berated in the street for wearing sashes across their chests with the word 'breast' written on them. It's been one of the great achievements of the women's movement and of programmes like *Woman's Hour* that we can now speak openly about cancers in the most intimate of places and have pressed for better diagnosis and treatment. It would have gone against every principle of openness I hold dear simply to slope off and not explain why.

*　　　*　　　*

It's now 28 December and I'm on my way to the hospital. I am, I have to confess, scared to death.

172

Nige the Knife has explained exactly what he will do while I'm in theatre. He'll cut across the breast horizontally, removing the nipple, all the breast material and the lymph node. He'll leave as much skin as possible and insert a tissue expander which will be pumped up with saline from time to time in the coming weeks and which will make it possible to have reconstruction at a later date.

It's reassuring to know that the surgeon is thinking about how I will look after it is all over. He apologizes that he can't make me look perfect naked—I reassure him that I haven't looked perfect naked for quite some time—but he promises that he can help me feel more confident in clothes. It also makes me think he might be telling the truth about the prognosis appearing good. Why would he waste his time and effort if he thinks I'm going to die?

It does, though, seem that losing a breast will be a painful and profoundly disturbing experience. To my astonishment, it is neither. The mind does marvellous things—helped along by generous doses of morphine—and I quickly convince myself that mutilation is infinitely preferable to cremation. There is some slight discomfort when I'm weaned off the drugs and given nothing more powerful than a few paracetamol, but it's all dispelled by the wonderful company I'm keeping. There is nothing more cheering than a whole bunch of women going through similar ghastly experiences and keeping their spirits up with filthy gallows humour. You would never imagine there was anything to giggle about in losing a breast or suffering the consequences of any of the gynaecological cancers, but I can honestly say the

173

only real pain I've suffered in the Christie is from laughing.

The nurses too are wonderfully cheery and supportive and one of my favourites suggests it might be a good idea to go and have a shower. Would I like her to come and help? I decline. If I'm going to have to look at it, I want to see it by myself for the first time. It's not pretty. It's a puny and pathetic little thing, but I'm neither shocked nor horrified by the sight of it. I am, though, curious and wonder what kind of strength it takes for a surgeon to take up the scalpel and slice into so potent a symbol of a woman's femininity. I guess you have to do some harm to save lives, and even this is definitely better than being dead.

*   *   *

It's 3 January. The drains which took waste blood away from the mastectomy site are out. David is waiting anxiously for Nigel to give him the go-ahead to take me home and then across the Pennines to the funeral tomorrow. I know he's hoping he'll say no, I'm not well enough to go. He's worried about the responsibility of taking care of me, but Nigel knows how important it is to me to be there for the funeral. He warns me to be careful, not to overdo things, and discharges me.

At home, I switch on the computer and write the address I'll give for my mother. I want it to be the best funeral oration ever, spoken with perfect articulation and resonance. I want her, if she can hear it, to be proud of me doing what I know she always thought I did best.

How does one get through the funeral of one's

mother? It passes in a deadened haze as I register little apart from my sons, smart and handsome in their black suits and ties, carrying their grandmother into the church as my father and I clutch each other. He and I sit close together as he trembles with grief and from somewhere I manage to find the strength to walk to the lectern and speak her praises loudly enough for my father to hear. It's not until I finish and touch her coffin as I pass that we both break down. It has been the most terrible day.

At the tea afterwards Dad seems to calm a little and begins, again, to look to the past and happier memories. He talks to the vicar about our relationship with the church where we'd just said goodbye to my mother. He and Mum were married there. I was christened there. The last time my father had walked down the aisle with me had been to give me away.

I met Brian Murray at the start of my second year at university. He was sitting in the Union, huddled over a pint and wrapped in a huge black coat that practically swamped him. He was alone and I'd gone in to meet friends who hadn't yet arrived. I was so drawn to a startlingly blue pair of quizzical eyes, I wandered over in his direction.

'Do you mind if I sit down here?'

'There's nobody else sitting there. It's up to you.'

There was an arrogance about him and a look of a little boy lost—a dead ringer for my favourite actor of the time, Robert Redford. I found him irresistible and from that point on, as my mother would have put it, quite shamelessly made all the running. It didn't take me long to move into the flat he occupied over a dry cleaning shop close to the university. We suffered terrible headaches for several months and smelled permanently of the fumes that constantly wafted up through the floorboards.

I kept my place in the hall of residence I'd moved into in case of a visit from my parents. It was just as well. Once they came back through Hull from a job Dad was doing in Czechoslovakia and it would not have done for them to find me 'living in sin' with a man. There was a panicked rush to transport clothes, make-up, books, toothbrush and toothpaste across the campus and by bus to the hall a couple of miles away, but the fury on my mother's part that would have been engendered had she found out Brian and I were living together would have been too much to bear.

The four of us went out to lunch—the first time they'd met Brian—and Mum seemed relatively content that I appeared to be 'settling down' with a young man with good prospects, architecture being more or less on a par with medicine or the law.

I can almost hear her talking to her friends in Barnsley and explaining in her posh telephone voice that 'Jen's going out with an architect and he's three years older than her, so she should be well looked after.'

I don't imagine she would have mentioned that he was a little shorter than she would have liked and came from a mining family from the County Durham pit village of Easington. She made it perfectly clear to me that she'd have preferred a six-footer from down south, but then, as she said, nobody's perfect, repeating her usual mantra that, as she'd always thought, I'd be lucky to find

176

someone as handsome and wonderful as Daddy. She really was the most awful snob.

Brian had another year to complete at college, then a year abroad and then his final year. It would coincide with my plans to spend a year in France perfecting my spoken language before my final year and graduation. Brian wanted to go to Israel, where some of the most exciting architects of the period were working. I too was intrigued by the country, drawn perhaps by the sense of my Jewish heritage which had never been mentioned since the visit to Auschwitz. All attempts to discover who in Dad's family was Jewish, when and from where were politely brushed aside.

I planned to spend the summer in Israèl, then go on to Paris. Dad was quite furious when I told him how I intended to manage, despite the fact that no mention was made of Brian and me travelling together. Dad's concern was that I seemed to be planning to abuse what he called my cursory Jewish inheritance. I'd explained that it would only be possible to obtain a work permit if I registered as a Jewish temporary resident and I would need to find a job for a few months just to live.

He pointed out that I really couldn't call myself Jewish because my connection came down the male, not the female line, and Jewishness can only be passed through the mother. It was one of the few occasions I recall when my father's views were completely at odds with something I wanted to do. He had always appeared more liberal than my mother, or perhaps he simply found it easier to leave all matters of discipline to her, but on this he would not be moved.

It didn't occur to me then, although it's perfectly

clear now that I have my own children to worry about, that he must have been desperately anxious about the political situation in the Middle East. The Six-day War had not long been over and there were frequent reports of bombings in the major cities. (In retrospect he was right to worry. I narrowly missed a bomb that exploded by the bus stop in the Tel Aviv station from which my bus had pulled away only seconds before.)

He never said he feared for my safety, but insisted instead that I would be taking work unfairly from a refugee who really needed it, and he refused any financial support for the trip. With the defiance and determination of youth, I ignored his warnings. He really had only himself to blame as it was my father, I now realize, who made me the independent, single-minded workaholic I became. While I always knew that if push ever came to shove and I was in serious trouble, financial or otherwise, he would be there to back me, I would never have begged him for help or approval.

Dad had always worked hard for anything he had and it always seemed to me the only way to be. I would never have wanted to feel dependent on a man as my mother had been for so long, to the extent that she'd been afraid to admit her wages in her part-time job were anything more than pin money. It never occurred to me that I should live the kind of life that women were supposed to lead. A man's life seemed far more attractive.

In order to earn some money for my year abroad I took the worst job I've ever had. Hull in those days was a thriving fishing port and the fish houses owned by Findus and Birds Eye were always

178

looking for workers. I was employed by Findus in the Pet Pack department. It meant putting coley that was not fit for human consumption into cardboard boxes ready for freezing. I rode there and back on my bicycle and the stench of the fish met you at least half a mile before you got there.

We wore plastic aprons and Wellington boots—the floor was awash with fishy-smelling water—and at the end of an eight-hour day I stank to high heaven. After I'd cycled home, Brian would meet me at the door to the flat and insist I stripped naked before coming upstairs, leaving the clothes on the doorstep ready for the next morning. A hot shower got rid of the worst of it.

Two things made the whole ghastly experience, which lasted only a month, worthwhile. My fellow workers were all women—only the bosses were men—and they were the fishwives whose husbands spent months away from home on the trawlers. It was their fate to spend their entire working lives in this terrible environment. They were responsible for contributing to the family finances, looking after the home and the children and they worried constantly about the safety of their men in the dangerous waters of the North Sea.

They worked long hours, were paid little and were expected to remain faithful and respectable while having no illusions about what their men might get up to with the 'ladies of the night' down at the docks. Yet they managed to retain a wicked sense of humour. Every hour we would spend a five-minute fag break in the ladies' toilet—the only official break we had was half an hour in the canteen for lunch—and it was then they told me their filthy jokes and teased me about the soft life I

179

was headed for. I learned more about feminist politics from them than I ever got from reading *The Female Eunuch*.

Then there was the wage packet. I earned the grand total of ten pounds a week, including overtime, but it acted on me like a drug. Financial independence. A reward for hard work I'd done myself. There's been nothing to match it, before or since. The flight to Israel was thirty pounds. After my four weeks' work and the sale of the most expensive books I owned—all three volumes of Glynne Wickham's *Early English Stages* brought the best reward—I had enough for the journey and plenty to keep me going for a week or so until I found more work. We were off.

*   *   *

Throughout the year I survived on the kindness of strangers. In Tel Aviv, through literally knocking on the doors of anything from cafés to travel agents, I was finally employed, just as my cash was about to run out, by Frank and Batya Meisler who ran a gallery for Frank's sculptures in the old town of Jaffa. My Hebrew was non-existent but most of the customers who came into the shop were American tourists, so language was generally not a problem. The Meislers treated Brian and me as family, even giving us a room to live in over the shop. We were sad to leave after three months.

Brian had decided to spend the rest of his year in Munich, working on plans for the new Olympic Stadium there, and I landed in Paris, again with just enough money to keep me in a hotel on the Left Bank for a couple of weeks, armed with a

180

copy of *Europe on Ten Dollars a Day*.

Again, I knocked fruitlessly on doors for a week or so in my search for work, ending up in near desperation in the darkness of a long winter's day ringing the doorbell of an English architect I'd found in the phone book. Theirs was a fancy address just off the Etoile in the eighth arrondissement and I didn't really expect they would have anything for an almost bilingual twenty-year-old with no discernible office skills.

Madeleine Keyte was Michael's French wife and ran the office of his one-man architectural band. She took me in, taught me how to cook steak and chips the French way, fed me, told me they couldn't employ me, but if I came back tomorrow she would teach me to type and help me find a job.

She was as good as her word and, on the first day of my typing lessons, came back from the shops triumphantly with a copy of the *New York Herald Tribune*. A travel company was advertising for French-speaking tour hostesses with English as a mother tongue to look after groups of American tourists. It was a bit 'Ah, it's Tuesday, this must be Paris' as their trip involved three- or four-day visits to the capitals of Europe. We picked them up from the airport, deposited them at their hotels, took them to Versailles and Fontainebleau and in the evening to the Lido and the Moulin Rouge and collected their handsome tips as we said goodbye at Orly. I have never had more disposable income.

I came home in the summer so bilingual I even dreamed in French and having learned the vital lesson that dogged determination will generally get you what you want and that you must never be afraid to ask, because eventually someone seems to

181

say yes. I had also written to my mother to tell her Brian had proposed during a visit to me in Paris and we intended to get married before the start of the new academic year.

In fact Brian had joined me in Paris for a couple of months to work with another architect he admired and we'd spent some time before our return to England hitch-hiking up through France from the south coast. Over dinner one night we had simply agreed that we couldn't face another year of a hole-in-the-corner relationship and living in fear of my mother finding out. We might as well marry. I'm not sure either of us really expected it to last for a lifetime.

We planned something small, but Mum went into nuptial overdrive. There were furious rows over Brian staying at the house during the preparations. My mother thought it indecent. I thought it simply practical, but rued the day I came down in my dressing gown—we were, of course, in

separate rooms—showing a mere hint of cleavage. Out came the accusations of sluttishness again and Brian was packed off to Grandma's.

I went along with the white dress and veil, persuading her at least to stay away from anything that resembled an iced cake and insisting on a simple dress and coat. The hair, now worn defiantly in the fashionable curtains she so hated, had to go up for the occasion and many hours were spent over the choice of her outfit as mother of the bride: a pink floppy hat and navy suit with a serious slit up the front to show off her wonderful legs. Even on the day that was supposed to be the happiest of my life she couldn't resist the temptation to compete.

Dad and I travelled to the church together with an unspoken anxiety hovering between us. I fretted because the whole idea of dressing up as a virgin for the day and being given away from the ownership of one man into the hands of another made me deeply uncomfortable. Dad worried because he didn't want to give me away into the protection of anyone but himself.

Mum of course was deliriously content. She didn't have to concern herself any more with the prospect of my disgracing her by getting into trouble. I would, she told me, get my degree, which would be something to fall back on after I had children, and I could settle down and be a good wife and mother. Job done.

I was all of twenty-one and had no intention of settling down to children or domestic servitude. I did, foolishly, take Brian's name of Murray and by the time I worked out how much I felt I'd lost my identity as Jenni Bailey because of it, it was too late to change back as I'd become known as Murray professionally. But I found out quickly how much I resented being somebody's wife. If the flat we lived in was a tip, no one seemed to consider it a reflection on Brian, only on me. If people came to dinner it appeared to be a given that I would have shopped, cooked and would then wash up. When the practice Brian eventually worked for held parties or social events, I was relegated to the status of wife and expected to chat about children and labour-saving devices with the other wives and secretaries. None of the architects was female. I hated it. The divorce was inevitable.

January

A new year begins and I am suffused with emotions that lurch this way and that. I hear my mother's voice at every turn and I find myself indulging in the truth of one of her favourite clichés: 'Love and hate—they're opposite sides of the same coin'.

There is unquestionable relief in the demise of the person who suffered so much, who haunted so many of my waking moments and could reduce me to a blubbering wreck with a single disapproving glance, but the depth of my grief surprises and shocks me. It's not a teary grief, but a bizarre sense of bewilderment. I am a motherless child, which seems an idiotic notion for a woman in middle age but is nonetheless a source of deep sadness. And I find myself looking back with guilty regret at all the times I ridiculed her, was cold towards her or told other people I hated her for her petit bourgeois small-mindedness. It's more than regret. It's shame. And it's too late to say I'm sorry.

Memories of specific incidents rush back. There was the time I picked her and my father up from St Pancras Station for a long weekend visit soon after we moved to London. As we drove towards Regent Street, she announced, 'Oh look, there's Garfunkel's.' I made her feel foolish at pretending knowledge of the capital by pointing out that Garfunkel's was a cheap chain of family restaurants that you could find all over town. I knew perfectly well that she was nervous of the city, of meeting friends of mine she saw as wildly sophisticated, and I should have been welcoming and sympathetic. There were numerous furious

187

rows, particularly at Christmas time, when she insisted on helping in the kitchen and spilled hot turkey fat all over herself and the floor. I knew that it was her fear of getting things wrong that made her hands shake. I never failed to respond angrily, 'For God's sake leave it alone, Mother, and go and sit down. I'll get on far better without you.' I should have cleaned up quietly and told her not to worry. Relentlessly, I hurt her feelings.

Just as I try to rationalize that there is no case for blame in the way she, as Philip Larkin put it so elegantly, 'fucked me up', explaining to myself that she was a woman of her time with only what she believed to be my best interests at heart, I endeavour to let myself off the hook of being an ungrateful child. I loved her and I hated her and I miss her so much. I even find myself picking up the phone to talk to her, forgetting for a moment that I won't hear that polite telephone voice say, 'Barnsley 291188', and then switch to a delighted 'Hello, love' when she realizes it's me.

Any dreams I might have had about becoming the focus of my father's undivided attention are quickly dispelled. He has disappeared into his own world of overwhelming grief and is unable to respond to any invitations to come and stay with us. He insists that he is most content at home where he feels close to Mum and instructs his lovely cleaner, Chris, to put nothing away that fulfils his fantasy that my mother is still present. Her underwear and stockings are still on a chair in the bedroom. There are curlers by her side of the bed. Her perfumes and potions litter the bathroom and her magazines and cookery books are still scattered around the sitting room.

He has ceased to take any interest in his own appearance. I suspect he was always a bit of a slob at heart, much happier in a pair of old jeans and a sweater than, as he put it, 'dressed up like a dog's dinner', but he made the effort for my mother's sake—or perhaps under her instruction. Now, when I arrive, I find myself taking on her bullying role.

He's often asleep when I get there, regardless of the time of day, his head slumped on the kitchen table. He hasn't done the dishes or been out for his paper—a ritual he's never missed in his life—but responds like the grinningly obedient husband he always was when I bark instructions for him to have a shower and shave and put on some clean and decent clothes before I'm prepared to take him out to lunch. He tells me I sound just like her. It seems to give him comfort.

As far as my little problem goes, it's obvious he can hardly bear to think about it. He asks me on each visit whether or not the doctors are happy with my progress, I reply that they are very happy, that the prognosis appears to be good and then the matter is closed. I really can't expect any more from him. He's endured quite enough illness and death in recent months, and coping with the worries of a daughter with cancer is quite beyond him. In many ways it's good for me too. My time is filled with concern for him and with devising ways of reminding him that he is surrounded by a family that cares for him and that is full of life and hope.

I don't have work, my usual distraction at times of crisis, to sustain me, as I've decided to take a little time off to recover from the op and the anaesthetic, but things are hectic enough with frequent trips across to Barnsley and regular appointments with Nige the Knife in Manchester to check the mastectomy site for healing and any signs of infection. He also drains away any gunk that still remains in there and inserts a needle into the port which gives access to the tissue expander, filling it week by week with the liquid that will keep what's left of the skin and muscle stretched, ready for reconstruction. He warns me never to allow anyone near the site with a needle or a pin, explaining how one patient during one of these procedures saw a different doctor who managed to pierce the expander and let all the liquid out. As if I would! I trust no one but him anywhere near it.

I find myself rather looking forward to these encounters and realize that I'm doing what every other woman in this situation I've spoken to has said happened to her. I'm falling in love with my surgeon. It makes no sense at all to be so drawn to the man whose scalpel has created such physical havoc, but there's an intimacy in the relationship that can't be denied. Nor can I explain to myself why, contrary to any other professional relationship I have had—dentist, accountant, GP, gynaecologist, where I have always looked for the services of a woman—for this, I actively sought a man. Can it be that even I, somewhere in the depths of my conditioning, actually believe that a man will somehow do a better job?

He's averagely attractive, charming, quite funny, snappily dressed and we share a passion for the crime novels of Tess Gerritsen (weird that, as the medical practitioners in her books are generally up to anything but good) but it's his absolute confidence in his skill and his ability to save my life

190

that, I think, makes him so alluring. Or maybe it's just that ever since *Emergency Ward 10*, through *Dr Kildare*, *Casualty*, *ER* and *Holby City*, I've been a devoted fan of the hospital drama and an absolute sucker for a God-like surgeon in a smart suit!

It's Mills and Boon writ large and, of course, safe as houses. He pays me close professional attention but there's no danger in it. It's hard to think of anyone finding me attractive in this condition anyway, least of all the man who's seen me flat out on the operating table—not, I suspect, a pretty sight.

David, who does his utmost to reassure me at every turn that he still considers me the sexiest woman on the planet, does not share my fascination with the man. I guess it's unsurprising that, when two alpha males meet and one has just removed the breast of the other's mate, they don't take to each other. David generally drives me to the clinic but prefers to wait outside in the car. So I know on this visit that something is terribly wrong when Nigel seems edgy, completely devoid of his usual unswerving confidence, and asks me if I'm alone. It's a sure sign he's about to deliver very bad news.

'No,' I say, 'David's here. He's in the car outside, learning his lines for the village panto.' What trivial nonsense one blurts out during times of extreme stress.

'I have the results of the post-operative tests on the tumour and it might be better if I explain everything to you both. It'll be easier for you to take it in and remember if I've told it to the two of you.' I'm slightly insulted that he thinks someone as well informed and calm as me can't take in bad

191

news by herself, but I call David on his mobile and he's there in a flash, his face contorted with anxiety.

Nigel confirms that the tumour had indeed been six centimetres across, was an oestrogen and progestogen receptor, grade two—all of which we'd expected. And then the bad news he's been putting off delivering. There had been evidence of cancer cells in the sentinel node—he'd removed that lymph node and four around it—and although there was no sign in any of the others, it was apparent that the cancer had been making its first attempts to take a trip to other parts of my body.

Then the statistics. After the extensive surgery I've had so far and with adjuvant therapy which would mean taking anti-oestrogen pills for five years, I will have around a 60 per cent chance of surviving for the next five years and possibly beyond. With chemotherapy that goes up to 75 per cent. It is, as the dread cliché goes, a no-brainer.

David, a mathematician and engineer, mutters darkly about lies, damned lies and statistics while I sit stunned at the thought that I will have to undergo a kind of treatment the very prospect of which fills everyone with horror, and might even then have only another five years to live. All my confident examples of women with much more rampant tumours who've lived for twenty years or more slide straight out of my head. Five years feels like no time at all.

I'm to go and see Dr Andrew Wardley immediately. I know the name. He's a medical oncologist who stuck his neck out during the Herceptin scandal. When NICE, the body responsible for sanctioning cost-effective

192

treatments on the NHS, failed to license Herceptin for women with a relatively rare but aggressive form of breast cancer called HER2, he did the unusual thing for a senior doctor and spoke out in support of the drug and the women whose lives might be saved by it. He was convinced of its efficacy, based on the results of trials in America, and talked to the papers and to *Woman's Hour* about it. It's believed his words had a positive impact and the government eventually agreed to fund Herceptin treatment for women who needed it. One of the good guys then.

I meet him at the Christie Hospital. He seems impossibly young to be a leading consultant in his field, which is sort of reassuring. A testament to his brilliance. I'm to receive four doses of a drug called Epirubicin which will be delivered intravenously every three weeks, then I'll move on to a combination therapy known as CMF. There'll be eight doses of that. A hit, then another the following week, then a three-week break and then the same cycle again. The drugs will attack the cancer cells, but will also do their worst with healthy cells. My blood will be tested on each visit and, if the white cell count is low, the treatment will be put off for another week. I work out quickly that this won't be over until at least the end of July. It feels like a life sentence.

I hit the internet as soon as I get home and only learn what I knew already. I will lose my hair, I'll suffer nausea, a depleted immune system making me prone to infection (which, one well-regarded website warns, can be fatal), tiredness, mouth ulcers, possible damage to the nails or nerves, headaches, aching muscles, pain passing urine and

193

diarrhoea. Death, I begin to ponder, may be a welcome release.

I have to explain to Dad that I may not be well enough for a little while to come over as often as I have been doing. I pop round to see his watchful neighbours, Frank and Pat, to tell them what's happening. Pat is retired now, but used to be a nurse. She knows exactly what I'm to face and reassures me that they will continue to keep a close eye on Dad and help with his shopping for food as they've been doing for some months now. I am again astonished at the community spirit that exists in the little close of bungalows my parents have inhabited for thirty-five years.

I'm more used to London, where it can take years to meet a neighbour, or the remote countryside where houses are so far apart it would be impossible to keep tabs on someone in trouble. I've rather liked the anonymity and self-reliance of the way I've lived my own life, and always found my parents' environment something of an intrusive goldfish bowl where people could actually see into each other's windows. Now I see the benefits of close contact and the old-fashioned way of being a good neighbour.

Dad hobbles to my car—his knee and back are causing him a lot of pain, both the result of long-ago industrial injuries—and looks askance at my convertible BMW. He does this every time I take him out, as if he's never seen it before. I open the door for him. The handle is stiff and the door is heavy. I take his stick as he slowly and painfully eases himself into the low-slung seat. I strap him in—his fingers can no longer cope easily with safety belts—and we roar off up the road. He

194

giggles delightedly at the power and speed.

'It's bloody difficult getting in and out, but it's like being in a plane taking off once we get going. I never thought a daughter of mine would have a car like this—least of all be able to drive one.' Grrr! Every time the same sceptical tone—and I know a son's ownership of such a car would have passed entirely without comment.

Our usual haunt for a meal out is the pub in the nearby village of Worsborough. It was a favourite of Mum's for Sunday lunch and therefore a place where Dad feels comfortable. His memory slips back frequently to fine Yorkshire puddings and treacle sponges they've consumed there over the years. The quality is not what it was, but it passes and Dad eats heartily. It's good to see him enjoying his food. He's lost a lot of weight and I suspect he barely feeds himself when I'm not there to supervise.

The chemotherapy question is dealt with quickly and without fuss or bother. My father is of the generation that has an instinctive dislike of doctors—memories of the years before the NHS when a family had to weigh up whether or not they could afford the fees—but an absolute trust in their ability to perform miracles. Which seems odd considering he's just experienced at such close quarters their complete impotence in the face of a wasting disease such as Parkinson's. He's quite sure that what the doctor has suggested is 'all for the best' and 'they can do wonders nowadays'.

His real worry is the one I inherited from his profound Protestant work ethic. How am I going to survive and support the family if I can't get on with my job? I reassure him that the BBC is, for now at

195

least, being as supportive as an employer can be.

'I've always been proud, you know, of the way you've managed to stand on your own two feet. I wouldn't want you having to go on the dole or anything like that. You only ever did that once and I wasn't best pleased about it.'

I remind him that the once was in the vacation after I'd married Brian. His terms at the School of Architecture were longer than mine and we had very few worldly goods with which to endow each other. Friends suggested I should pop down the Department of Health and Social Security as it was called then (known to us as the Department of Stealth and Total Obscurity) and claim benefit for the rest of my holiday until term started and the grant came in.

It was one of the more humiliating and infuriating experiences of my life. I queued up for an age, filled out the relevant form and then sat in front of a woman clearly trained to be as obnoxious as possible.

'I can't give you any benefit,' she said, bluntly.

'Why not?' I asked.

'It says here you're married.'

'That's right,' I explained, 'but he's a student and I don't have any money coming in and there's not enough time to get a job before my own university term starts, so it's only for a couple of weeks.'

'No,' she sighed, 'I don't think you understand. You see, you're married. You have a husband and he's legally bound to keep you.'

It was one of those moments when the feminist light bulb shone brightly and undoubtedly contributed to my long-held suspicion of the

196

marital state. Being a kept woman was the last of my ambitions. I remind Dad I never did actually get any money from the state and bore him yet again with the impact the episode had on my thinking and the development of my feminist politics.

'Oh yes, I forgot. You and your funny newfangled ideas!'

We move on to safer territory—how he's going to manage if I am too ill to keep popping over to see him as regularly as I have done.

'I'll be all right, love. You concentrate on getting better. I get the paper again now and I try to do the *Daily Mail* crossword, but I never finish it—not like when your mum and I used to do it together. Pat and Frank pop in a lot for a chat and I've got the telly and the radio. I don't listen much, though, when you're not on it, there doesn't seem much point.'

While Mum always worried about how I would combine work and family life—never quite sure that it was right for a woman to go out to work when she had a husband and a home to look after—Dad was an unequivocal supporter of my workaholic tendencies and was always thrilled to hear again the story of how I wangled my way into the BBC.

I applied during the final year at university through the conventional route. There were two graduate training courses at the time. The news division took on three or four trainee journalists each year. I was advised by the careers department that there was no point even applying, despite my extensive experience of writing for the school magazine and working in the university's TV and

197

radio studios, and my thoroughgoing knowledge of the politics of the Middle East after my travels in Israel. You didn't stand a chance, they said, unless you'd got an Oxbridge First and were male.

They were, though, occasionally taking women for the studio managers' course. It would involve knowing how to cut tape, wire up a studio, balance sound and keep your head when all around were losing theirs in the heat of a live broadcast. It wasn't what I wanted, but it was a way in. I applied and got an interview.

What I didn't know about the way a microphone worked when I got to Portland Place for the first time was really not worth knowing, although I was pretty shaky on wiring and plugging systems, despite my father's attempts to teach me. I'm still so scientifically incompetent I find it astonishing that my voice can go into a mike in London or Manchester and be picked up virtually anywhere in the world, but I blagged my way confidently through the interview, feeling I was doing pretty well, until the final question.

'What is the Prime Minister doing today?'

I hadn't a clue. I'd spent the entire train journey mugging up on Broadcasting for Beginners and had forgotten the one crucial thing—read the papers!

'We do require all our employees at the BBC to be au fait with current events,' said the interviewer and I knew I'd blown it. Back to the drawing board.

With the poor typing skills I'd learned in Paris I thought I might just get away with some sort of office work and went along to the Brook Street Bureau employment agency. I had no shorthand, my typing was slow and wildly inaccurate and filing

198

has never been a strong point.

'I'm really not sure I can send you to an office,' said the interviewer, 'but you have great personal skills and we are looking for an interviewer to work here. Would you be interested?'

Wouldn't I just! The pay was good, the training a doddle and I'd have access to information about any more interesting work that came in. My rise within the company was rapid. Within weeks I was managing the Bristol branch, all the while scouring the jobs, temp and permanent, to see if there was anything more suitable to my skills and ambitions.

Eventually it came. HTV were looking for a temporary copy taker in the newsroom. It would involve typing up any stories that came in from stringers or the emergency services and passing them on to the journalists. It was the lowliest job in any newsroom, but I knew at once it would be a start. I sent myself for the two-week assignment, arguing I had no one else on my books who was free or suitable.

The atmosphere was thrilling. I felt I was at the centre of my small universe. The journalists didn't seem to mind that my typing was far from perfect—they managed to read the information I passed to them and it was great fun hearing from the police, ambulance and fire services about crimes and disasters before anyone else got the news. It was the perfect environment for an inveterate nosy parker. I loved it.

Halfway through the assignment my fellow copy taker mentioned that she'd been listening to local radio that morning and they had put out an advert for a copy taker. It would be a permanent position. She thought I was doing rather well at it and could sell myself on the experience I'd gained at HTV. The news editor agreed to give me a reference, so I sent off an application.

I'd walked past the BBC in Bristol so many times and was determined to do one of two things. I'd either get a place at the Bristol Old Vic Theatre School to study on their postgraduate acting course or get a job at the BBC. The BBC was favourite as I knew in my heart that I didn't have the talent to compete with the greats on the stage. But I knew I could be a broadcaster, which would combine my interest in journalism with my passion for showing off and performing.

I was sick with nerves when I went to the interview, but there are times in life when everything comes together and this was one of them. The manager of the station was a man called David Waine, who'd already employed Kate Adie—she was then the farming producer—and Michael Buerk, who was one of the journalists. David was young and energetic and only too aware that the world in the early seventies was changing dramatically and that women would be part of broadcasting's future.

I joined in 1973. There were no female newsreaders on television and it would not be until the following year that Sheila Tracey became the first female newsreader on the radio. Susannah Simons, who did manage to get through the studio manager interview I failed so miserably and had her training in the early seventies, told me that the course consisted of all the technological work for which I was so well prepared and trainees were also tested for their abilities as announcers. The women were invariably given a B grade or lower.

Only those with A grades were considered suitable microphone material. Just as well I flunked it really. I'd have been permanently blazing at such open discrimination.

It was Susannah who told me that when she began at the BBC, only a couple of years before me, women were not allowed to wear trousers unless they worked in the Arabic service. She decided to flout the rules and bought herself a trendy trouser suit—bell bottoms and jerkin—but was confronted in the lift by her line manager, who told her she was in breach of her contractual obligations. With enviable quick thinking, she took off the pants. The miniskirt, it seemed, was more than acceptable to him!

Local radio in the early seventies was a relatively new and reasonably well-resourced arm of broadcasting, although the staff was small and there was a lot of air time to fill. I learned quickly that the way to get on was to volunteer for everything when they were short of someone to do a particular job. 'I can do that' became my mantra. It was also necessary to be just bad enough at the job you'd been employed to do, while charming the pants off everyone in charge, to climb the greasy pole. From copy taker with poor typing, I was promoted to newsroom secretary.

After a disastrous incident when I managed to send letters intended for Labour candidates in an election to the Tories and vice versa, I had to be promoted again to a position in which neither typing nor filing nor the addressing of envelopes would be required. I became a station assistant, responsible for studio management duties and some broadcasting. I'm not sure whether it was my

talent in front of the microphone or inadequacies in the technical department that got me the job as producer and presenter of the 9 a.m. to 12 magazine programme, but I had it within eighteen months.

I know it always saddened my father that he missed out on so much of my childhood because of his work commitments. He never attended a parents' evening, didn't see the school play and it was always my mother who took me to my weekly elocution lessons and sat in the audience while I stood on stage and recited poetry at any number of local music festivals. His pride in any achievement of mine was always second-hand. He would gaze admiringly at any certificate, medal or trophy I brought home and say how much he wished he could have been there to see me win it. I never resented his absence, nor thought to question it. It was simply a given. Daddies went out to work early in the morning, came home late in the evening and handed their pay every Friday to the matriarch of the household, who managed the bills, the insurance, the shopping, cleaning, childcare and cooking in order to enable the patriarch to carry out his role as breadwinner, untrammelled by any trivial concerns.

Any time my father and I had together was restricted to sleepy kisses good night as he rushed up to my room when he got home from work. Bedtime was non-negotiable from my mother's point of view. I had to be in bed at seven until my teens and no amount of begging to stay up to see Daddy when he got home would sway her from what she thought was right. There must have been many occasions when I was so fast asleep I was completely unaware of his presence.

All my memories of magical moments with my dad centre on the holidays we spent together and those early mornings picking up the paper before waking Mum; occasional Saturday nights out at a restaurant—designed, as my mother explained, to teach me how to behave properly at table in public—and the sickeningly exciting anticipation when he came home from a trip abroad, tanned, handsome and loaded with presents. I still have the vast collection of dolls he brought me from all over the world, silver bracelets from India and amber from Poland.

He also brought home records. Perry Como's 'Catch A Falling Star', Tommy Steele's 'Little White Bull', Cat Stevens's 'Jennifer Juniper' (I couldn't believe someone had written a song with my name in it!), Addinsell's *Warsaw Concerto* and an LP of Strauss waltzes. He always found a little time on a Sunday morning, between breakfast and tending his beloved garden before lunch, to put the Strauss on the record player and waltz me around the sitting room.

I stood on his feet. He was a terrible dancer with no sense of rhythm and counted every step—'one two three, one two three'—but it was a father's duty, he said, to teach his daughter how to dance so that she could always wow young men on the dance floor when she grew up. I'm not sure his inept shuffling stood me in any sort of stead, but I loved being in his arms.

Perhaps it's true, as my mother would have put it, that 'absence makes the heart grow fonder'. I adored this rather distant figure in my life and don't remember ever feeling angry with him. I missed him terribly when he was away, but there was never tension between us as there was with my mother and on the whole I was always on my best behaviour when he was around.

But three was always a crowd—to use another of my mother's favourite clichés—and she usually managed to spoil our intimate moments together, calling from the kitchen for me to go and help with the cooking or do the dishes.

'The sign of a good, efficient cook is that her kitchen always looks immaculate even during the cooking process, which means washing up as you go,' she'd say. No wonder I became irritated with her and lavished affection on him. To her, a dutiful daughter was one who did her jobs in the home and knew her place—and it was not at her father's side.

It never occurred to me as a child that this traditional way of running a household might have caused my father untold misery. It was only as I got older that I would see the sadness in his eyes when he spoke about the time he and his friend Eric had tried to set up their own electrical business. From

204

trips we took together around Barnsley, it seemed there wasn't a house or a public building they hadn't been responsible for wiring.

But all this labour—including the paperwork that had to be carried out at home—had been done during evenings and weekends. Neither of them ever had the courage to give up their day jobs and, of course, the business folded when Dad was offered work which meant travelling around the country or abroad. It's only now I realize what a miserable and lonely time he must have had, staying in boarding houses or bachelor flats and missing the comfort of home. It was time he would have preferred to spend as a hands-on dad, but such was his ambition—and that of my mother—to rise in the world and to ensure his family had only the best of everything, he buried himself in his labours. He never quite admitted out loud to wishing he'd spent more time with his family, but an air of regret always hung around him.

During those early years of mine as a journalist and broadcaster, when I was in my mid-twenties and he was still only in his late forties, he must have decided that he was going to put right some of the mistakes he felt he'd made in our relationship. When the job in Turkey was completed, he asked to work in England for a while. The company was swayed by his claim that there were medical reasons for his wanting to be here for a bit.

He'd contracted a severe form of dysentery in India which had recurred a couple of times in Turkey and he felt his body needed a chance to recover from working in conditions of extreme heat. He called me (by now my mother had conceded that having a telephone was perhaps useful and not simply a potential harbinger of doom) and announced with delight that he'd managed to fix up a contract in Avonmouth. I was in Bristol. He'd be a mere half-hour away.

He would never have presumed to ask to stay with me. Having now understood that the degree of tension between my mother and me could be partly put down to the fact that two females and one male are unlikely ever to feel entirely at ease in one household, I also realize that Dad was never quite comfortable with me and any of the men in my life. He would bristle at the slightest hint of criticism of me that Brian might utter and his eyes would harden if he felt I was being put upon domestically. It was me he wanted to spend time with, not me and Brian.

The company, he explained, had found him a room near the site, but perhaps we could meet up from time to time? He especially wanted to come and watch me at work. I was in seventh heaven. During his first few visits to the station, I was responsible for opening up Radio Bristol at five thirty in the morning, presenting the first half-hour of records and chat and then handing over to the presenter of the morning news and current affairs programme. It was then my job to sit on the other side of the glass from the studio and handle the technical aspects of the programme—editing and playing in tapes and opening and closing microphones as required.

Dad would be there on the dot of five twenty-five and not leave until eight, which just gave him time to get to his own work. He would sit in the control room watching me broadcast, then, as I took over the technical side of things, conducting wry conversations with Dave, the station engineer. I was, they agreed, something of a jinx when it came to anything electrical. Things have always broken down in my presence. I argued that they should be grateful; it was people like me who kept people like them in business. The banter was invariably good-humoured and I don't remember my father ever uttering a critical word about my performance. He made me feel confident and clever.

He was not in Avonmouth for long after I got my promotion to producer/presenter and from then on it became much more difficult for him to find the time to come to the studio. Our programme went on the air at nine and finished at twelve, so if he was to come and watch he had to find an excuse to take some time off from his own job.

The programme was called *Compass* and, together with a colleague called David Eggleston, I'd taken over from a terrific old broadcaster called Dougie Chalmers, my professional dad. Dougie left local radio to move to London and join the BBC's radio training unit, then housed in what is now the Langham Hotel in Portland Place, but before he took on the role full time he'd spent many hours coaching me and nurturing whatever talent he'd spotted in me. It was he who gave me the best piece of advice about broadcasting I've ever had.

'Jenni,' he said, 'just before you open the mike or someone opens it for you, smile. The audience will hear it.' I still remember those words every day.

Sadly, David Eggleston and I didn't work together for very long. He married during the first few months of our partnership and went to Africa on honeymoon. We learned of his death early. It came through to the newsroom's rip 'n' read direct from Victoria Falls: 'Local radio man dies in tragic accident.' He'd been taking photographs at the falls and had stepped back to get a better shot. He fell over the edge and died instantly.

His death was the first ever to touch me closely. His funeral was also the first I ever attended and I will never forget the pale, haunted face of his young widow. It made me determined always to get the best out of life every day because it could end so suddenly. It also made me quite cautious about taking physical risks and, as my own children have grown up and embarked on adventurous journeys abroad, a very nervous parent. I know now why my mother so feared the telephone as a potential harbinger of doom.

David's place was taken by Geoffrey James, a charming, funny and creative companion with whom to spend long working days. Together we gave the programme a little more edge than it had before. We kept the service items such as the daily swap shop and achieved some spectacular successes on the social side of things. I've always seen local radio as the equivalent of a village shop or a Roman forum—a place where people can meet and converse with each other in an age where the old methods of meeting your neighbours physically in such central venues as a market place or church have largely disappeared.

We were responsible for setting up one of the first mother-and-toddler groups in Yate, a new

208

suburb built outside Bristol and teeming with newly arrived young families who had no means of getting to know each other. One young woman called the programme to say how lonely and isolated she felt and by the end of the broadcast there were dozens of others all in the same boat and ready to create some form of network.

We also set up a local weekly *Any Questions*, where people would phone in to discuss the issues of the day with a panel of local dignitaries. The then Bishop of Bath and Wells gave us one of the most heart-stopping moments of my broadcasting career. He arrived on time to take part as a panel member and had the most debilitating stammer I've ever heard. I looked at Geoffrey despairingly and he looked at me in fury. Each of us thought the other had checked out the bishop on the phone. In fact, we'd both spoken to his secretary. There was nothing to be done. We couldn't turn him away at such late notice.

I was presenting that morning—Geoffrey and I took turns to produce or present—and I did my best to avoid throwing a question to the somewhat puzzled-looking bishop. Eventually he chipped in and spoke with absolute clarity and articulacy. In the coffee break after the phone-in—we had fifteen minutes each day when we took *Waggoners Walk* from the network—the bishop grinned and, stuttering, explained that he had trained himself to overcome his impediment when speaking in public. Amazing!

Dad was determined to be around the day we had Tony Benn. Every Monday morning, before they had to be back in London for the start of the parliamentary week, we held an MP's 'surgery of the air'. Each of the region's MPs in turn would spend the first hour taking questions from constituents. For my Conservative-voting father, Benn was the devil incarnate. For me, then as left wing as it was possible to be without joining the Communist Party, he was the next best thing to God.

My father was patient with my political ranting, often quoting Denis Healey who said something to the effect that 'If you're not a communist in your twenties, you are heartless. If you're still a communist in your forties, you're an idiot.' And, of course, both men were right. My political views have been toned down with age.

On the morning of the broadcast Dad arrived bright and early, sipping coffee and muttering about 'the inverted snobbery of the man—who'd give up the title Viscount Stansgate to be mere Tony Benn? The man's mad.'

I ordered him to sit quietly in the corner and make no comment. I didn't want my broadcast messed up by any animosity. He behaved himself perfectly and said nothing about Benn's production of his own flask of tea and his pipe in the few moments before we began—although he did later say he saw the drinking of tea in the morning as a mark of Benn's adoption of working-class credentials to which he had no right. He would not accept that maybe the man just liked tea made in a certain way, which was why he brought his own.

I was dreadfully nervous. I'd never before interviewed someone who'd risen as high as the cabinet and, while I admired Benn's politics and erudition hugely, I knew it was my job to show no

210

bias. I needed to challenge his opinions on behalf of the listeners. I opened the programme with a long history of his credentials, found him utterly charming and delightful with the listeners who called in and at the end of the hour felt immensely grateful when he ended an answer in perfect time, giving me the fifteen seconds I needed to thank him, identify the station and introduce the news.

He came into the control room for another cup of tea before he left and I now felt safe to introduce him to my dad.

'You must be very proud of your daughter,' Benn said. 'She's doing a very good job. Although,' and he laughed, 'I did think her introduction of me sounded a little like an obituary.'

Dad had the good manners to wait till he'd left the building to say, 'If only!'

Throughout my broadcasting career my father was my greatest fan. He made trips to visit whatever studio I was working in, lauded me for every tricky question I put to a difficult interviewee and I would occasionally overhear him showing off to friends about the 'hard time' I'd given to men and women in politics.

During the years before his retirement and after I'd become the presenter of *Woman's Hour*, he would often call to tell me he'd been late for a meeting because he couldn't leave the car until a particularly gripping item had finished. This was in the days when the programme was broadcast at two in the afternoon.

'What excuse did you make?' I would ask.

'Oh, I just told them I was listening to *Woman's Hour*. They think I'm weird! It's good. It scares them and puts them on the wrong foot.'

Perhaps it was his experience as the youngest of a large family that taught him to work at making an impression. Maybe it was all those years of living with me and my mother—an exercise in peacekeeping that would have qualified him to run the United Nations. It could have been a career as a foreign contract engineer—swooping in to sort out problems in multi-million-pound developments and juggling the quirks of people from vastly varied cultures. Whatever the source of his talent, he was ever the wise tactician.

February

Oh, what horrors. More than a month has passed since Nigel delivered the news about the diagnosis and I'm back in his consulting room, top and bra off, an NHS cape, made of a material not unlike a J-cloth and open down the front, draped around my shoulders. Happily the room is warm and I'd prefer to be without the ridiculous cape—any modesty has long been abandoned—but the nurses have great concern for form and respectability so I wear it for their sakes. I'm due another top-up to the tissue expander.

First he begins his examination and, again, his face darkens with alarm. He's scrutinized his handiwork closely and stroked what's left of what used to be my right breast with infinite tenderness. It reminds me of myself in my fanatical horse-riding days, learning gently to skim my hand over an animal's legs, feeling for heat—a sure sign of lameness or infection. I know he's felt the slightly raised temperature and noticed a hint of reddening in the skin.

'I'm so sorry,' he says, 'there is an infection here. We must hit it hard and speedily. Chemotherapy starts this week, doesn't it, and it could be dangerous to begin it with an infection.'

He can't explain how it's come about a month after the surgery and when everything seemed to have gone so well, but he prescribes powerful antibiotics in the form of tablets which might well have been suited to a horse. They're enormous and they make me violently sick.

Another antibiotic is prescribed. This time it's to be delivered by injection and needs to be done

215

every day. Which is unfortunate, because I've just agreed to go back to work. I'm to do three days a week when I feel up to it. Not working Monday or Friday will give me time to catch my breath over a long weekend and will also mean I can travel to London on a Monday rather than a Sunday night. It seems to be generally agreed that abandoning the horrible, overcrowded and invariably 'delayed due to engineering works' Sunday evening trains is a good policy for someone with a greatly diminished immune system—the inevitable consequence of the chemotherapy treatment.

I am as angry as ever with the rail system in Britain. Other countries seem able to run trains at reasonable prices at times when ordinary people need to travel. Our network is entirely geared to the business traveller. The fares are ludicrously expensive and at the weekends or on public holidays, when families, friends and lovers simply want to spend time together, there are delays and hardly any hope of finding a seat unless you board at the station where the journey begins. Even having a booking makes little difference when you're faced with marauding Manchester United fans, often the worse for drink after a Sunday game, who have no regard for the fact that you had pre-booked the seat they've occupied.

I remember once travelling just before the Christmas holiday. My son Charlie had been in London with me—we'd been shopping together—and we had seats booked at Euston. The train filled quickly. There were people sitting in the spaces between the carriages and along the aisles. We broke down at Stoke-on-Trent with no information about when we might set off again.

The guard disappeared into his cubby hole and refused to face the dozens of irate passengers who fought their way through the crowds towards the end of the train where he hid. One girl sobbed that her boyfriend might not wait at the station. Another cried that she was attending her grandmother's funeral and might miss it. A young man was engaged in a furious mobile phone conversation with his ex-wife. It was clear that if he didn't arrive at the agreed time to pick up his son, a former spouse still stinging from an acrimonious divorce would take great pleasure in denying him access to the boy. Why, I wondered, have we so failed to see a cheap and efficient system of public transport as a vital social service?

Despite the infection and the inadequacies of the railways, I don't want to put off my return. I know I will go quite bonkers if I'm forced to stay home with nothing to think about but the cancer. Is it still trying to attack other parts of my body? How absolutely ill will I feel with the chemotherapy poison coursing through my veins? I want to feel independent again and am anxious to give David a bit of a break from feeling responsible for my care. I have to get back to work.

Dad says he couldn't be happier that I feel fit enough to begin my commuting again and is looking forward to tuning in to *Woman's Hour* on his wireless and reassuring himself that I'm all right. It was always, he says, the way he and Mum felt they were in touch with me, even on the days when I failed to make a phone call. Again I feel ashamed that I was not a more dutiful daughter when I had the chance and now I do call him every night on the days when I don't go over to visit—

whether I'm on the radio or not.

The delivery of the antibiotics by injection to get rid of the infection presents a bit of a problem. It has to be done daily and I'll be away from Monday night to Wednesday afternoon, coming back to Manchester for the Thursday programme. I persuade Nigel to give me the medication to take with me, assuring him that there will be someone professional at the BBC who'll be capable of delivering the jab.

One of the young producers knows Dr Mark Porter. He's a GP and presents *Case Notes*, one of Radio 4's medical programmes. She agrees to call him and ask if he's prepared to give me the Gentimicin. It's all highly unorthodox but I assure Mark that my consultant has said it's OK, so he's happy, although I know I've given Nigel the impression that the BBC has a medical centre in-house and that it'll all be done under the best professional circumstances. In fact, the BBC did use to have nurses and a doctor on the premises, but no longer, so the arrangements will necessarily be a little Heath Robinson.

Getting back to London after an absence of a little more than a month is slightly daunting, but exhilarating. I meet friends at my local brasserie for dinner and find myself laughing for the first time in what feels like ages. I sleep well in my funny little London basement flat—Wuthering Depths—wake at five thirty and arrive at the office, as usual, at seven.

The welcome back is wonderfully effusive and once we've got over the hushed 'How are you?'s and my somewhat brusque 'Fine's (it quickly becomes obvious to all concerned that I don't want

218

to be mollycoddled or fussed in any way) I begin, deliciously, to feel like my old self again.

What I laughingly call my office in Broadcasting House is more of a cubby hole, but it does the job. Some presenters prefer to be in the open-plan area alongside the producers and the noise and bustle of the working day. Perhaps it's being an only child who's always had somewhere quiet and uninterrupted to work, but I find it incredibly hard to concentrate if there's activity going on around me. I can't write if there's chatter or music in the background, so I need a space, however small, that's cut off, and the producers come to me, knowing that my temper will shorten if they interrupt my flow with any conversation.

We begin the day just after seven. I read emails and the newspapers—*Daily Mail* and *Guardian* first to get opposite ends of the political spectrum, gossip, sensation and solid analysis, then skim the others. At eight we begin to prepare the programme. I've read the research notes for any interviews or discussions the night before and the writing process follows a familiar pattern. Serial introduction first, then the lead-ins to any taped items, then the second menu which appears in the middle of the programme and says what's coming up, then the menu for the start of the programme, then we prepare the live items. I write the intro with the relevant producer on hand to check we've got all the facts right. I write down the questions I want to ask in a structured form (always ready to deviate from the grand plan if something unexpected comes up during the programme) and by nine forty-five we're ready to go to the studio to begin the broadcast at two minutes past ten.

It's a deeply satisfying way of working and I'm surrounded by an excellent small team of producers who are bright and brimming with fresh ideas. Most of them are young, but the editor and I are of an age and bring years of experience and common sense to the table. It's a fruitful combination. I've always likened the relationship between the producer and the presenter to that between a solicitor and a barrister. The solicitor does all the legwork and prepares a brief based on thorough research. The barrister absorbs it, works out how to present it and goes off to court and shows off. Just like a presenter in a studio!

After the programme there's a post mortem to analyse how it went and what might have been done better, then planning for the following day. After that I'm done until the notes for the following day ping on to my BlackBerry that evening. So it's after the post-mortem meeting that Dr Mark Porter fetches up in my office. It's small, as I said, there's not much room for manoeuvre and it's surrounded on two sides by huge windows. But we're on the fifth floor and the building opposite is still under construction, so it doesn't occur to us to close the blinds. In any case, it's horribly murky in there if they are closed. We shut the door for some privacy.

The injection has to be delivered in the posterior, so Mark suggests I bend over the chair. He stands behind me, delivers the jab painlessly and without fuss and it's only as I rise to an upright position that I notice the line of builders ranged along the adjacent floor of the skeleton of the building opposite, jaws collectively dropped. We seem to have confirmed the widely held but generally mistaken suspicion that broadcasting is a hotbed of sexual shenanigans. I pull up my trousers hastily, give them a wave and Mark and I look at each other in embarrassment.

'You don't suppose any of them had a camera?' he hazards anxiously. I reassure him that there was no sign of any photographic equipment, privately feeling oddly flattered that it might occur to anyone that the young and undoubtedly handsome Dr Mark Porter might have had the slightest interest in a rather overweight middle-aged woman, innocent though our encounter had been. I thank him profusely for his help and we agree to check the tabloids the next morning for any hint of scandal at the BBC. Happily we escape unscathed.

On my return to Manchester, Nigel declares the infection under control and OKs the first chemotherapy treatment. I'm to go along to the Christie after Thursday's programme in Manchester, see Andrew Wardley, the medical oncologist, again and then face the first dose.

I'm so afraid I don't want to go alone. Charlie agrees to meet me from work and take me there, keeping me company until I have to go in for the treatment. I don't want him there while it's going on as I have no idea how I'll react. David says he'll pick me up afterwards. I hardly sleep during the night.

I need to be a little cautious about how I describe the Christie Hospital as my care there was so tender, attentive and professional that I would hate to hurt the feelings of any staff or question its reputation as one of the world's great centres for the treatment of all forms of cancer. Nevertheless, for the frightened patient walking through its doors for diagnostic tests, surgery or treatment, it feels like the confirmation of a death sentence and an imminent one at that.

The outpatient department buzzes with activity and is crowded with patients in various stages of their illness and treatment. Some are waiting nervously for confirmation of their diagnosis, others have just received the news and sit with anxious relatives in stunned silence, some with tears of despair coursing down their cheeks.

There are those who are well into their treatment, be it radiotherapy or chemotherapy. Some look quite well. Some are thin and ravaged by the disease that's eating them away. Some are brave enough to wander about with their bare heads uncovered after chemotherapy hair loss, while others wear elaborate and elegant scarves or hats to cover their baldness. They stroll around like old lags, accustomed to the atmosphere and putting the bravest of faces on the worst of situations.

In the corridor I bump into Sue—a lovely woman who was on the ward with me at Christmas time when I was having my surgery. She's sixty, has two grown-up daughters, a devoted husband and loves her job as a student counsellor at one of the universities. She had ovarian cancer the year before, had chemotherapy, but had been on the ward for more surgery as the cancer had spread to other parts of her reproductive organs. She smiles, says hello and asks how I'm doing—tells me I look really well. I say the same to her, although her face is as strained as I suspect mine is. She explains that she's just had her dose of chemotherapy and is on her way home now.

But she's also spoken to her consultant and the cancer has spread to her liver. With chemotherapy, she tells me, he gives her a few months. Without it, it's a few weeks. She carefully considered whether a shorter life with some quality—in other words without the ghastly after-effects of the drugs—was better than putting up with nausea and exhaustion just to gain a little while longer and she'd decided she wanted as much life as she could get. We promise to call each other and perhaps meet for coffee—just like normal. I know we never will.

I can't stop the image of a painting by Hieronymus Bosch leaping into my mind. It feels as if I've entered hell on earth. I decide that a bitter sense of humour is probably going to be the only way to cope with regular visits, and dub the place the Poison Palace. It's entirely unfair to the staff who try to make it all as pleasant as possible, but hey, it helped me to picture it as something from a particularly malevolent fairy story and I was one of the ones trying to make herself feel better—so, sorry folks, but there it goes.

Charlie is almost as scared as I am and comes with me to see Andrew Wardley, breaking a little of the tension by asking him to feel his glands which he thinks are a bit swollen. What is it about guys that gives them the ability always to upstage even the most serious illness their womenfolk might have? Andrew kindly stands up to comply. Charlie is well over six feet tall and built like the proverbial brick. Andrew, standing in front of him, has to stretch to reach his neck. The situation is so ludicrous I can't help but laugh. He declares the glands absolutely fine, sends my blood test to the lab and packs me off for a chest X-ray with a note for the radiographer which says, 'R mastect. ? L.'

Ha! I see through his shorthand immediately—it means 'Right mastectomy—query lung cancer.'

I spend the next forty-five minutes or so in a flat spin. Finally, I return to his consulting room clutching the films and blurt out, 'Well, has it spread—do I have it in the lung?'

'Good heavens, no. It's just one of the routine tests we carry out before starting the treatment. Like the blood test. Just checking you're fit enough to cope.'

I point out to him it might be wise to explain to patients in advance that this is a routine procedure that everyone goes through and does not indicate suspicion of any kind. It might save a few from ending up in intensive care with a heart attack. He sheepishly agrees.

I'm declared fit enough to face the chemotherapy suite and Charlie leaves, hugely grateful that he can at last escape.

In a nearby waiting room, I join the queue. No one speaks—a fair indication that even those who have experienced the treatment before are too apprehensive to find the energy to chatter. My name is called by a young nurse who leads me through to a clinically sterile small room in the centre of which is a huge leather armchair. She indicates I should sit. Even now, as I write about it, I can feel the nausea rising. The mastectomy and node removal were on the right side, so it's to be my left hand that will receive the dose. The right side will always be prone to infection without its full complement of lymph glands.

She identifies a 'good vein' on the surface of the

hand and sticks a needle into it. To this she attaches a saline drip which helps wash the chemotherapy through apparently. Next she takes an enormous tube containing a pink fluid—rather a pretty colour for such a powerful substance. This is the Epirubicin. She wears a rubber apron and gloves, not wishing to drip any of the nasty stuff on to herself. She attaches the tube to the needle and slowly begins to inject it into my vein. I feel as if ice-cold concrete is running through me. It takes about twenty minutes for the whole dose to be delivered. I clutch a paper bowl under my chin and throw up. The sick feeling is horrible. She gives me anti-emetics and steroids, reassuring me the nausea will pass and the steroids will help me find the energy to get through the next couple of days.

Now I know why Alan Bennett wrote in his memoirs that he never got on to friendly enough terms with chemotherapy to shorten it to chemo. It is entirely counter-intuitive to sit passively while someone injects a corrosive poison into your veins—except of course that you know it may be the thing that will save your life. I am so glad to get out of there, knowing I don't have to come back for three weeks.

David is waiting and seems surprised that I look reasonably human still. We decide to go and eat in the centre of Manchester. Already I'm learning that steroids make you very hungry (and consequently very fat—a result I need like a hole in the head) and very cross. Outside the hospital, there is a gale and a wild rainstorm. The traffic is appalling and it takes us two hours to complete a journey that would normally take twenty minutes. We have to stop twice for me to go to the loo.

Sensible old body is doing its best to eliminate the nasty substance. I peek into the toilet before flushing and, yes, the leaflet was right, it is pink. I wonder how it can possibly be doing any good if it runs through the system so fast. I spend the rest of the journey shrieking at passing motorists and wanting to kick the car. Poor David slips into strong and silent mode. We eat and I'm desperate to go to bed. It's not long before I know for sure that it's working on the cells. I feel like lead and could sleep for a week.

Once we get home I stagger up the stairs and ring Dad. I don't give him any of the gory details, just tell him I've had the first treatment, I'm home safe and it wasn't too terrible. He sounds tired and sad, says he's not doing too well, but is relieved that it all seems to have gone OK. I promise to see him over the weekend, although I'm not convinced I'll have the energy to drive there and back and give him the attention he needs. At least the anti-sickness pills are working. Dave puts a bucket by the bed just in case and I crawl under the covers.

A friend has sent me a copy of *Cancer Vixen* and, a few days later, I manage to muster enough concentration to read for a while. It's a graphic novel by a New York artist, Marisa Acocella Marchetto, who was diagnosed with breast cancer a month before her wedding. Her representation of her cancer cells as little, angry green blobs sticking out their tongues and giving her the finger raises a feeble laugh in me. Her pictures of herself undergoing chemotherapy and looking grey and washed out already have the smack of familiarity. I feel sorry for her and there's always comfort in recognizing that someone is worse off than you.

226

Her chemotherapy means she'll be infertile. She's much younger than me and will never have her longed-for baby. I can be grateful that, at least, I have my children already.

And I love her attitude. She wears her killer *Sex and the City* heels when she goes for treatment and being a vixen rather than a victim makes absolute sense. But I envy her her mother's ministrations. Her mum is what she describes as a 'doctor-a-day' New Yorker who always turns up to Marisa's treatments or appointments with her specialist saying something is wrong with her. Maybe sons and mums have to invent their own complaint to make you feel they are coming out in sympathy or to take your mind off your own woes. Marisa describes her mum as her Smother. I only wish I had mine there to hold my hand and drive me crazy.

My mother would, of course, have been completely hopeless in such a crisis. As a child I was fantastically accident-prone and a familiar figure in the Barnsley Beckett Hospital casualty department. There were broken limbs from falling out of trees, grazed and bloodied knees from tripping over in the road and there was a particularly nasty incident involving the staples taken from the centre of an exercise book in which I'd been writing stories.

Mum would cope admirably with flowing blood or blistering skin from burns until a professional arrived in the form of a paramedic or the district nurse or calm and efficient Dad with his car. The moment someone else took over the responsibility, she would pass out. Her most dramatic faint came in the waiting room of the casualty department a week after the staple incident had turned my finger septic. It had gone a very nasty black and blue and was horribly swollen. The doctor had said it would need a little operation to relieve the pressure and I'd been put to sleep and sent home heavily bandaged.

The following week we returned to the hospital to have the dressing changed. I went in alone to see the doctor, dreading the removal of the yellow, criss-crossed piece of lint that was always used in those days next to the wound. It was impregnated with antibiotic, saving the sufferer from infection, but it invariably stuck fast to raw and broken flesh. The doctor diverted my attention from the procedure with an 'Oh, look over there' and whisked the stuff off entirely painlessly. Good tactic. He told me my finger was healing well and sent me out to Mum to wait for a nurse to put on a fresh bandage. I examined his handiwork closely, turning the finger back and forth, and couldn't see any fingernail.

'Mum, look, I think they took my nail off,' I exclaimed.

Mum didn't even look at the finger. She simply passed out, collapsing on to the floor of the casualty department, and everyone's attention was immediately focused on her. I personally never did learn the trick of feminine fainting and I generally preferred it if Dad was around to support me in the face of any disaster. We seemed to have an unspoken understanding that the person who was truly suffering should get all the consideration.

I was very small when he went to the dentist to have all his teeth out. It was common in those days to have teeth removed and dentures put in at the

228

same time to save problems later. I went with him, held his hand, guided him out into the street and took him to the cinema to see Mario Lanza in *The Student Prince*—Dad was a huge fan of the singer. When I needed a filling or an extraction he came with me if he could and afterwards we'd go to a movie of my choice. Pain then pleasure was our maxim. If Mum had been there we'd have had to go straight home and put her to bed.

I suspect her squeamishness was a learned response to my grandmother's depression; a way of attracting her attention when Gran was really in no fit state to give it. But regardless of her inability to cope with the pain and distress of anyone else around her and her constant denial, until those last months we had together, of the seriousness of some of my grandmother's symptoms and the terrible effects of the electroconvulsive therapy she'd been given, there are times when only a mother can provide the comfort you need. I miss her fussing—and the fact that she would have given me the great distraction of simply feeling irritated with her.

Having had to face so much difficulty in the past year, I am grateful for the degree of independence her crazy ideas about pushing children away and giving them the impression they're unloved forced upon me. Her motive was to ensure that I never felt tied to her apron strings in the way she had felt forced to be by her mother. But she had taught me a very good lesson from which my children have benefited. I learned that you can help your children become independent and confident by letting them go, but you should never ever allow them to feel they are unloved. I tell them I love them all the time and miss them when they're away. I'm convinced I've done the right thing because they keep on popping back, something I never wanted to do when I was younger.

The sad thing about my mother's and grandmother's generations is that they were really living without a map that placed them as anything other than the keepers of house, children and family respectability. As women they were to be handed from the ownership of their father to that of a husband and patronized in the same way as children if they fell off the straight and narrow. It's difficult to imagine now, but my grandmother was born in 1902, sixteen years before women won the limited vote in 1918, granted only to those who owned property, and twenty-six years before universal suffrage. (I always get angry with young women who ask me, 'When were women given the vote?' and I tend to shriek rather testily, 'We were not "given" the vote. We had to fight bloody hard to win it!')

It was only when my grandmother was a young woman—twenty-seven years old, married and a mother—that women were officially declared 'persons' with all the legal rights that definition brings. It was at the specific request of the Privy Council after pressure from a group of five women in Canada who came under British law and had not been allowed to stand for election because of their lack of legal status. Perhaps the best British example of how women suffered from this lack of status was what happened to the eminent scientist Hertha Ayrton, the first woman to qualify as an electrical engineer. She was invited to become the first female fellow of the Royal Society, but at the meeting of the rest of the members in 1902 it was decided to withdraw the offer because she could not be defined as a 'person'.

But, while these issues and the antics of the suffragettes may have made the news in London and the major cities like Manchester, for a young girl raised in the Yorkshire countryside by a father steeped in the ideas of Edwardian patriarchy and a mother who, by the time she had her twelfth child—my grandmother was the youngest in the family—had little energy to concern herself with her daughter's education or intellectual development, there was no place for newfangled ideas about women's rights. While my grandmother was lucky in her choice of a gentle and kind man as a husband, it never occurred to her to question the tough treatment she had received at her father's hands.

She would tell me stories about the days she was expected to help behind the bar in the pub her family owned. She was allowed to say, 'Good evening and what can I get you?' She could pronounce the cost and say please or thank you, but no other words were to pass between her and the men (and it was only men who came to drink) she served. On the rare occasions she was caught engaging in any further conversation her father would slap her face and literally kick her up the stairs. It was, she thought, just what fathers did to preserve their daughters' reputations as respectable and suitable marriage material.

So it's unsurprising that, when it came to facing her illness, my grandmother simply took whatever the doctors told her as gospel. And for them a woman suffering from a nervous disposition and

231

behaving in a neurotic manner was only to be expected, given the weaker and less reliable constitution most women were assumed to possess. She took the tablets they gave her without question and meekly accepted the electroconvulsive therapy—an unproven and barbaric treatment—even though I would point out to her that it didn't seem to have any long-term benefit as the depression returned frequently, and it had a disastrous effect on her memory. She was able to recall events that took place in her childhood, but couldn't remember what we'd done the day before.

I know that, regardless of my constantly harassing her to ask more questions and make enquiries about side-effects, she never challenged the paternalism of the doctors who cared for her. For much of the later part of her life she was zonked on tranquillizers—the great scandal of the sixties and seventies when so many women became addicted to the tablets that so successfully kept them quiet and of no trouble, but led to addictions which ruined lives.

The women's movement changed everything for my generation. We read hungrily publications such as *Our Bodies Ourselves* and, while there was much comedy to be found in consciousness-raising classes which were said to encourage women to look at their genitalia with hand mirrors in the company of other women, we did learn to know our bodies and ask questions about how we should control our fertility, how we might give birth and what treatments were useful and woman-friendly, rather than accepting what a predominantly male medical profession thought might be good for us.

232

Happily I never personally came across any of the more radical consciousness-raising encounters but do remember devouring Germaine Greer's *Female Eunuch*, in which she urged us to find out more about how our bodies worked and to revel in being female. I was shocked (still am, to be honest) that she urged us to taste our menstrual blood and it was one of her orders with which I steadfastly refused to comply, but I determined never to conceal a tampon in public when I was on my way to change one in the loo—another of her suggestions. Quite an advance for a young woman whose mother had always hidden her sanitary protection, even from her own daughter, and for whom menstruation was a dirty word.

While my grandmother was too late to benefit from what I was learning from the pioneers of second-wave feminism in the seventies, my mother was—at times—ready to listen and act upon some of the new ideas. She too must have been shocked by the brutality of my grandmother's treatment for mental health problems, although she never admitted it to me, but I do know the memory of my birth and the way she'd been left to labour alone, almost to the point of death, was burned in her mind. She was certainly appalled at the callousness of a hospital in-patient system that banned children from visiting close family, kept parents away from their sick children and fathers from their new babies.

Given my mother's reticence about matters such as periods and any carryings on 'down below', I was astonished in the mid-seventies to receive a phone call from her telling me she was going to have to go into hospital herself. She had been told by her doctor that she must have a hysterectomy. I told her to hang on—to do nothing—and I would come home and we'd talk about it.

I was still in my early years as a journalist, but already interested in getting what were then so often dismissed as 'women's issues' into the mainstream of broadcasting. *Woman's Hour* was, of course, doing a brilliant job, as it had since the late forties, in bringing women's health out of the dark ages, although not without some consternation on the part of the controllers of the then Home Service. In 1948 there was a now famous exchange between the editor of the programme and a controller following a series of broadcasts on the menopause, in which Dame Josephine Barnes had graphically described symptoms and solutions. The memo from the controller read, 'We do not wish to hear about hot flushes and diseases of the ovaries at two o'clock in the afternoon. The women in my office agree.' The archive of correspondence from the listeners suggests otherwise.

It was not so easy to get these subjects on to the radio programme I produced and presented in Bristol, although I had managed to sneak in an interview with Wendy Cooper, the author of the first well-researched book on the menopause and the new hormone replacement therapy to be written by a woman. It was called *No Change*. I took my copy with me on the train to Barnsley, suspecting that it might be menopausal symptoms that were causing Mum's problems. I had severe doubts about whether hysterectomy was the right solution if that was all that was going on. I'd made a programme about the operation—one of the most common in women at the time—where I'd followed a woman whose only symptom was heavy bleeding in her late forties. I had been horrified by the impact her hysterectomy had had on her sense of herself as a woman and on her sexual relationship with her husband as she recovered.

At home, I persuaded my mother to talk openly about what had caused her to go to the doctor in the first place. She was embarrassed, but she said her periods had become unmanageable. She never knew when one was going to start and the flooding was so bad she never dared to wear light-coloured clothes in case a stain appeared. She'd seen a specialist and there didn't seem to be anything seriously wrong. He'd just said it was the sort of thing women should expect at the change of life when 'everything went haywire' and he booked her in for the op saying, 'Just have it out, dear. You don't need it any more and you won't miss it. It'll give you no more trouble.'

I advised her to put off the appointment and gave her Wendy's book to read. A few weeks later, she called to tell me she had gone back to the GP and told him she'd been reading about HRT, that she thought it might help control her symptoms and would he please prescribe it. He must have been pretty shocked to be faced by a woman who'd rejected conventional wisdom, informed herself as to what treatment might be available and asked for what she thought was right.

Nevertheless, he gave her the prescription and she was one of those lucky women who hit on the right HRT straight away. Almost immediately her symptoms calmed and she carried on taking the tablets happily until she was in her seventies. She never ceased to be thankful for my advice and

appeared to develop a new respect for me. At last, she seemed to think, I have a daughter who knows something useful.

March

This chemotherapy ain't for cissies.

Already, after only the second cycle of treatment, I'm familiar enough with the way the drug works to know exactly what to expect. The first week after a dose is crippling. I've never known such exhaustion, nor such a constant sense of nausea, despite the powerful anti-sickness tablets I consume religiously, counting the hours until the next one is due. Already I'm developing cheeks that wouldn't look out of place on a gerbil—a side-effect of the steroid use. I've lost the ability to concentrate for more than five minutes on a book—a terrible blow when reading is your favourite pastime and a vital ingredient of preparation for the kind of work I do.

I can't bear to watch television because it seems there are references to the size and allure of 'tits' in every comedy programme and drama. The adverts are a nightmare—nothing but models flashing their embonpoint and tossing their gorgeous hair. I seethe with barely concealed aggression. The cats scatter as I enter the kitchen. A few days ago, they saw me kick the rubbish bin and they have an acute sense of self-preservation.

Poor David has to put up with me ranging from feeble to fuming with no in-between, but he's patient and calm and continues to reassure me that my attractiveness to him is undiminished. He shows no fear or revulsion at the naked me with the oddly mutilated right breast and is as tactile and sensuous as ever. He doesn't get much response, but the cuddles are a great consolation and I can't quite believe how lucky I am to have found such a good man. I hear terrible stories of rejection from other women in a similar position and can't imagine how one would cope with this onslaught on one's body and psyche without the unconditional back-up I seem to have.

After five or six days I begin to feel a little better and agree that I'll take off the first week after each dose and then come back to work as the white cells start to build again and a little energy returns. Two weeks out of every three will keep my hand in and contribute to keeping me sane. All I have to do now is learn to face the world without my hair.

Olivier, the lovely French hairdresser I found in Manchester—every bit as good with the scissors as any of the fancy London ones I tried and half the price—has done his best to cut it as short as possible without making me look too butch, but it's really not enough. Already, after such a short time on the treatment, I'm finding clumps of hair on the pillow and scattered around my shoulders. David offers to take things a step further using the clippers Ed bought from Boots during a teenage phase when he favoured the Number One, a virtually shaved haircut. They'd saved us a fortune on barbers' bills and now would keep my own humiliating crop within the privacy of my own home.

I sit on a stool in the kitchen, festooned in and surrounded by towels to catch what remains of what had always been my crowning glory, requiring monthly trips to the salon, excellent cutting, artistic colouring and half an hour each morning for the wash and blow dry at which I became quite expert. It kept me looking young, professional, smart and did wonders for my confidence. I cringe as I feel

240

the cold metal on the back of my neck and begin to sob uncontrollably.

David, also upset, tries to get by on black humour. He reminds me he was ship's barber in his early days in the navy, so I can feel confident that he'll do a good job of making me bald.

When he's finished he strokes my shiny scalp and says, 'Come on, slaphead, you don't look too bad.'

I am fresh out of humour and just carry on weeping. He hugs me and tells me it'll be OK. I can get a good wig and it will grow back when the treatment is over. I still go on crying like a baby.

I am not alone in this extreme response. Lisa Jardine, professor of Renaissance studies at Queen Mary, University of London, and a formidably determined and courageous woman, tells me a similar story. She, like me, decides to cut off her own hair in anticipation of total loss as her chemotherapy drugs kick in. She goes to her hairdresser for the complete crop and breaks down in the salon.

Neither of us has shed a single tear through the diagnosis, the mastectomy or the news that we need chemotherapy because our cancers have been attempting to go on a trip through the lymph nodes under our arms. We reassure each other that our response to hair loss has not been trivial. It's not a sign that we are underplaying the trauma of having the disease in the first place, but we've somehow gritted our teeth and got on with what was necessary to save our lives. So why is it losing our hair that's reduced us to such abject weeping and wailing?

It's partly, I think, because a bald head on a

241

woman is a sure sign that she's a cancer patient. It tells the whole world that you're sick, no matter how hard you've tried to carry on as if nothing was the matter and have stuffed your bra to look as normal as possible. It's also that hair is a mark of a woman's femininity. We spend huge amounts of money getting it cut, primped and dyed—up to £600 a year according to one research project—and nothing upsets us more than a 'bad hair day'.

So, unlike men, who rather expect to go bald and are seen as pretty potent and sexy without their hair—think Bruce Willis or Yul Brynner—a woman who's bald is seen as mad, bad or tragic—anything but alluring. I find myself back on the internet again reading whatever I can find about women, baldness and what it all signifies.

As far back as cave paintings there are pictures of youthful women of childbearing age with long flowing hair. The zoologist Desmond Morris thinks that modern women who style their hair to be clean, beautiful and a little wild—the kind you see in every television ad for hair products—are sending out the same clear sexual message as our prehistoric ancestors. The hair is a secondary sexual characteristic and suggests a degree of availability. It's not by chance that a fairy story such as Rapunzel depicts a beautiful young woman locked up at the top of a tower by a jealous crone. It's only by letting down her long, flowing locks that she attracts the attention of the handsome prince who rescues her and leads her off to the happy ever after.

The evolutionary biologists and psychologists say that thick, glossy hair or fur is seen as a sign of good hormonal health and it's one of the outer

242

signs that both animals and human beings use to select a mate. It's why Joan of Arc said she chose to shave her own head, arguing that it helped deter men who might otherwise have made sexual advances towards her while she was trying to further a military career. It's also the reason certain orthodox religions insist a woman covers her head and why a nun is traditionally shaved before she dons her wimple, lest a hint of free-flowing locks sends out the wrong message and drives some man wild.

I guess it's also the reason why it's now common for a post-menopausal woman whose hormonal health may well have declined to put that regular visit to her hairdresser to erase any signs of grey near the top of her list of priorities. It's one of the simplest and most affordable ways to present a more youthful image to the world. I certainly hadn't seen my natural colour for nearly twenty years. The first sign of a grey hair had sent me rushing to the salon.

It's interesting that, at the same time as I'm being shaved in my kitchen, Britney Spears is getting rid of the flowing blonde locks that marked her out as a sexy pop diva, and I read the press coverage with rising alarm. She's done it, it's said, because of the difficulties of seeing her sons after her separation from her children's father. She's described as 'frenzied', 'teeth bared', 'wild-eyed' and 'bald'. All the reports claim that the shaving of her head signifies that she has become deranged, thus emphasizing her status as an unfit mother. What sane woman, the press appears to be suggesting, would choose to mutilate herself in such a way?

Sinead O'Connor received similar opprobrium when she shaved her head. Her action was seen not as empowering or flouting the rules of what's considered acceptable in a woman, but as a sure sign that she was a lesbian or that she had severe psychological problems. Even Gail Porter, who lost her hair as a result of a medical condition, alopecia, and bravely chose to face the world without a wig, didn't escape the suggestion that she was suffering a breakdown. The sexy shots of her that had appeared in the lad mags were replaced with close-up pictures of her appearing to fall apart.

And, of course, shaving the head of those considered mad or criminal has been a common practice throughout the ages. Sigourney Weaver played Ripley in *Alien 3* with no hair—she was living with a crew of convicts—and Natalie Portman, who revealed a shaved head in the 2005 film *V for Vendetta*, openly admitted that people would think she was a neo-Nazi, a lesbian or had cancer. Emma Thompson, who was shaved for the TV film *Wit*, in which she played a cancer patient, said, 'I'll be bald for months. I'll be sleeping in pyjamas and a hat—no chance of any sex.'

Shaving her head has long been a way of condemning a woman for her sexual behaviour. In the Bible, in Deuteronomy, it says that a man is allowed to marry a woman he has captured after a raid on a city, but only if she shaves her head and he leaves her 'untouched' for a month. The hair is cut to render her unattractive and confirm her position as a captive during a period of mourning for the men lost during battle. Similarly, in France after the Nazi occupation, a woman who was believed to have fraternized or collaborated with German soldiers had her head shaved. She was stripped of her sexual identity and punished for it.

The only example I can think of where the removal of the hair is seen as a brave, strong and determined move is in the film *GI Jane* where Demi Moore, training to be a US Marine, sits in front of a mirror and commits the act herself. The face of the pretty girl, framed by beautiful long hair, is transformed into that of a hard-bitten soldier. She succeeds in her ambition, but only by looking exactly like one of the boys.

So it's not surprising that Lisa and I, and I'm sure thousands of other women who've gone through a similar experience to ours, are finding it profoundly upsetting to be bald and will immediately go to great lengths to conceal the fact from those around us. I battle my way through the Manchester traffic and the awful task of finding a parking space to visit a shop that works closely with the Christie Hospital and specializes in wigs. Cancer patients are given a £50 allowance to make the purchase, but you need to pay a little more than that to get one that looks even remotely natural.

The women in the shop advise against real hair—it doesn't look like the real thing once it's made into a wig and is difficult to care for. Instead they recommend an artificial one by Revlon and spend ages solicitously finding the right shape and colour. I donate my £50 and pay a total of £180 for one that people tell me looks really good. It's of a similar length and cut to my own hair and convinces me that I might, in future, get away with a reddish dye. The colour seems to suit me.

It is, though, desperately uncomfortable to wear—itchy, tight and will be unbearably hot in the summer. As an alternative, and I'm lucky in that turbans are the height of fashion this year, I buy a headpiece in black cotton that has a hint of the thirties movie star about it. After a few outings in it, I'm getting heartily sick of the number of times I get asked if I'm ready for my close-up!

Hairdressers are now beginning to wise up to the need for assistance during this tough time. Trevor Sorbie has launched a wig-cutting service where he'll style a wig to suit you and Anita Cox, who has salons in Clapham, Chelsea and Essex, is running workshops to help with preparation for hair loss, cutting short or shaving, wig styling and dealing with hair growth at the end of treatment. She assures me that regrowth happens at the rate of half an inch a month, that the damage to the hair follicles caused by the chemo drugs may give it a different texture from before and may cause it to grow back curly, but says that, as long as the doctor says it's OK and you have an allergy test at the hairdresser, it can be coloured as soon as you want it. I prefer her approach to that of some of the cancer charities, who advise waiting six months before attempting to use permanent colour.

I will, of course, take advice from Andrew before lurching into colour when this is all over, but I can't bear the thought of my hair growing back in that terribly ageing pepper and salt mix that's reminiscent of my old miniature schnauzer, William. Nevertheless I resolve that the only dyeing (the pun works if you say it) I'm planning to do is back with Olivier and Kelly who does the colour. I'm counting the days.

David volunteers to drive me over to Barnsley to see Dad. I'm not sure he quite trusts me out alone and certainly not behind the wheel of a car. He makes sure I'm carrying the card that says 'I am a chemotherapy patient' and has the emergency number of the Christie's chemotherapy suite. I feel more or less OK, but I suppose it's best to be on the safe side. Not that I'm planning to do any of the things you're warned against. One of the advantages of being subject to such a powerful and potentially dangerous drug is that you don't have to do any dirty work—so weeding, pruning and cleaning up, anything that might cause a cut and the entry of bugs into the system, is strictly off limits; which is fine by me. Every cloud and all that.

Dad is pleased to see me, although he looks tired and sad and his mobility seems to be deteriorating. He gets up stiffly from his chair, he's unshaven and his hair is unkempt. His lovely face is pale and drawn. He's lost a lot of weight in a short period of time. He assures me he's eating. The neighbours, Pat and Frank, are still bringing him his favourite Italian ready meals from Marks & Spencer and he pops down to the baker in the village every day for his bread and bilberry pie.

I check the fridge and the freezer and it does seem they are not overloaded with provisions—so he must be consuming what's been bought. I begin to worry about why he might be losing weight if he is eating properly and urge him to go and see the doctor for a check-up. He brushes my concerns aside, says he's feeling fine and totters, painfully, across the sitting room to the bathroom. He's going to shave and tidy himself up ready to go out to lunch. He even throws me a grin.

'Don't worry,' he laughs, 'I won't shame you by going out looking a sight. I know that look that says for goodness' sake smarten yourself up, Alvin. You got it straight from your mother.'

It's not until we're sitting opposite each other, tucking into steak and chips with treacle sponge and custard to follow, that he seems to notice my appearance has changed. I'm wearing the wig and I have put on weight. For the first time in my life he makes a critical comment on how I look.

'You're a bit heavy, love, maybe you should give the treacle sponge a miss. It can't be good for you to put on more weight, not in your condition. But your hair looks nice.'

I explain about the steroids, feeling slightly irritated that, in this at least, he seems to have taken over my mother's role. He always told me I was beautiful regardless of how scrappy I might have appeared. She was the one who took it upon herself to meet me at the door at every visit and dash my confidence in an instant with comments on how I was too thin or too fat and how, no matter how I'd done it, my hair was a sight. 'You look like you've been dragged through a hedge backwards' was her favourite.

I tell him that the 'nice' hair is a wig and that underneath I am bald as a coot. I explain that I'm lucky to have kept my eyebrows and lashes, which isn't always the case, and offer to show him what's under the wig. His face is a picture of absolute horror as he begs me to do no such thing. Maybe I was wrong all those years to think he thought me perfect regardless. Perhaps he simply sat back and let my mother express a distaste for my imperfections they both shared—anything, as he

248

often said, for an easy life.

The great thing about being on the radio—with apologies to Woody Allen who applied the definition to masturbation—is that you don't have to look your best. During my years at Radio Bristol, I learned that it was probably wise to dress cleanly but casually. A presenter owes it to a guest to look as if they've made some sort of effort, but appearing too trendy, too smart or too expensively dressed is likely to be intimidating. And the last thing you want to achieve is to make them feel uncomfortable from the outset.

And, of course, being on local radio, many miles from my mother's critical eye and ear, meant I could pretty much go my own way without any fear of comment from home. It seemed to be enough for her to be able to show off to her friends that 'Our Jen is working for the BBC.' She didn't seem to feel the need to follow my career in such close proximity as Dad did. It was only much later that I discovered Dad and Dave the engineer had conspired to make recordings of a wide range of my activities—interviews with politicians such as Tony Benn, the pets phone-in where I'd collapsed into helpless giggles at a call about a toad that was mating in the back garden of a house in Clifton and seemed to be inextricably attached (the toad and its paramour became quite a saga. It later died and I was roundly ticked off by the caller for not taking it seriously enough) and a series of short stories I wrote and performed for Radio Bristol's children's programme. It makes me laugh to hear them now as I sound so posh, but Mum and Dad clearly spent many a proud and happy hour boring their friends with the aural equivalent of a slide show.

As I rose up broadcasting's slippery pole my father congratulated me on my ambition and tenacity, my mother fell into her usual confusion about what a woman's role should be—worker or foundation of a family—and Brian became increasingly irritated at my absences from our marriage. Success meant long hours at the office and evenings spent making contacts at civic receptions and meetings or tripping around the region speaking to groups from rugby clubs to the WI to raise the profile of the station.

I learned to drive at the BBC's expense— probably the only perk I had from a job that paid me at the outset some £850 per annum—and bought myself a tiny and ancient Fiat 500. It more or less got me from A to B without mishap unless I tried to park it in a multi-storey car park. It had no synchromesh on bottom or reverse gear and couldn't make it up a steep incline, nor would it go backwards. Luckily, it was small and light and I was then fit enough to get out and push it with my shoulder while still managing to operate the steering wheel. It gave me a tremendous sense of freedom and independence.

But I was not the wife Brian had hoped I would be. By this time, we'd been married for four and a half years and we'd bought a house very cheaply at auction. It was in a fabulous location in an up-and-coming part of Clifton, but it needed a phenomenal amount of work. It had been let as bedsits and the pervasive scent of spicy food and the décor suggested it had long been occupied by immigrants from the Indian sub-continent. There was an awful lot of bright blue and gold gloss paint where there should have been emulsion, which was a demon to get off.

Brian's talents as an architect and a DIY practitioner suited the project perfectly. But no matter how hard I tried to share in the enterprise, I could never get used to climbing over cement bags to get to work in the morning or coming home to cooking and then being builder's mate. It was during one of Brian's most demanding tasks— restoring the intricate plaster cornices to their original glory by scrubbing the old paint from every crevice with a toothbrush—that it became apparent this was not for me.

I was nearly twenty-six, loving the work I was doing, being encouraged by the station manager to move on and upwards, and getting increasingly irritated by Mum's hints about grandchildren and her constant criticisms of my standards of housekeeping. The marriage had developed in exactly the way I had dreaded it would, with an assumption that my ambitions would necessarily be secondary to those of my husband. After a flaming row one night when I'd been out to dinner with some friends from work while Brian had stayed home getting on with remodelling the kitchen, I packed a bag and left.

I stayed with the friends until I managed to find my own small flat and it was weeks before I plucked up the courage to tell my parents what I'd done. My mother was shocked and angry and tried to encourage me to come to my senses and go back to my husband, where she said I belonged. What, she wondered, was she going to tell her friends? Dad, to whom I spoke only briefly—he was never big at chatting on the phone—was calmer and

251

much more supportive. It had to be my choice, he said. If I was truly unhappy in the marriage I was right to get out. I suspect it was a natural paternal response—a sense of relief that his little girl was extricating herself from the clutches of some man of whom he'd never really approved; not, I think, that any man would have been good enough for him.

Curiously, my mother did eventually come round to my decision, announcing that divorce was perhaps not the shockingly immoral act she had at first believed it to be. On 15 March 1976 it was announced that Princess Margaret and Lord Snowdon were to divorce after fifteen years of marriage. I remember quite plainly my mother calling me after she'd watched the evening news, asking me if I'd heard about it and actually saying, 'Well, it seems you're in good company.' A royal divorce had magically made what I was doing respectable enough to gain my mother's approval. She and the Queen Mum—in the same boat!

I doubt very much I would have entered quite so blithely into the marital state had I realized how much I would hate what it would mean to be defined as a wife—from the woman in the social security office in Hull who told me I had a husband who was legally bound to keep me, to the various building societies I approached when I came to buy my own first house.

Each one rejected my application, explaining a lone woman could not be granted a mortgage without the signature of a husband or a father to guarantee the repayment of the loan. They were unmoved by the fact that I had a job and a salary that was patently adequate to cover the amount I

252

needed. I went back to my rented home after this series of humiliations seething with fury, until the provisions of the new sex discrimination legislation, enacted in 1975, suddenly slipped into my brain. I went back, threatened them with legal action and got my mortgage.

Things were changing—it was already possible to leave the 'obey' clause out of the marriage service and it would soon become common for a married woman to retain her own name and call herself Ms, rather than defining herself as unmarried or married—Miss or Mrs—just as men—Mr whether attached or not—have always been able to do. The only woman I've ever interviewed who had steadfastly called herself Mrs was the obstetrician and gynaecologist Wendy Savage, who explained that she'd insisted on her title being Mrs to show that it was possible to be married and a mother and a consultant surgeon! But things were not moving quickly enough for me.

It would take me another thirty years before I embarked on marriage again and even then I was appalled to find myself signing a register that included my father's name and profession and my partner's father's name and profession, but when I suggested our mothers should be included we were told by the registrar that such information would not be required. Even in 2005, marriage remained a patriarchal institution which ensured the legitimacy of children through the male line and wrote women out of family history.

Quite apart from the political ramifications of embarking upon marriage and divorce at such an early age, I had not anticipated the personal pain of extricating oneself from a relationship to which one had made such a public commitment. Brian and I didn't own much, but we tried to be as civilized as possible in dividing what little we had fairly and amicably. The day I finally walked out with my share of the record collection and my books was agonizing. We hugged each other and cried, knowing there was no alternative to our separation, but acutely aware of how much of our early years as young adults we had shared. We are still in touch. No one but Brian remembers my grandparents or my parents as relatively young and active people. I'm the only one who really knew his parents, or his younger brother who died young after many years of battling the effects of spina bifida. I still regard him as part of my family.

It was soon after our separation that the manager of Radio Bristol, David Waine, suggested it was high time I moved on. The BBC in those days operated a system of attachments under which you could try out a new field without a permanent commitment being made on either side. David's motive was to ensure that all his employees acquired a broad set of skills in an industry which notoriously gobbles up talent and burns it out. I thought I would like to move up to Radio 4—the arts programme *Kaleidoscope* was then my ambition. David insisted I should try television. If journalism was to be my career, he said, I needed to get experience in radio, television and print. He fixed it for me to spend a summer month presenting and reporting for *Look North* in Leeds.

Personally, it was a tremendous relief to leave Bristol and the possibility of bumping into Brian at every turn. Chance meetings were upsetting for both of us. Professionally it was a great move. I was thrown in at the deep end with only a half-hour of training in reading the autocue. We'd begin the day around nine with a planning meeting, set off on the road with a camera crew to cover anything from industrial disputes to skateboarding ducks, rush back in the early afternoon with the film, wait for it to go through 'the soup' for developing—this was long before digital cameras made the whole process quicker and easier—sit with the film editor constructing the pictorial story and then manically type out a script to fit. Then it was down to the studio, change into a decent top (we were behind a desk, so the bottom half really didn't matter), cake on some slap and then into the studio for a 'Good evening and welcome . . .'

I found to my surprise that I was entirely comfortable in front of a movie or studio camera, although I'd always hated having to pose in front of a stills camera. You don't get that rabbit-frozen-in-the-headlights look when you can keep moving as the pictures are recorded. I loved the deadline adrenaline rush of getting the story and putting it on air that night, and the competition shared with the other reporters—who could get a story that might make the nine o'clock national news that day?

There were drawbacks. For me, words had always been my business—as a child writing stories and poetry, at school for the magazine, academically in English and French, on the stage, learning and speaking other writers' wonderful lines, and then in radio where the words and the tone of voice are all you have with which to communicate. In television the words were subservient to the pictures. It took a while to adapt to the discipline of writing three words per second to fit the pictures exactly.

Then, of course, there was my mother, a devoted fan of her regional news magazine programme and now able to switch on at six and see her own daughter there five nights a week. She began a pattern which was to continue long into my career on TV. After the programme had ended, there would be the immediate and inevitable phone call.

'Hello, love, it's Mum.'

'Oh, hi, what did you think of the story about the miners?'

'Oh, did you do a story about the miners? I can't say I noticed, but I did think that red shirt was not really suitable. You've got such rosy colouring it makes your face look too ruddy. And I did think you could have done something a bit better with your hair. I know you have to rush to the studio, but you could have spent a bit more time on it and I really think you should make an appointment with the hairdresser and get that fringe cut, it flops in your eyes and they really are your best feature and you know they say television puts on about half a stone, well, I think that's right because you do look even plumper than you look normally, so I think losing a bit wouldn't go amiss . . .'

All this, despite the fact that at this period of my life I was the thinnest I've ever been apart from a short time after the birth and breastfeeding of my children.

I would eventually send her a copy of Susie Orbach's *Fat Is a Feminist Issue*, in which I recognized myself as both a consumer of comfort

256

food and as the daughter of a mother who obsessed about whether or not I conformed to her perception of the perfectly slender feminine ideal. She ignored the book and I never quite managed to learn the Orbach advice of eating what I wanted if I was hungry, stopping when I was full and being happy with my natural physique. I did my best to listen to my appetite but found it to be a subject on which I was consistently and profoundly deaf.

On and on it would go. Even after I graduated from local broadcasting to London and the national networks and became a presenter on *Newsnight* she would phone, regardless of the lateness of the hour, with the same tedious and confidence-sapping diatribe.

'Oh, did you interview Norman Tebbit/Margaret Thatcher/Arthur Scargill—I can't say I noticed who you were talking to, I was just looking at your hair/top/make-up and . . .'

After Leeds I had a period in Southampton and a proper job as presenter and reporter on the regional programme *South Today*, which covered an area between Reading in the north, Weymouth in the west and Brighton in the east and which mercifully took me far away from her prying eyes and constant criticism.

It was in the seaside and sailing town of Lymington in the New Forest that I bought the first house of my own. It was rather tweely called Smugglers' Haunt and was a tiny cottage with the kitchen, bathroom and dining room on the ground floor, two bedrooms in the middle and the sitting room and balcony on the top. But it was close to the sea and the forest where I could walk and ride horses and I had a view of the Solent, which gave me endless happy hours on a Sunday afternoon watching inexperienced sailors battle their way around the Isle of Wight ferry.

I'd successfully bullied the building society into giving me my own mortgage and persuaded a rather shocked local solicitor to find a way of describing me on the deeds other than 'spinster'. It's a word I've always hated, suggesting as it does a rather sad, greying, dried-up and unloved old crone. After much coercion on my part he came up with 'feme sole', an acceptable term in English law deriving from the French *femme seule*. Woman alone—much more pleasing and precisely what I intended to be for some time as I found my own feet and learned the true independence of being responsible for no one but myself.

It was, I think, one of the proudest days of my life when I invited my parents to come for Christmas to my own home. My grandparents had died that year—my grandmother first from a sudden stroke and my grandfather less than a year

later. He'd been having a pint in his favourite haunt, the working men's club, popped out the back (his euphemism for going to the toilet) and collapsed with a heart attack. He'd died in the ambulance. Our little family was reduced to three and my mother couldn't bear to have Christmas at her house without them—throughout my life we'd had Christmas Day at ours and Boxing Day at Grandma's. So it made sense to shift the whole operation to new territory.

Dad had always been quite clear that once I was through university he would have no more financial responsibility for me, so there was never any point in asking for a sub or a loan. I suspect if I'd been really desperate he would have willingly bailed me out, but he was delighted that I was established with a job and a house that I'd achieved entirely by myself. Mum worried about whether I'd be able to pay the mortgage. Would I be safe, living alone? Why did I insist on buying old furniture—wouldn't new be so much nicer? And why couldn't I have bought a modern home? She spent most of her visit scouring the place for imaginary damp patches. Nothing could diminish my enthusiasm.

I spent three hugely amusing years as the 'girl' reporter, rushing around the region, covering both hard and soft news, enjoying the company of various casual boyfriends and failing professionally on only two counts. I'd covered the Newbury air show and was offered a ride in a First World War biplane by a mad RAF pilot, dressed in leather jerkin, hat and white silk scarf, who warned me as I climbed into the cockpit not to push my feet through the delicate fuselage. I sat in the seat behind him.

Another man climbed in, moved me out of the seat, told me he was the gunner and instructed me to sit on the floor. There was no seat belt. He assured me I needn't worry about falling out. He'd hold me down by the shoulders if necessary. Two minutes into the air and the pilot looped the loop, then flew along the route of the M4 to Bristol and back, performing more aerobatics as we reached the airfield again. I vowed never to get into a small plane again and when I was asked to do a parachute jump as part of a story, I refused, only to be hailed as a wimp when I got back to the newsroom.

My second failure was in 'doing the dunk'. A number of the stories we covered in Southampton involved shipping and sailing accidents and the air-sea rescue and naval helicopters were always on hand to ferry journalists out to the site of any disaster. But, during my time as a reporter there,

there had been a terrible accident in Weymouth Bay. A chopper had gone down with a pilot, co-pilot and a number of journalists on board. Only the two professionals and one experienced cameraman had survived. They were the only ones who knew how to escape from a sinking helicopter. After this we were all expected to undergo training.

The drill is to wait until the inside of the vehicle fills with water, then gently push on the doors. It's only when the pressure is equalized that they will open. The dunk involved a visit to one of the naval bases where there is a simulated helicopter cabin in a swimming pool. I turned up with some of my colleagues, put on my costume and stood at the side of the pool. I could not bring myself to get in—the thought of waiting until I was completely submerged and unable to breathe filled me with horror. I never flew over water in a helicopter again—and was inevitably designated a weak and feeble woman!

Generally, I avoided the navy. Other women who'd worked as reporters in the seafaring regions had developed quite a reputation after relationships with naval officers and I was determined never to be branded the Forces' Sweetheart. I did, though, accept an invitation to a party arranged by one of the young officers I'd met on a story who was house-sitting the beautiful home of an admiral. There would be dancing in the garden—it was a balmy summer's evening—and possibly swimming in the pool. I had just had my thirtieth birthday, spent with old friends in Israel, and was feeling particularly bronzed and lithe. I couldn't resist.

It was a great party and most of us stayed overnight, being in no fit state to drive ourselves home. Over breakfast I sat opposite a dead ringer for Marlon Brando—broad-shouldered, square-chinned, a little moody (might have been the hangover), but with sparklingly amused eyes. We competed with each other in a joke-telling session and went our separate ways. The next day the phone rang after the programme with an invitation to dinner.

David and I have been together from that day on, and even my mother seemed relieved. At last I appeared to be 'settling down'.

April

'If Winter comes, can Spring be far behind?' The line from Shelley's 'Ode to the West Wind' has always cheered me in the depths of the dark season and here, at last, is a little something to brighten the misery of the past months. The days are getting longer, the daffodils are bursting out bright yellow and there are mornings when the sun rises over the hills and bursts into my bedroom window, dangling a prospect of hope for better times to come.

Life is still something of a struggle as I lurch from work, to family, to bouts of treatment which seem to get harder with every dose and play havoc with my metabolism.

I watch Julie Goodyear being interviewed by Piers Morgan on late night television when I can't sleep, my night-time insomnia the result of having worked all morning and died, as David would say, as soon as my feet hit the pillow around lunchtime. I wake around 9pm, pick at a takeaway curry (which the chemotherapy leaflets strongly advise against, but it's a little of what I fancy, so how can it do me harm?) and flop on to the sofa unable to cope with anything more taxing than undemanding TV.

Julie is a rather reticent Mancunian whose life history seems quite dreadful. Awful childhood, men who've left her in the lurch, a child to raise alone and a career playing Bet Lynch on *Coronation Street* that's had more ups and downs than the Pepsi Big Max at Blackpool Pleasure Beach.

'How,' asks Piers, obviously sympathetic, 'have you managed to get through it all, while at the

265

same time putting on such a brave face? Do you smile your way through every setback and disaster?'

She fixes him with a determined stare. 'It's not a smile, love. It's a lid on a scream.'

Despite the small pleasures I find in the arrival of spring, nothing could describe my current mood better. When I'm not smiling my way through Oscar-winning performances at work, I'm staying resolutely cheerful for David, Dad and the kids. Charlie is soon to set off on his travels around the southern hemisphere before starting university later in the year, Ed's about to do his finals at vet school, and David is juggling his job and doing all the cooking and shopping, most domestic activities being beyond me.

I've tried to drag myself around Waitrose—for some reason my favourite supermarket, possibly since I heard a Radio 4 comedian describe the purpose of Sainsbury's as 'a way to keep the riff-raff out of Waitrose' . . . not that I'm snobbish about these things . . . well, maybe I am—but I'm now so physically depleted that I can barely totter around while clutching the trolley for support.

Then, of course, there's Dad. My trips to Barnsley are becoming more frequent. I seem to need constant reassurance that he is doing OK and nightly phone calls are not enough. Unlike those of his slap-happy daughter, Dad's financial affairs are in perfect order and part of his motivation for keeping going through his grief is to ensure everything is sorted out and done properly. So we often have appointments with building societies and the family solicitor as we deal with Mum's estate and Dad satisfies himself that I won't have any problems or inheritance tax to pay when he goes.

I've spent years refusing even to discuss such matters with him—not ever wanting to think about the death of my parents—but now he insists I take it all on board. His greatest dread seems to be that he'll leave a single penny to Gordon Brown and it appears that through careful arrangements of his and my mother's wills and long-ago-fixed legacies for the children, we'll come in just under the limit. The news is the most pleasure he's had in a long time.

We spend far too long in the formal boardroom of the traditional firm of lawyers Dad's been with for ever. Dad sits at the head of the long, wide table while the charming Mr Wilkes and I sit opposite each other under portraits of the original Victorian partners, who look down on us rather grimly. I try to hurry things along, even, despite my atheism, agreeing to swear the signature of documents on the Bible, as affirmation, I'm told, will take a little longer. Not only am I hating the whole process of mopping up the affairs of people I never wanted to lose in the first place, but I've been conditioned to see a meeting with a solicitor as a mountingly expensive occurrence, not a counselling session.

I'm not a mean person, but I am a Yorkshire woman, and as I watch the minutes tick by I see the bill accumulating. Dad, normally the most careful of spenders, sees Wilkes as a willing and relatively new audience for his stories, so, each time, we go through the wonders of Mum, me and my public profile, Charlie's prowess on the rugby field and Edward's imminent graduation as a vet. I can't bring myself to interrupt Dad's proud catalogue of what he, after all, sees as his lifetime achievements and sit patiently through every word, as does Wilkes. I'm sure it's out of generosity of spirit and not greed.

It's a slow and painful journey from the offices to the car park as Dad shuffles along, claiming his arthritic knees are giving him gyp and his old back injury is playing up. He stops from time to time to catch his breath, pauses for which I'm ashamed to say I, twenty-four years his junior, am more than grateful. There's the usual fuss about the car.

'Eee, I feel like a fighter pilot getting into this bloody thing. Strap me in, love. Now, let's go fast. I never thought a daughter of mine . . . !'

I must be maturing. I've learned to make no comment on his heavily loaded remarks about daughters, fast cars and driving. We arrive at the pub and I rush round to the passenger side to help him unravel himself from the seat. I take his stick from the boot and we make our decrepit way into the restaurant.

He orders his usual—steak, chips, peas and treacle sponge with custard—but pecks at the food. I eschew the treacle sponge to avoid the danger of any disparaging comments about my ballooning weight, bemoaning dryly to myself that I couldn't have had one of those weight-loss cancers. I recall Liz Tilberis, the former editor of US *Vogue* and one-time size 14, telling me breezily about the benefits of the ovarian cancer diet. She'd gone from a 14 to an 8 and, for a short time, was able to wear the sample suits that came into her office from Chanel. Sadly she died not many months later, but managed to keep her sense of humour to the end. I'm trying to do the same, but it tends to be rather darker than most people can take, so I generally keep the thoughts to myself.

Suddenly our conversation takes an unexpected turn.

'I've made a decision,' Dad announces. 'I really don't want to go on living without your mum.'

I try not to show how much this hurts me, but point out that while I know how upset he is and how much he misses her, he has family who love him and want to care for him. I talk about the boys and how much they admire him. I tell him we have plenty of room and he can come and stay with us for as long as he likes. He loves the hills that surround our house. It's the reason I love them so much too. One of the great joys of my childhood was to be taken over the Pennines on one of his trips to the Stockport office. I'd wait patiently for as long as his meeting took, reading my book, until it was time for us to drive up into the hills and walk, our feet sinking into the purple heather and squishing through the peat.

Again, he insists that he doesn't want to leave home. It's where he feels closest to my mother. He still hasn't moved any of her things—shoes, curlers, stockings—from where she left them. He explains he's very grateful for the offer and he likes it when we pop over to visit, but he's fine where he is. He never expected to outlive my mother. She'd always seemed so much fitter than him whereas he'd always been a creaking gate. And she would have managed alone so much better. She'd always made friends easily and found plenty to do, but his world had revolved around her. Finally he admitted he wasn't doing too well by himself.

I sigh. He really is the most stubborn person I've ever encountered. But then, I've always known that was where I got it.

'No,' he says quietly, 'I shan't be moving, not at this time of my life. Anyway what I've decided is this. I'm going to make it to eighty this month— none of the others got that far. Norman made it to seventy-nine, but Arnold, Reuben and Eileen all died younger. Your mum would have wanted me to outlive my brothers and sister—she always said she looked after me better than any of them were taken care of, so I don't want to let her down. So I'll get to eighty, then I'm off.'

His eightieth birthday is only a week away and I feel a sense of terrifying shock that he really means what he's saying. Nevertheless, I try to make light of his lifetime commitment to planning ahead extending even to his choice of when to make his departure, and he smiles, secretly and indulgently. I have no idea what he's plotting, but I try to work out what he means.

We've had long discussions about assisted suicide in the past. We both agree that choosing the time of one's own death is a human right that should be respected. Neither of us had ever brought ourselves to the point where we would talk about it together during the last months of Mum's horrific illness and I doubt she ever asked him to help her die, although she had whispered her desperation to me frequently.

She knew, I guess, that he would never have been able to help her go—not for fear of any consequences arising from an illegal act, but because he couldn't bear to face life without her. I think I could have helped to save her from more terrible suffering, had I had the knowledge and the means, and hope fervently that when my turn comes there will have been a change in the law to enable doctors in Britain to act in the humane manner they are able to do in Switzerland, the Netherlands and Oregon in the United States. The last thing I want is to suffer the loss of quality of life my mother was forced to endure. Nor would I ever want my children to go through the agony of watching a parent in great pain and only partly in command of their precious faculties slowly starve to death.

But Dad has no medical or dental friends, has never asked me for help and, as far as I can tell, there is no alcohol or paracetamol in the house, although he has taken up smoking again with a vengeance. He had always been a heavy smoker, but he gave up, allegedly, in his early fifties when the ENT surgeon he met on a flight to Belfast spotted his deafness and offered to replace the old, useless stirrup bone with a plastic one. Dad had the op in secret and came home hearing and, he said, a non-smoker. He claimed to have given up in hospital. It was only a few years previously, during one of Mum's stays in the Barnsley orthopaedic ward after she'd broken a hip, that I discovered he was back on the fags.

Mum's rings had been removed in casualty and when she came round from the op they were nowhere to be found. Dad insisted he had no knowledge of where they were. I suspected he'd been so distressed at Mum's condition he had simply forgotten what he'd done with them and at home I asked if he minded my checking through the pockets of his overcoat. He agreed and I found

271

not only the rings—the precious ones I'm wearing now that make me feel closer to her—but a packet of cigarettes as well.

He looked as shamefaced as a teenager who'd been caught out by a parent, but claimed it was the stress of looking after Mum that had driven him back to nicotine. His friends Mary and Eric suggested otherwise. He'd often gone down to see them for a sneaky one while Mum was cooking supper and his frequent long walks with their dog had, it seems, had an ulterior motive. I began to understand his passion for Polo mints, although I can't believe Mum never knew. She had the most acute sense of smell.

Now that he needn't worry about her reaction—her fear of him dying from a smoking-related disease had long been an obsession of hers—he's smoking openly and furiously. A death wish, possibly, but hardly a suicide plan. I ask him what he aims to do.

'Nothing,' he tells me, 'but they do say you can die of a broken heart.'

I put it down to wishful thinking and, as usual, do my best to jolly him along. I quote Oscar Wilde's Lady Bracknell to him, putting on my best Edith Evans voice. 'To lose one parent . . . may be regarded as a misfortune; to lose both looks like carelessness.' I manage to raise a laugh.

My next visit to Barnsley is with Charlie, who's leaving for Thailand on the 17th and won't be back for six months. Dad thoroughly enjoys his company and they part with big hugs and kisses. Charlie promises postcards and phone calls to keep in touch and they both say how much they're looking forward to seeing each other again in September.

272

Charlie wishes his grandpa a happy eightieth birthday, says how sorry he is not to be able to be there on the day, but assures him he'll be thinking of him. It's a sad parting with an air of finality about it that they both find distressing.

The next week is always a busy one. David's birthday is on the 16th, Ed's on the 18th and Dad's on 20 April. Our celebration is to be a joint one, on Friday the 20th. We range his cards along the mantelpiece and lunch is to be at the pub as always—Dad's choice, not mine. I wanted something a little more special, but he's a creature of habit and opts for familiar surroundings.

I'm still concerned at his lack of appetite and today he makes no pretence of ordering his usual quantities. He asks for the old age pensioners' lunch, which has smaller portions than he's used to consuming, and he hardly touches the food. Nevertheless, he claims to be enjoying himself and delights in watching Ed demolish a huge plateful. We go back to the house for champagne with neighbours and friends and he goes to bed a little tipsy, having congratulated Ed on being twenty-four and Dave on reaching fifty-three and obviously happy to have reached his goal.

Later that evening, as I relax at home, I remember the day Ed was born and how much David and Dad had teased each other about whose birthday he would share. Ed's due date was in fact 16 April, but in the diplomatic manner which has characterized most of his life he decided to arrive bang in the middle, keeping both his father and his grandfather happy.

The biological clock was ticking fit to deafen when I met David at the age of thirty and it was a

273

given from the start of our relationship that we had each found a breeding partner. We had similar northern backgrounds—mine in Yorkshire, his in Cheshire—parents who had made the first steps towards middle class and we each had a failed marriage behind us. I try not to toy with the idea that David shared a star sign and a profession with my father. It feels too weird to contemplate the idea that I may have been subconsciously trying to replicate my parents' marriage, but they were both electrical engineers, and shared an Aries birth sign and a calm, quiet and kind temperament, so make of it what you will.

We moved in together with what my mother would have regarded as alarming abandon had she known about it and, for a while, played the separate houses game, David moving into naval quarters for the weekend whenever she came to visit. Even after we jointly bought a house in the sailing village of Hamble, the fact that we were living as a couple was unspoken between my mother and me, although it was obvious we were building a nest that would be big enough to accommodate any addition to the family.

David, at that time, was weapons officer on a nuclear submarine, based partly in Plymouth and partly in Gosport and spending the occasional long period at sea. The boat would leave for a two-month top-secret tour, during which time he'd be incommunicado. It was just before the start of one of these trips—David was to go to Faslane in Scotland and then goodness knows where—that I began to suspect I might be pregnant. The night he left, I hadn't mentioned my suspicions. I didn't want to worry him when he would have no means of staying in touch and monitoring progress.

I went to dinner alone at a friend's house and began to feel decidedly ill. Soon I was sick and doubled over with pain. I went home early and went to bed, but couldn't sleep. The pain got worse. By dawn I was seriously worried that I might have appendicitis. I called an old friend in Bristol who was the only person I could think of who might have an idea what was going on and would be available early on a Sunday morning.

He was a genito-urinary surgeon or pox doctor, as he preferred to describe it, who, when asked at parties what he did for a living, would always respond, delightfully, 'I save private lives.'

He answered the phone at once and asked me to describe the symptoms.

'Look,' he said, 'I'm not going to make a diagnosis over the phone, but my advice would be to call for an ambulance and get yourself to hospital immediately. From what you're saying it could be serious.'

I took his advice and will always be grateful that his sense of urgency may well have saved my life. I was pregnant, but it was ectopic—the foetus had lodged in the fallopian tube. An immediate operation would be necessary to remove it. I managed to make a call to the base at Faslane on the off-chance that a message might get to David and put myself into the hands of the NHS.

Twenty-four hours later as I was regaining my faculties after the anaesthetic, the door to the ward swung open and David arrived at my bedside.

'Move over,' he said, 'I need to lie down.' It was the worst case of male upstaging of female indisposition ever recorded, I suspect. He had,

275

apparently, been diagnosed with a condition called labyrinthitis—an infection of the inner ear which causes a loss of balance. It had only shown itself when the submarine dived on its way to Scotland and he keeled over. He'd received my message, hightailed it to Southampton on the train and taken the lift up to the ward. The lift had had a similar effect to the diving of the submarine, hence his desperate need to lie down until the giddiness passed.

There were certain benefits to his condition. It meant he was grounded for a long period and able to stay with me as I adapted to what the gynaecologist grinningly described as 'firing on one cylinder' after the loss of one fallopian tube. I've had a deep suspicion of short, male gynaecologists ever since. The other plus was there was no question of David being sent to take part in the Falklands war.

The lack of sensitivity on the part of those who organized the ward where I spent a week in recovery was more than staggering. I, having just lost a longed-for baby and full of fear that the loss of a tube would make it difficult to conceive again, found myself next to a woman who had been trying for years to get pregnant and was part of a trial of a new infertility treatment called ICSI, which involved her husband's sperm being injected directly into an egg. She had already been through a number of failed IVF cycles and felt she was in the last chance saloon. On the other side was a fourteen-year-old who thought she was around twenty weeks pregnant. It was only as her body began to swell that she'd realized what was going on, had not told her mother, had pretended she was going on a school trip and had referred herself for a termination.

The nursing staff were less than supportive to the poor child. She was taken to a side ward in the early evening, hooked up to a drip and left to give birth to a dead foetus alone. Her screams were heartrending. My neighbour and I got up, staggered across the ward—we were both in a good deal of pain—and sat either side of her for what felt like several hours, holding her hands and reassuring her. We were asked to leave when the nursing staff finally came to attend to the end of her ordeal.

The experience was the foundation of my commitment to honest and effective sex education for all young people, regardless of their parents' wishes, as well as easy access to contraception and early abortion by sympathetic staff for those who slip up. No youngster, indeed no woman, should have to go through what that kid endured. When it was all over, we persuaded her to contact her mum. We were right in our assumption that her mother would be cross and very upset, but we were confident she would come through for her daughter in the end, as indeed she did.

My one cylinder worked spectacularly well and within six months I was pregnant again. I waited until three months had passed and there seemed little danger of anything serious going wrong and then decided it was time to tell my mother that David and I were living together and, at last, she was to become a grandmother. Her response was not the joyful one I'd anticipated.

'I knew you'd disgrace me in the end. Did I really have to wait all this time—thirty-two years—

for you to become an unmarried mother?' And she put the phone down.

It rang a few minutes later.

'I'm sorry. I'm sure you're pleased about this and so am I—but what on earth am I going to tell my friends?'

I was speechless.

'Listen,' she went on. 'Would it be OK if I told them you're going to have a baby and that you and David didn't want a big wedding because you'd both been married before so you just went off to the register office and did it quietly with a couple of friends? That way I can explain why I haven't been to a wedding.'

I was stunned at her readiness to lie for the sake of her idea of propriety and, to my shame, agreed to let her say whatever she liked. I should have stuck to my principles and explained that David and I had been living together for nearly two years, that we jointly owned the house and had no intention of getting married—I because I had developed a deep aversion to the institution which was rooted in my political beliefs about the status of women, and David because he really didn't care too much either way and respected my conviction.

Instead, I left her to get on with whatever she chose to do, while I concentrated on making the enormous adjustment from 'feme sole' to mother. Nobody warns you of how ambivalent you may feel about having a child once it starts to grow inside you. Indeed, I remember reading Lionel Shriver's book *We Need to Talk about Kevin*, and thinking how courageous she was to be the first writer to dare to say out loud what an alarming prospect a developing pregnancy can be.

On the one hand I was thrilled to be having a baby, but, at the same time, as Shriver's character, Eva, describes, I felt I'd been invaded by an alien that might eventually burst out of me and be terrifyingly unpleasant. I absolutely detested ceasing to be me and being seen only as a receptacle for my precious foetus. I gave up drinking, smoking and eating Brie and resented my friends for blithely continuing to consume whatever they chose in front of me. I bit off the head of anyone who had the audacity to pat my stomach uninvited—and many do—trotting out such arrant nonsense as 'Ah, lucky you, you're going to have a baby and I'm sure it's going to be a footballer. I can feel it kick.' It was as if I didn't exist.

I had sleepless nights worrying about giving birth to a monster. On the nights I slept I would wake suddenly in the early hours of the morning in a blind panic. Would I be able to take care of a child? What impact would it have on me and the things I still had left to do? Would it be possible to juggle an infant and a journalistic career? How would I find a decent nanny who could be trusted? Would I be forced into that box marked 'mother', designed to contain women who are rarely seen to have got anything right?

I spent hours—generally at night—arguing with myself: if you retain your independence it's neglectful and wrong. If you stay at home you're a failure as a unit of economic usefulness and a waste of an expensive education. If the child turned out a wrong 'un, I knew no one would ask whether it might have been the working father's fault, but a working mother would surely get it in the neck.

As the bump burgeoned, I carried on reporting and presenting *South Today*, buying ever more voluminous frocks in a vain attempt at concealment. It seems surprising now that pop and movie stars are photographed proudly showing off a naked pregnant belly or appear in public with a tight T-shirt barely covering the bump when, only twenty-four years ago, there was so much pressure to hide the evidence away. It was also very rare to see a heavily pregnant woman in so public a place as a TV studio. Sue Lawley and I were probably the first to do it. I remember Sue hid her evidence behind a desk. I didn't. I was out reporting or walking around the studio and the response from viewers was generally extreme. Some would write in offering their congratulations and knitted bootees or jackets. The majority of letters were abusive.

'How dare you appear in public looking so disgusting?' or 'How dare you carry on working in THAT condition, taking a job away from a man? Do you not have a husband to keep you?' Ah, the irony in that!

I determined to turn the whole affair into a project, partly to take my mind off all the things that caused me either anger or anxiety and partly because I felt I had to prove my mother wrong and show that actually having the baby could be a pleasant and satisfying experience in itself. All I'd ever heard from her was that it was the most painful and terrifying thing to which a woman could be subjected.

I had the benefit of natural childbirth campaigners such as Dick Grantley Reid and the

National Childbirth Trust, Mrs Wendy Savage and Sheila Kitzinger. I read their work voraciously and held firmly in my head a comment made by Kitzinger on the question of pain. The English language, she explained, is poor. We have only one word for pain, but the feeling comes in many different forms. There's the pain of a road accident victim whose limb is severed in the crash. Their agony is destructive and signifies loss. Then there's the pain of the marathon runner who, at the end of the long race, finds every muscle screams with agony as she pushes herself towards the finish line. It's a positive pain with a triumphant outcome. That, she said, is the 'pain' of childbirth.

I wanted a home delivery, but it was impossible to arrange. The GP said she'd never done one—it just wasn't part of their training any more—and she advised that a first-timer who also happened to be defined at the age of thirty-two as a geriatric for the purposes of childbirth really should be in hospital in case anything went wrong. There was nothing to indicate that anything might be amiss—I was healthy and fit, and I did yoga regularly to keep myself supple for the marathon ahead—but I conceded that maybe she was right.

The next step was to engage the support of the chief midwife—a woman who'd been trained in the days when midwife-led home delivery was a common occurrence—and that of the young registrar who was as passionate as I was about trying to make delivery a less technical and traumatic experience wherever possible.

We agreed I would have a birth plan—no induction, a bean bag to bend over and the bed lowered to floor level for a squatting delivery (the hospital insurance wouldn't cover us to dispense with the bed altogether). I would not have an episiotomy, where the perineum is cut to ease the passage of the head and from which thousands of women suffered much more painful after-effects than those caused by a small tear. There would be no drugs apart from a whiff of gas and air and I would not lie on my back or be connected to any monitoring machines. The midwife would keep track of the baby's heart rate in the old-fashioned way, listening through a kind of ear trumpet, and I would remain as upright as possible to let gravity do its work.

I did some charity work to raise money to have a room in the hospital wallpapered and curtained in a welcoming and warm pattern. There would be quiet, low light and no members of staff rushing in and out of the room. Should the midwife judge there to be anything amiss, I would willingly subject myself to whatever the obstetrician thought might be necessary to deliver a live and healthy baby.

About a month before my due date the registrar told me I had to see the consultant obstetrician with whom the buck of responsibility stopped for every woman under his care. It would not, I was warned, be an easy meeting. He was a high-tech man working in a brand new maternity hospital with all the best equipment at his disposal. He had little sympathy with the natural birth movement, believing it should be consigned to the dark ages where it belonged.

His attitude was aggressive from the start, confirming my suspicion that he was absolutely the wrong sort of person to be looking after frightened women at one of the most vulnerable times of their lives.

'So,' he sneered, 'I gather you're one of these primitive women who think they could drop their babies in the field, sling them over their shoulders and carry on working.'

'Not at all,' I responded, much more calmly than I felt. 'I'm a great believer in hygiene, midwifery and technical expertise for when things go wrong. But I also think that women are a little like animals in that they want to give birth to their young in a dark and quiet environment, free from drugs that might adversely affect the baby's feeding response immediately after birth, and free to move around so that gravity helps the passage through the birth canal rather than being humiliated by shaving, enemas and being strapped on their backs to a bed with their legs in the air, which seems to me to be of no benefit to anyone except the obstetrician who gets easier access.' I barely paused for breath.

'Fine.' He fixed me with a cold and angry eye. 'But on your head be it. If this baby dies it will be entirely your fault.'

He was alarming, but I was never one to be bullied. If anything, his behaviour made me more, not less, determined to make my way work. I knew instinctively that the majority of women are perfectly capable of doing what comes naturally and that the high-tech medical empires should be reserved for those who are at risk from dangerous conditions such as pre-eclampsia or breech— although Mrs Wendy Savage, one of the great exponents of woman-centred delivery, was even ready to give a breech baby the chance of a natural birth. Above all, I was absolutely determined that I

283

would not repeat the ghastly experience that my mother had endured and been so damaged by.

And so it went. In the early hours of 18 April serious contractions began. David packed his sandwiches, a flask of coffee and an Evian water spray for cooling me down and wetting my lips if I became dehydrated but too nauseous to drink— thank you again, Sheila Kitzinger, for such practical advice for birth partners who may well get hungry, but have no time to wander around seeking out the cafeteria—and we made our way to the hospital.

Everything proceeded exactly as planned and I look back on Ed's birth as one of the most pleasurable and satisfying experiences of my life. It was intimate, calm (except during some of the more powerful contractions when David claims I became a vicious tigress and swore like a pitman when all he was doing was rubbing my back in an attempt to give comfort) and, sure enough, at the end of the great marathon when every muscle screamed out for it to be over, a beautiful, healthy baby emerged.

There was one shock. Just as my mother had carried her imaginary David Robert around for nine months, I had carried Eve. I gave her the name of the first woman and had such plans for helping her grow up into a confident, powerful creature who would never be told she was too fat or too thin or her hair looked awful. I had assumed that as the only daughter of an only daughter I would simply replicate what had gone before, so imagine my astonishment when the midwife cried, excitedly, echoed by David, 'Oh, it's a boy. It's a big strong boy.' I have a terrible suspicion that, had it

284

been a girl, there would have been a much more muted tone and different words. 'Oh, look what a sweet, pretty little girl.' And thus the nurture of gender difference begins.

*   *   *

He fixes me with the bluest of eyes and gurgles. I'm in love in a way I never thought possible. My heart literally wants to burst out of my chest. Did my mother feel like this for me, I wonder, or was she so distressed by the trauma of my arrival that she was simply grateful to have survived? The pair of us take to breastfeeding like the proverbial ducks to water and David hops around the delivery room, the nearest such an undemonstrative man can get to hysterical delight. We are a family and we are inordinately pleased with ourselves.

The maelstrom of emotion pinging around the room was broken by practicalities. The registrar arrived to put a couple of stitches into the tiny tear

the delivery had caused—thanks again to Sheila Kitzinger for advising the breathing in of gas and air to dull any pain from the stitching process. Only one problem. Entonox is what used to be known as laughing gas and I giggled my way through the whole procedure, making the job much harder for the poor professional at the business end.

'Please, Jenni, will you stop laughing or my embroidery will be a mess,' he pleaded with me more than once, but eventually declared the job well done.

David had gone off to find a phone to ring the parents. We'd agreed I would stay in hospital overnight, then we'd like one night at home, just the three of us, to get used to each other and after that mums and dads would be more than welcome to come and stay. I knew David's parents wouldn't rush us. They'd had six children of their own and Ed was their fourth grandchild. It would need to be made very clear to my mother that we really did want a little time to ourselves.

I felt so sorry for David being packed off home in the evening to face a lonely house by himself, leaving his precious baby behind. There's pressure now for fathers to be allowed to stay in hospital overnight for those first crucial hours of getting to know the child and taking on the pleasurable job of sharing care with the mother. It's a move I would wholeheartedly support.

It was when I was left alone in a room with no one to fall back on—the nurses were gathered in the dayroom, making cups of tea and smoking cigarettes—that the magnitude of what I'd done really hit me. Ed lay sleeping in a plastic cot more suited to goldfish than babies, snuffling and wiggling his fingers. I couldn't take my eyes from him. The sense of responsibility that gripped me was fearsome. Until that moment I had been able to change anything in my life at will. Difficult mother—leave home. Unsatisfactory marriage—divorce. Dull job—move on.

But this was for ever. I was his mother and the overwhelming feelings I had for him would never leave me. Even should something terrible happen and his death precede mine, I would grieve for him until it was time for me to die. I would want to protect him long after he was too grown-up to need me. I felt entirely inadequate for the task. I hadn't even been too good at changing his nappy and the thought of having to bath him the next day without drowning him filled me with woe.

A kind young nurse came to my rescue. She'd heard me sobbing, said what I needed was a cup of tea and some adult company. She assured me it was OK to leave him sleeping for fifteen minutes just to pop to the dayroom. I reluctantly agreed.

There was a jolly atmosphere of normality in the dayroom. I had my tea and a biscuit and one of the nurses offered me a cigarette. I took it without thinking and was halfway through it before I shrieked, 'But I don't smoke. I gave up.' But I finished it, savouring every puff, and wouldn't give up again, unfortunately, until four years later when Charlie was conceived. Like father, like daughter, I suppose.

David was there first thing to share the bathing lesson, which went off without too much of a hitch, although clinging on to a soapy infant who revelled in slithering about in the water was not the easiest of tasks. We dressed Ed, wrapped him warmly and

287

were held up only for a few minutes by a contrite consultant who had come to apologize. He had heard how well things had gone and how much the staff had enjoyed doing things the old-fashioned way, and would not object to anyone in future who wanted to try to do things quietly. We stepped out into the wide world, triumphant, and set off for home.

We had lunch and made our way upstairs to bed for the afternoon. I needed the rest and David couldn't wait to snuggle up with his son. We'd been tucked up for about five minutes when we heard the back door open and determined footsteps on the stairs. The bedroom door was practically flung off its hinges and my mother threw herself into the room. My father followed, sheepishly, a few steps behind. She said nothing, but raced around to my side of the bed and removed Edward from my arms. She held him aloft, her hands carefully cradling his back and his still wobbly head. Then she spoke.

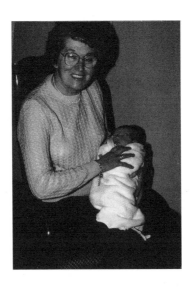

'At last, my boy!'

I managed to spit out a response.

'Actually, no, Mother, he's MY boy.'

She was undeterred, offered no words of apology and showed no signs of remorse. In four short words, *at . . . last . . . my . . . boy*, she had wiped me out.

May

I'm now into the fourth month of treatment and the chemotherapy regime has changed, but not for the better. I've had four doses of Epirubicin and I've now moved on to CMF, which some fool described to me as chemo-light. Ha! Where the Epi hit came once every three weeks, giving me some time to recover before the next injection, CMF is delivered on one Thursday and then the following Thursday and then a break of three weeks. I'm out cold after each dose. One of the tubes is a sickly, yellowish colour, the rest is clear—no pretty pink to admire now—and light it is not.

The method of delivery is exactly the same, so I turn up religiously to the chemotherapy unit, head covered by the cotton turban as the wig, attractive though it may be, is simply too uncomfortable to endure except for a few short hours. I am full of trepidation at the knowledge that I will soon be feeling absolutely wretched.

The nurse takes some blood, which is sent off to the lab to check that I still have enough white cells left to prevent me from collapsing altogether. I dread the result. If it's low, I'll be sent away for another week to build up some strength and the end of the treatment will move even further away.

It comes back OK, so more of the poison can be dripped into my hand. The nurses do their best to make the experience as palatable as possible. They're friendly and funny and offer drinks, soups and fruit salads, none of which I can face. They are frighteningly practised and efficient, but it's getting harder to find a suitable vein in the back of my hand that isn't screaming out for a break from the nasty, corrosive liquid. We find one in the wrist and I discover the inside of the arm, just as it joins the hand, has far more pain sensors than the back of the hand. The insertion of the needle used to deliver the CMF is agonizing.

That feeling of nausea and of cold concrete coursing through my veins grips me again. Then the anti-emetics and the steroids go in intravenously and the sickness diminishes. I leave after the second hit of the cycle knowing that for a few days after the steroids are done—they only allow me a couple more days, I suppose to suppress the aggression—I can expect to feel more listless than I ever imagined possible, barely able to crawl under my own steam from the bedroom to the bathroom. It means an extra week away from work, staying home and feeling sorry for myself.

There is, though, something to look forward to. My birthday is 12 May and every year three friends and I, Norma, Jane and Sally, take ourselves to a first-class restaurant for lunch. This year it's to be special. Norma's brother is to lend us his house just north of Nice in the south of France. The date falls on what I expect to be a good week chemotherapy-wise, the flights are booked and Dad seems happy that I'm to have a weekend of pleasure just for me. It's a little sign of hope on the horizon of much misery.

The weekend before I'm due to go away I spend in Barnsley with Dad, who is still not eating as well as I'd like. He's lost even more weight and seems to have little energy or enthusiasm for anything. Not even a half-pint at the pub. His throat sounds a little rasping too and I wonder if he's picked up some sort of bug. He's thrilled because Charlie has called from Bangkok and sent a postcard, but I'm worried when I leave him, making him promise to go and see the doctor about the husky voice. He agrees, kisses me goodbye and wishes me a really good weekend. He strokes my cheek and tells me I deserve it.

For the rest of the week I call every evening. Of course, he hasn't been to the doctor and, even though his voice is now reduced to a tiny whisper which I can barely hear on the phone, he assures me he's feeling fine and it's probably just a bit of a cold.

It's a working week, so I finish the programme in Manchester at Thursday lunchtime and make my way home full of excited anticipation. I'm to pack my case, David will pick me up from home and drive me to the airport at Stansted where I'll meet the others. We're to stay overnight in a hotel, catch a ridiculously early flight and then all that lies ahead is warm spring sunshine, a pool, fabulous food and wine and the girly giggles I've missed so much. The four of us really do seem to regress to teenagers with a couple of glasses inside us and generate nothing but laughter.

Just as I'm shutting the case and can hear David's car coming up the driveway, the phone rings. It's Chris, Dad's cleaner. She comes in once a week. My mother hated hiring another woman to do her dirty work, but, as her illness took its toll, she had to acknowledge that she couldn't keep up with the housework by herself. Chris had been a playmate of mine as a child, so my mother knew and trusted her. She persuaded Mum that someone else really could keep the house as sparkling as she would have kept it herself. They'd become good friends.

Chris explains it's taken her an hour to rouse Dad from his bed. She's rung the bell and banged on the windows. For some reason Dad would never part with a key—even I didn't have one until he was on his own and recognized it might be necessary. Dad managed to get to the door and let her in, but he's barely able to walk. He's back in bed now and, she thinks, desperately ill.

I'm stunned and anxious but most of all, to my shame, I'm fuming. Why now, just when I'm so looking forward to a short break away from it all? For a second I contemplate telling Chris I'm about to leave for the airport and I'll be away for the weekend. She should call the doctor and make sure he's OK. I'll be over on Monday. But, of course, I can't leave him alone when he needs me. Instead, I tell her I'll be there as soon as I can get across the hills. She agrees to stay with him until I arrive.

I call Jane and tell her the weekend's off for me.

'But the whole point of going is for your birthday and to give you a break,' she protests. 'Surely he'll be all right?'

I sigh, feeling guilty for having ruined their weekend, but have to stay firm. 'Chris wouldn't have called me unless it was really serious. I have to go to him. Enjoy yourselves, raise a glass to me and give me a call to let me know what a wonderful time you're having.' I can't keep the edge of jealousy out of my voice.

David will drive. He bundles me into the car together with the bag I've packed. It looks, he reckons, as if I may have to stay for a few days. I'm nervous about what I'm going to find. My father has never needed me before. Yes, he's wanted my company, but has always prided himself on his complete independence—a trait I've inherited—and I'm afraid that my great rock will now want me to be his support. Will I match up to what he needs and, maybe, expects?

Chris is in the sitting room, together with my mother's great friend, Dorothy—the only person Chris could think of who might give her some support until I arrived and took over. I rush past them into the bedroom and there is my father, lying quite helpless on his side of the bed. His face is grey. He's unshaven. His hair is dirty and unkempt. The room smells of incontinence.

I kneel by the bed and cup his face in my hands. His voice is no more than a grating whisper. He tells me he's fine. There was no need for me to come. Chris is making a fuss about nothing. His skin is dry and cool to the touch. I tell him we need the doctor. His eyes flash with alarm.

'No,' he says, 'I don't want any doctors. Just leave me be.'

And then I realize what he's doing. He's trying to die. He is skin and bone. I doubt he's eaten since I last saw him at the weekend. He hasn't drunk. His lips are blackened and cracked. He has worked all this out. He knew I'd be going away for the weekend. He figured he would be alone. He is trying to starve himself to death, thinking it could all be over by the time I get back from France. But he has miscalculated. He forgot about Christine coming on a Thursday. He is, as always, trying to stick to his stubborn plan. 'I'll get to eighty, then I'm off,' he'd told me. It's less than a month since his eightieth birthday.

I explain that I'm sorry but I can't let him stay in this mess. I tell him I love him. He says he knows, but he's had enough. Why can't I just leave him be? I fetch lemonade—his favourite—from the kitchen and with a straw, reluctantly but thirstily, he sips.

I call the doctor on my mobile from the bedside. It's in my list and is one of my most phoned numbers of the past years. Dr Sykes, who I know best, is away. The new doctor will be there as soon as possible. David thanks Chris and Dorothy and releases them from responsibility. I sit on the floor next to my father, running my fingers through his hair and clutching on to his hand. I feel two years old again—wanting my big, strong daddy to tell me everything is going to be all right.

It's a sign of age when the doctor looks as if she's a contemporary of your own children, but, if this is the way they are training young doctors nowadays, boy, are they getting it right. She enters the bedroom with humility and a warm smile, acknowledges me and introduces herself to my father. She refers to him as Mr Bailey and asks his permission to examine him. Never once, even though he occasionally loses concentration and drifts off, does she address her questions or concerns to me, except when she has asked for and received his permission.

She declares him dehydrated and too weak to get up. She isn't able to diagnose the source of the problem and recommends that Dad go to hospital. He is adamant that he will not leave the house. I know he's telling me he wants to die in his own bed.

It is, I suppose, what we all would like—to die at

home, surrounded by those who love us—but I don't want him to die. I want him to go to hospital and get well, unrealistic though it seems. But I also know I can't take care of him myself. He's thin and shrunken, but he's still a big man with a heavy frame. I couldn't possibly manoeuvre him in the bed. Nor would he want me to. I'm his daughter and he is a very private man. I have never in my life seen him naked. Neither of us would be able to bear it if I were forced into a position where I had to perform the most intimate functions for him.

The doctor picks up on the tensions in the room and agrees to wait overnight to see what progress we make. She'll arrange for a team of emergency nurses to come round at once and clean up the mess. She'll return first thing in the morning before surgery begins. I'm not to try and persuade Dad to eat if he doesn't want to, but I must insist he drinks. The dehydration he's suffering is serious and dangerous.

The nurses arrive, all bustle and efficiency, eject me from the bedroom and get on with what they have to do. The bed is stripped and clean sheets put on. Dad is wrapped in incontinence pads as there's no question of him making it to the toilet. He'll be fine, they reassure me, until morning, so I shouldn't need to do anything until more help is forthcoming. I see them out, pushing the dirty, foul-smelling linen into the washing machine as I close the back door.

David pops out for fish, chips and peas and I peck at them. Dad can't manage so much as one chip, but is drinking his lemonade. David has to get back home as he's working early the next morning. He offers to stay and take the day off, but it's a new job, working with schoolchildren, and I know he would prefer not to let them down. I assure him we'll be fine.

I sit until late by Dad's bedside, holding his hand and speaking soothingly about the past. Occasionally he responds with his own memories, even the odd joke. 'Bless you, love,' he whispers. 'Your mother always used to say you're no Florence Nightingale. I think she was right. But I'm glad you're here.' Most of the time he drifts into a fitful sleep or simply loses track of what's going on. But we are close and I tell him over and over again how much I love him.

I sleep the way I used to when the babies were small—cat-napping in the bedroom next to his with one ear cocked for any worrying sounds. Around three in the morning I hear his voice—weak but worried. I rush into his room and he's half fallen out of bed. He wants to go to the toilet, but I know we can't get him there. I reassure him, tell him not to worry, he's wearing a pad. He grimaces and spits out 'Nappy!' but allows himself to be tucked up again and falls asleep. I crawl, gratefully, back to bed.

At six I'm up, dressed and making coffee. The doctor is due at seven. Dad seems pleased to sip at a cool, milky, sugary one and rallies a little with the liquid and sweetness inside him. I wash his face, brush his hair and plump his pillows. He doesn't look quite as bad as he did yesterday.

The doctor arrives on the dot and notices that I seem as frazzled as Dad does. I'm also wearing nothing on my head, so the chemotherapy giveaway is clear for her to see. Again, she addresses her concerns to my father.

'Mr Bailey, you seem a little better today—your daughter has obviously looked after you well. But I really do think you should consider going into the hospital. That way we can find out what's really going on. I can't make a diagnosis without proper tests.'

Again, that look of alarm. The soft brown eyes, blurred with age, light upon me appealingly.

'Jen, no hospital, please.'

I know I have to play the mother card.

'Dad, you know what Mum would say in these circumstances. She'd say, "You're not well, Alvin, don't be so stubborn and silly and do what the doctor says. Go to the hospital." '

It works like magic. The doctor asks again if he is happy to go to hospital. He slowly nods his agreement. And then everything happens incredibly fast. The paramedics are there in a flash. He recognizes them from the many times they've turned up at the house to take Mum to casualty after one of her falls. They're cheerful and competent, wrapping him in a blanket and carrying him out in a kind of pushchair as easily as if he were a child. They urge me to follow later and bring things for his stay.

I strip the bed and put the washing machine on again. His car is in the drive. I find the keys, search high and low for the one pair of pyjamas I know he owns—he was never much of a pyjama man—put washing and shaving kit into a bag with a couple of towels and a hairbrush and climb into his vehicle. It's unfamiliar and I manoeuvre it with great care out of the narrow drive. It's pretty new and I know he'll be displeased if I so much as scratch it.

By the time I've found and paid for a parking

space, identified that he's in an emergency ward for new and undiagnosed conditions and made my way to his bedside, he's sitting up in bed wearing a hospital gown. It's taken me a couple of hours, but there's little evidence of anyone having troubled to clean and tidy him up. I brush his hair and ask him what's happened. He seems bemused and isn't hearing well. He understands me all right, but I've had long experience of making myself clear to him during the years of my childhood when he was deaf as well as in recent years when his hearing has deteriorated again. I have, of course, forgotten his hearing aid, so he has no idea what's been said to him or what's been done.

This, as it turns out, is a blessing. I'm sitting at the side of his bed, having had no joy from any of the nurses on what progress we've made. They seem to be busy gossiping to each other about their social activities and pay scant attention to patients or their relatives. Eventually there's the recognizable scurry which signifies consultant alert and a young man—probably in his late thirties—pauses briefly at the end of Dad's bed.

'You must be the daughter.' His voice is clipped, unsympathetic. He barely looks at either me or Dad. 'Lung cancer. Advanced.' And he walks away.

I cannot be more shocked. Dad hasn't been coughing, he's kept his strength together until a week or so ago, he's not breathless—the only symptoms I've recognized are the weight loss and the husky voice. But he's had an X-ray and that's the diagnosis. Brutally delivered. I mean to complain about consultants who appear to have had their bedside manner amputated, but I don't have the energy.

302

I can't help but gaze at this old warrior and marvel at his strength and self-possession. He asks me what the doctor said. I hold his hand and tell him, as gently as I can, that it's lung cancer.

'But Dad, it can be treated,' I rush on selfishly, thinking not of what he wants but what I want. 'You could live for ages if we get it treated. I'll find the best specialist.'

He pats my hand.

'I knew, love. I just wanted to go, quietly, without all this fuss. I'm sorry, but there's nothing to be done. Just take me home.'

I remind him how impossible it will be to look after him at home, and what trouble we had trying to get care for Mum. He agrees and tears roll down his cheeks as he says he'll never see his garden again and begs me not to put him in a home. I promise, not knowing what on earth I'm going to do.

I leave him reluctantly in the evening, assuring him I'll be back the following day. He's to be moved to the chest ward and that's where he'll be the next morning.

I spend the night alone in my parents' house, racking my brains for a solution.

The following day I'm back at the hospital, seeing the chest specialist, who is kind and gentle but doesn't pull any punches. He's astonished that Dad has been independent for so long and says he gives him two or three more weeks at the most. I ask to see the palliative care team.

Sara heads the Macmillan nursing team and she's with us incredibly fast. She quickly organizes a new hearing aid—Dad thinks he's lost the old one—and sits down to discuss where we go from here.

I tell her about the brainwave I'd had in the middle of the night. Barnsley has a hospice and I had done a fundraising lunch for it some years ago when they needed money for an eight-bed in-patient unit. I ask Sara if she thinks Dad would be a suitable candidate for hospice care. She thinks it will be perfect and she says she'll find out right away if they have a bed. They do. He can be admitted the next day.

'So it will have to be a home,' Dad mutters despondently.

'No, Dad,' I reassure him, 'not a home, a hospice. I think you'll find it very different from what we had with Mum.'

The moment I walk through the door of the bright, modern building I know we've made the right choice. There is no unpleasant smell of urine or faeces. Everything is clean. The staff wear uniforms and there are lots of them. I'm shown into Dad's room and only an hour or so after being admitted he's a different person. There are fresh flowers on a chest of drawers in the corner, a TV with a remote that's easily accessible—ditto an emergency bell. There's even a radio tuned to Radio 4 so that he can listen to me when I'm not there. Obviously he's been quick to point out who his daughter is, and the staff seem to know quite a bit about his grandchildren too.

He's been shaved. His hair has been cut and brushed. His face doesn't look pale or strained any more. They call him Alvin but I know they've asked permission for the more familiar form of address, and he preens himself delightedly as one of the nurses teases him about how handsome he

304

looks—like a movie star, she says—and he does.

His room, like all the others, is on the ground floor. It has its own bathroom and glass doors leading to a patio covered with pots of bright flowers. The gardening is all done by volunteers. Fifty per cent of funding comes from the local primary care trust, the rest is raised by charitable work. The place is a miracle. I'm shown to the kitchen where I can make myself tea or coffee and to the room where, if I need to, I can stay overnight. I have a long chat with the sister on duty, who makes it plain that they are as concerned for close relatives as they are for the patient, and says I am not to hesitate to ask for help or advice. For the first time I feel somebody understands how tough this all is.

In Dad's room I range photographs I've brought from home—his wedding, his favourite picture of Mum, the children when they were small, me as a baby. He asks if I could bring in the one of me with the Queen when I was awarded the OBE. He wants to show me off. I promise I'll bring it the next day. I help him eat supper. He shows little interest in the beautifully cooked savoury dish but wolfs down the pudding, grunting appreciatively at the quality of the cuisine.

As I leave him for the night he thanks me for finding such a lovely place for him to stay, grinning and saying it's like a five-star hotel. As I get to the door he calls me back.

'Give us another kiss,' he smiles. 'I love you. And, by the way, you haven't got a fag on you, have you?' Incorrigible!

'No, Dad, I haven't and, even if I had, this is a hospice and you have lung cancer.'

'Wouldn't do me any harm then, would it?'

I should have mentioned it to the nurses. Apparently, I discover later, they're quite relaxed about it and would have wheeled him out to the patio to enjoy his cigarettes. I shouldn't have denied him his pleasure.

Next day I arrive to find him full of cheer, joshing with the nursing staff who've warned me there might be a bit of a funny smell in the room. It's brandy, they tell me; someone had brought in a bottle the night before and Dad had enjoyed a drop, but a bit had been spilled. I ask him about his new drinking habit—he's never been one for alcohol.

'You know what they say,' he laughs, 'a bit of what you fancy.'

I'm not sure what it is, but something is clearly doing him good and the hospice is fulfilling its aim of making the end of life as pleasurable as possible.

Comparing the facilities here with what Mum had to put up with in a commercially run nursing home makes my blood boil. This is the kind of care to which every one of us should be entitled in our old age.

My phone rings, which makes him laugh again. My ring tone is *The Archers'* theme tune and he hums along, 'Dum di dum di dum di dum.'

It's Charlie calling from somewhere in Thailand and wanting a quick chat with his beloved grandpa. He feels terrible being so far away when his grandfather is dying and even discusses flying home. I manage to persuade him Grandpa wouldn't want him to spoil his travels, which Dad confirms on the phone. There's talk of rugby and Dad reminds Charlie there's a Test match on—then they say goodbye.

Dad turns to me.

'Such a shame that lad never got into cricket. He could bat and bowl like a demon when he was little—he could have played for England, you know.'

What a fulfilment of a great ambition that would have been. Rumour has it that a visit to friends in Lancashire had been planned around the time of my birth, but Dad insisted we must stay in Yorkshire 'just in case'. 'David Robert' would have to be born in Yorkshire to qualify for the county cricket team—so I guess, even though he never expressed it quite so clearly as my mother did, my sex was a disappointment to him too, especially as I was to be the only one. I spent much of my childhood on the boundary making daisy chains, watching Dad and my grandfather play for local teams or accompanying the pair of them during TV marathons whenever a match was on. I loved their company, but never learned to appreciate the game. Dad said it represented everything that was great about being British—calm, strong, elegant and fair. I thought it was boring—and still do.

Imagine his disappointment when I managed to produce not one but two sons, one born in Southampton, the other in London, one of whom had no interest in any sport apart from riding horses and the other whose passion for rugby outweighed all other enthusiasms.

That Charlie would be sporty was evident from the moment of his birth. This time I was determined to have my baby at home. My GP was reluctant, never having had any experience of home births, but was ready to pass me on to an old GP nearby for the duration of the pregnancy. Dr Goldenberg had delivered lots of babies, but still insisted that I should see the consultant at St George's Hospital in south London.

308

I arrived, armed with statistics about the relative safety of home delivery versus hospital birth—very good, as long as no abnormalities are predicted—and sat down in his office ready for a fight.

'Now,' he said, 'we can offer you a range of options—there's domino where you simply come in to us for the delivery, or you can stay overnight or a bit longer if you like. Whatever suits you.'

'I'd like a home delivery, please.'

He glanced down at his paperwork.

'Very straightforward delivery last time. I don't see a problem. So, yes, that's fine.'

It was as easy as that.

Throughout my pregnancy I worked on the *Today* programme. We'd moved to London two years before as I'd got a job as a presenter and reporter on *Newsnight*—a move which I'd found quite daunting. I remember watching women negotiate their buggies across traffic-filled roads and wondering how on earth I could subject my little Ed to such hustle and bustle. Nor could I quite believe that a hick from Barnsley could possibly survive in the shark-infested waters of the

London media scene. It was only when I met another family with a child exactly the same age as Ed, who lived in Clapham and had plans for playgroups and who assured me there was a very good local nursery and primary school, that I felt easy about making the move.

By early June we were in the thick of the '87 election. I was to interview Norman Tebbit on a Thursday morning *Today* programme about some row that was going on between the Tories and the Labour Party, and Brian Redhead—a great mentor and a man of whom I was extremely fond—patted my enormous bump (only he would have dared— only he would have got away with it) and said, 'This must all seem so trivial to you, with that little life inside you.'

'No, Brian,' was my response. 'It's because of this little life that all this matters so much. It's this little life's future we're concerned about, isn't it?'

That shut him up. And so to Mr Tebbit—the rottweiler of the Conservative Party—known for tearing inadequate interviewers limb from limb. I was nervous, but well prepared.

He took one look at me, several inches back from my side of the desk, and gushed, 'Oh my dear, you look as if you're likely to pop any minute. But don't worry, if you should go into labour now I know exactly what to do. I was there when my children were born, you know.'

I reminded him we were about to do an interview. He switched off the avuncular mode for its three-minute duration, we gave each other a combative turn and then he oohed and ahed again, wishing me luck and assuring me what pleasure children brought until he was ushered out of the

310

studio.

I kept going until the Saturday morning programme with a mercifully unemotional John Humphrys and on the Monday afternoon, during a shopping trip around Marks and Spencer's, I felt the first twinges of contractions.

At home around 6 p.m. the midwives came and assured me it would be tonight, but there was a long way to go. They would nip out for some supper and come back. I watched the start of the nine o'clock news and went for a bath, leaving David with our dentist friend, Norma, chosen for her medical knowledge in case of emergency, to look after Ed.

I lay happily in the bath until, around nine forty-five, I felt the head crown. I called for David, who rushed into the bathroom panic-stricken, and at that moment the doorbell rang. The midwives had got lost in the maze of streets 'between the Commons' and apologized for their late arrival.

They hustled me out of the bath and into the bedroom. One of them knelt down and caught Charlie as he shot out like a rocket. He was born as he meant to go on.

A little later, Ed and Norma came to say hello. Ed thought he'd rather watch the end of the *Star Wars* video in which he'd been engrossed and eventually our little family settled down together to get to know each other. It was the perfect way to do it.

Mum and Dad arrived the next day, as instructed, and greeted the new arrival with a little more subtlety than the last, although my mother couldn't fail to go on about how I had managed to produce not one but two strapping sons. Our brilliant nanny Jeanne adapted quickly to having two children to care for and five days later I was back at work. It's known as freelance maternity leave. If you don't work you don't get paid and we needed the money.

Working on the *Today* programme with a new baby was surprisingly easy. I'd get up at three thirty—around the time Charlie needed to be fed—express enough milk for David or Jeanne to feed him at breakfast time and be home around nine thirty. I did, though, feel a little like a one-woman milk marketing board and Mum never failed to voice her disapproval of my failures as a mother and homemaker during her frequent telephone calls. Curiously, some years later, she was equally disapproving of a significant change in our childcare plans. Jeanne decided she'd like to work in a school and we were unable to find a suitable replacement, so David suggested that one or other of us might consider becoming a full-time parent.

By now I had transferred from *Today* to *Woman's Hour* and was loving my new job. David hadn't found anything he felt passionate about since leaving the navy, so it was obvious to us both that he should be the one to be at home with the boys. It was, though, a tough call in the late eighties. He was the only father at the school gates and was viewed at first with deep suspicion as a potential paedophile. Even when he became a familiar figure he was denied all the usual social networks to which mothers have easy access. No woman is going to invite a lone man back for coffee.

Nevertheless he stuck to it and helped to lay some of the foundations for what is now a strong movement in favour of fathers taking a more active role in the care of their children. My mother never quite got the hang of it, though, constantly asking him when he was going to get a job. Dad, not one to interfere, simply never mentioned it, but clearly thought there was something very strange about a man who would let his wife be the family breadwinner.

Not, of course, that I was David's wife. Another subject that was studiously ignored by my deeply conventional parents. Until, of course, I wrote THAT article in which I set out my arguments against the marital state. Immediately the *Daily Mail* described me as the most dangerous woman in England, and the *Evening Standard*'s billboards cried '*Woman's Hour* presenter says marriage is legalized prostitution.'

Not that they had got that quite right, of course. It was, as I wrote in the article, Mary

313

Wollstonecraft who defined marriage as legalized prostitution in her *Vindication of the Rights of Woman,* written almost two hundred years to the day before my article was published. I did, though, urge women to hang on to their financial independence for fear of suffering what I had seen too many times: a loyal and dependent wife dumped for a sleeker model when the children had flown the nest and it was too late to get back into the workplace.

I had not anticipated the flurry my article, written for a fairly obscure women's magazine, would cause. To his credit my ex-husband, besieged by tabloid journalists looking to dish the dirt on what a terrible wife I had been, turned down the offers of vast sums of money and told them there was no story to tell. And to my astonishment, my mother, equally bombarded with requests, saw them off with an 'I don't agree with my daughter's views, but I would defend to the death her right to express them.'

314

It was, however, another matter during the acrimonious telephone calls I had with her. How, she wanted to know, could I have done it, when she had told all her friends that David and I were married? For the first time in my life, I really stood up to her. I explained that we had to accept that we had very different views, and that she could no longer silence me. I felt it important to put these ideas out into the public arena so that people could discuss them and make up their own minds about what path they would choose to take.

I had so often felt gagged by my fear of offending her and her moral standards. Now the press, in its violent reaction to what were perceived as subversive thoughts, also sought to silence a radical woman by demeaning and ridiculing her. I wasn't going to play the game and stay quiet any longer and I would like her to respect that. We moved, I think, into a new realm, where she finally realized that her daughter was an adult. I was forty-two.

When David and I did finally wed, after twenty-odd years of unmarried bliss, it was with my father's sound financial advice ringing in my ears. Property does not pass between unmarried couples without inheritance tax being due. If either of us died, the other would probably have to sell our family home in order to pay the taxes. It seemed a very expensive way of sticking to one's principles and very unfair to the kids.

We planned the most basic ceremony at the Macclesfield Register Office with the boys and Norma in attendance. Charlie was too young to act as witness, but Ed and Norma were enough to fill the bill. There was to be no mention of bride or groom, no flowers, no music and no romantic guff. This was a business partnership and we would say only what was legally required.

The whole thing went off in a fit of giggles.

'We are here today to join David and Jennifer in front of their family and friend,' the registrar intoned. Charlie began to titter at the singular 'friend', which Ed and Norma caught as did David and I. We were ticked off by the registrar, who thought we should take things a little more seriously.

My parents were not there. My mother was already too ill to travel and I had thought seriously about not telling her it was going to happen, thinking what she didn't know she wouldn't miss. Ed was outraged at the suggestion, rightly pointing out that I would not be best pleased if he went off and did something so significant without telling me.

I went over to see her before the event and told her of the plan.

'Hmmm,' she grunted, 'and not before time.'

'At last, some financial sense,' said Dad.

It had, I suppose, been unrealistic on my part to expect a more enthusiastic response after so many years of disapproval and I had not exactly sold the occasion as one of romance, hearts and flowers. I was a little afraid myself that tying the knot legally might have a negative effect on the relationship between the two of us. Had we, I wondered, succeeded in staying so solid because neither of us felt trapped?

It has made no difference at all. We still refer to each other as partners, rather than husband and wife, and neither of us feels there are any chains around us from which we need to break free. We never actually spoke the words 'till death do us part', but we're a couple who love each other and who created a new family that matters to both of us more than anything else, so I guess it's a given.

June

Friday 1 June and something good has happened for a change. Ed has passed his final exams and is now a qualified vet. My maternal pride and absolute euphoria seem to surpass even the ghastly effects of yesterday's second dose of CMF chemotherapy and continuing worries about Dad. It's twenty-two years since Ed first announced he wanted to be a vet, when he came with me to the surgery to see our old dogs, William and Mary, have their annual booster jabs. He was two years old and said, 'Mummy, I want to be a dog doctor.' He never wavered from his ambition. The news is the sun in the dark sky of this damp and depressing summer.

We decide that the three of us, David, Ed and I, will go over to see Dad together today. We're longing to tell him about Ed's success.

Dad's condition over the past few days has not been good. Sometimes we can hold a conversation, but more often he's sleepy or he appears awake but his mind is somewhere else and I'm unable to reach him. I know Ed's youth and energy will bring life into the room where, I'm forced to acknowledge, my father is dying.

Dad has been moved to a new room, identical to the other but a little closer to the nurses' station, which I know is a sign they're needing to keep a more watchful eye on him. He's no longer really capable, I suspect, of summoning help if he needs it. He rallies a little to our greeting and smiles at the news—holding Ed's hand and whispering, 'Well done, lad, I'm proud.' I'm struck, as I have often been since Ed began to mature into an adult, by how similar the two of them are. There are pictures of Dad in the army in his late teens and early twenties which could be pictures of Ed as he is now—gentle eyes, straight nose and sensuous mouth—and they share the same calm, solid temperament. It's consoling to see Dad's line continuing.

One of the doctors pops her head around the door and asks me to come and have a word. The staff here are so gentle and considerate without being in the slightest bit sentimental. We sit together in comfy chairs in a room reserved for private conversations and she explains that, while Dad is in no pain and for the most part is not distressed, his condition has indeed deteriorated. He is at times upset and troubled and the staff think it is maybe time to give him the means to receive a constant stream of drugs which will help him relax and relieve his anxiety.

I explain my dread that I will have to watch him die a slow and protracted death, steadily starving under the influence of powerful narcotics, as I did with my mother. It seems such a selfish thought, now I look back on it, considering my benefit rather than his, but I really don't feel I can bear it again. I don't want my last memory of my hunk of a father to be like that skeletal image of my mother that will not be dispelled from my mind. The doctor assures me Dad will not be allowed to starve, but insists that the medication will help give him peace of mind. We spend an hour together chewing over the pros and cons and in the end I agree. I have so much trust in the staff of the hospice. They give me time and I know they don't bullshit.

We spend another hour or so at Dad's bedside, talking to each other about the past and about Ed's future. I suggest to Dad that I might stay the night, but he's quietly insistent that I should go home with my family and celebrate the future. He wishes he could be with us. He wishes he could be there for the graduation next month, but he doesn't think he'll be well enough. He drifts off to sleep, half opening his eyes as David and Ed say their goodbyes. He pecks my cheek as I whisper, 'Dad, I'll see you tomorrow,' and drifts off again.

The three of us are silent for the whole journey back. It feels as if final goodbyes have been spoken.

To my great relief, there is no dreaded phone call during the night. David and Ed volunteer to come with me to Barnsley again. They're worried, I can tell, about the state of my health. It's the second day after the most recent hit of CMF and I'm still just about surviving on steroids and anti-emetics, but I seem to be dredging up an untapped energy source from somewhere. Instinct insists that I must make this journey alone.

I drive faster than usual. I have a sense of urgency, the source of which I cannot place. It's not a conscious act, I'm just driven to get there as quickly as I can. I arrive around lunchtime, park hurriedly and badly and rush through the security procedures to gain admittance. I want to be at my father's bedside.

He's sleeping when I finally sit down beside him. I grasp his right hand. The left one has the contraption which is delivering his drugs. His hand is the same big, dry, slightly calloused one I've always hung on to in times of trouble. I remember it from as far back as memory goes—the most steadying, reassuring thing I've ever known. I can't bear to let go.

I talk—it's what I do—it's what my mother always did—rattling on about everything and nothing, telling him stories to make him laugh, recalling incidents from the past to jog his memory. He would always tease us for the chatterboxes we were, and he never was. He was a man who never said much unless it had depth and moment, but he enjoyed his women twittering around him. Strong and silent, we called him—such a cliché, but so true. Now he is simply silent, his breathing shallow and barely perceptible, but I chatter on, hoping he can hear.

One of the doctors, a different one from yesterday, pops in to say hello and ask me how I am. She asks if I'd like some company and I find that, for a little while, I would. She sits down next to me as if she had all the time in the world, even though it is a Saturday afternoon and she must have family to be with and things to do. We talk about the drug Dad is getting and how peaceful he's been since he started taking it. We discuss him and my mother and what it was like being an only child, looking at the photographs that are ranged about the room.

Ely, the nurse with whom Dad's formed the closest bond—the one who tells him he looks like a movie star and takes so much care over his appearance—looks round the door and asks if I'd like a cup of coffee. She brings it through and I sip it, more out of politeness than thirst, and the two women seem to sense I need to be alone with my father. They leave the room.

I want so much to lie down on the bed next to my dad and have him hold me and tell me everything's going to be all right. Instead, I pull my chair closer, put my head next to his hand and lift it so it rests on the back of my neck. I'm wearing the ridiculous turban. There is no hair there for him to run his fingers through as he's done so often and his hand is limp and heavy, but the weight and warmth of it feels so reassuring. I sit there, listening to him breathe, as I used to as a youngster. His hand on my head, the smell of him, the breath going in and out, making my breaths match his—was there ever anything more soothing? I wonder if he can sense how much this 'little' girl loves him?

I have no idea how long I've been in this position, but I'm woken from a trance-like state by his hand slipping down heavily on to my shoulder. I hold it again for a moment and lay it gently by his side. My mouth is dry. I sip the coffee which is now cold. Ever the dutiful visitor to the hospice, I get up to take the dirty cup back to the kitchen and wash it up.

I'm gone only a few minutes. I wander back into Dad's room and stand for a moment at the end of the bed, watching his chest slowly rise and fall. All of a sudden his eyes open.

'Dad,' I cry loudly, 'you're awake.' I feel overjoyed that he's with me again. He's looking straight into my eyes and he's smiling. His eyes close. There is one ferocious exhalation of breath, then nothing. I rush to his side. Clutch his hand again. It's warm, but he's not breathing. I don't remember shrieking, but Ely is quickly by my side, her arm around me.

325

'He's gone, hasn't he?' I barely recognize the voice that chokes out the words.

'Yes, love, I think he has, but don't worry, you can stay with him as long as you like.'

I sob on her shoulder, then take my father's hand again. Warm, dry, dependable, like always. I kiss his hand. Lean over and kiss his cheek. I once saw a puppy sniffing and licking at its dead mother, willing her back to life. I want to breathe life back into my father. But there is nothing there.

My heart wants to stay at his side for ever. My head makes me stand up and walk out on to the patio and into the fresh warm air of the summer's afternoon. I call David, Ed and Charlie in Australia. Again Charlie wants to come home. Again, I reassure him that Grandpa would not have wanted him to break into his travels and come such a long way for his funeral.

I return to his room and look down at the lifeless body of the man I have loved longer than anyone else in the world and can almost hear his voice urging me to be sensible and practical, telling me there's nothing more to stay for. The doctor who spent time with me earlier in the afternoon arrives and carries out the tests she needs to perform. I watch her check for the non-existent pulse and heartbeat. Tears roll down my cheeks.

For a moment I consider staying and helping the nurses wash Dad and ready him for the arrival of the undertaker. They used to call it laying out when I was a child. Some cultures do it as a matter of course, out of love and respect. It feels as if there should be some ritual for me to observe to mark the passing of such a potent spirit, but I know he'd be embarrassed to think I should see him with his dignity stripped away. He'd berate me for being mawkish.

He has no belief in God or an afterlife and neither do I, but I want nothing more than for him to be somewhere hearing me say, 'Goodbye, Dad. I love you,' as I turn my back on him and leave the room. The nurses urge me to stay, have a cup of tea, recover my senses before embarking on the long drive. I brush aside their kindness and tell them I'll leave him in their care. I give them the name of the undertaker. I just want to go home.

* * *

I have never felt so lost and lonely as I feel on this terrible drive back across the Pennines that he and I loved to wander so much. My father is dead. I remember all the times he urged me to sit down with him and discuss his will, the provisions he'd made for the children, what he wanted me to do with whatever money he had left, and I steadfastly refused to talk about it. I could never bear to think towards a life that he and my mother would no longer inhabit. It never seemed possible that I would be without them. And now they're gone. I'm a middle-aged woman, a wife and a mother, tough, resourceful and independent, and I am as much a bereft orphan as a small child. I wish I had a brother or sister with whom I could share these feelings, but there's no one.

I am now more experienced than I would ever have wished to be at the testing round of practicalities that follow a death. Off I go again to Barnsley knowing there will be no one there I care about. First stop, the Town Hall to register the death, having first made an appointment. The registrar has spectacularly long, red nails and a stunning, huge diamond solitaire. I compliment her on her exquisite taste. It's a bit flash, I know, but I'm afraid it's one I share and her diamond is even bigger than mine. She hurries to tell me that she only bought the diamond last year; she'd saved up for years. Like me, she hadn't met a man rich enough to fulfil her gaudy dream. I saved up and bought mine too.

She asks me if I'm Win Bailey's daughter. She remembers her from the days when Mum was receptionist for the Council.

'She was here the day I started. She was such a nice woman, so good at her job and always so nicely turned out. We all looked up to her and we missed her when she retired.'

It's still a small town, just like when I was a kid, and everybody knows everybody else's business. Where I would have been embarrassed as a child, I'm now delighted that Mum lives on in people's memories. The registrar expresses her condolences for my loss, says she remembers Dad and what a looker he was and I leave bearing several copies of the death certificate. I know that one is not enough when there are building society accounts and insurances to be wound up.

Then I go home, where I unlock the door myself for the first time in my life. Dad's cigarettes and lighter are on the mantelpiece where he left them, his underpants still drying on the radiator. Soon I'll have to sort everything out—a whole lifetime of possessions. But not yet.

The vicar arrives. She knows from talking to Dad about Mum's funeral that he had no religious conviction, but agrees to preside over the ceremony at St Thomas's Church then at the crematorium, and yes, she'll keep the service simple and as non-denominational as possible. We choose a favourite hymn, 'The Church's One Foundation', which he used to sing as a choirboy, and she agrees to make up an order of service with photographs and a poem, just as she did for Mum.

It seems slightly hypocritical to be fixing things in the house of a God neither Dad nor I believe in, but the setting and the atmosphere will be just right and the vicar is a delight. I know it's what he would have wanted—it's exactly what he chose for my mother. She was a believer, or so she said, although I never recall her going to church for anything other than hatching, matching or dispatching, but the crematorium is a cold and soulless place—cheaply decorated, more bright community hall than venue for grief and drama. The bells, smells and gothic darkness of the church will be much more fitting. The vicar doesn't seem to mind at all.

Next on the list of appointments is the undertaker. I haven't gone with the Co-op this time. They are generally the funeral directors of choice among Barnsley's aspirant middle classes, but I found them a little over-melancholy and formal in my dealings with them at the time of Mum's funeral and the sight of a woman in top hat, black suit, purple neckerchief and high-heeled shoes teetering up the cul-de-sac in her role as chief mourner as the cortège set off almost reduced the boys to hysterics. The heels were dreadfully out of place. This time I've found a young man just starting his own business. He's friendly, efficient and doesn't speak in hushed, lugubrious tones.

We fix a date, confirm the venue for the ceremony and the 'tea' and get down to the nitty-gritty of selecting a coffin. It hadn't been a problem for Mum—we chose a simple wooden box which she would have found tasteful and suitably expensive. Dad wouldn't have worried about the aesthetics for himself, would definitely have considered the cost an unnecessary extravagance—'burning bloody money'—and, as the keen gardener he was, had often expressed irritation at the waste of trees 'for nothing but show'.

So we discuss the ecological alternatives—wicker or cardboard. I look at the pictures in the catalogue. The undertaker has a little warning about the wicker. Very practical, extremely environmentally sound, but displaying a tendency to creak as it was carried down the aisle. I rule it out. And, honestly, can I really send my dad into eternity in a cardboard box like a pair of old shoes?

I can't and order instead the exact same coffin we'd had for my mother. I suspect that what was going through my mind was my mother's voice: 'Hang the expense. Don't you dare shame me by looking cheap. It's just not done.'

* * *

The funeral passes in a haze of emotion. Charlie, of course, is missing. He's taken my advice about not flying halfway across the world for it, but calls in the early morning to send his best wishes and tell us he's thinking of us. Ed acts as a pall-bearer, ramrod straight and serious, and David spends the whole day holding me up when I fear at any moment I may fall down. I sob my way through my eulogy. I can't decide whether these rituals are an essential part of making sense of the cycle of life and death or a form of public torture, but it's certainly not the case that the practicality of a funeral lays the horrors of grieving to rest.

I find myself doing things which are patently stupid. I absent-mindedly pick up the phone in the evening to make my nightly call and am beginning to dial before it hits me that he's not there any more. I wake early on a Saturday morning, ready to take myself to Barnsley, and again am halfway out of the house before I remember I don't need to go. And I think obsessively about death, asking myself what is the point of it all when so powerful a personality can simply be snuffed out.

People trot out the old comforts. 'Ah, he was eighty, well, he'd had a good life.'

But had he? Had she? They lived through a terrible war and all the hardships it brought. They worked hard all their lives and paid their taxes, never wanting to be any trouble to anybody, least of all their wayward, headstrong, self-obsessed daughter. And, just as I began to realize what heartache a seemingly ungrateful or uncommunicative child can bring—mine were hitting their teens just as my mother began to suffer from Parkinson's—and regret my own behaviour, the years of travel and pleasure they had planned for their retirement came to a shuddering halt and there followed ten years of falls, fractures and grappling with the NHS. When the care services for which they had paid and which they were due were needed, any concept of being

331

looked after from the cradle to the grave had been blown out of the water.

I am sad, frightened and most of all angry. Angry at a so-called society that spends so little money on the old and weak and pays them such scant attention, and angry at myself for all the little slights and moments of forgetfulness. Why didn't I let them know if I was going to appear on *Call My Bluff* or *This Morning*, instead of leaving it to friends to tell them they'd seen me? Why didn't I visit more often and bring their grandchildren to them more frequently? Why didn't I persuade Mum to put her fears aside and accompany Dad on the trip that was his lifelong ambition?

For their fiftieth wedding anniversary we had a party at their favourite hotel in Barnsley, the Queen's—now closed and converted into flats. There was a cake and I gave a speech and the boys dressed up in their best bib and tucker and put on their most charming personae for the occasion, but something much more exotic had been Dad's plan. He wanted to sail around the world on the *QE2*. He had saved up the money. He was ready to go to the travel agent and book. Mum was still well enough to endure the rigours of the journey. He talked about it all the time. He wanted to see New Zealand and Australia, the Caribbean, the South Pacific. He was full of excitement.

Literally the night before he was due to go and pay his deposit, Mum said she'd like to go to the cinema. She'd heard a lot on the radio about a new film that was said to be very good. It was called *Titanic*. My mother was never much of a swimmer. As a small child she'd been having swimming lessons when a couple of bigger girls had asked to use her for life-saving practice. They were not practised enough and, she told me, she was coming up for the third time in the deep end when my grandmother spotted what had happened and dived in, fully clothed, to rescue her.

My mother had never forgotten her fear of drowning. She would force herself to come and watch me at school swimming galas, but would pale and catch her breath as she smelt the chlorine. She'd tried to overcome it when she retired and attended special classes for fearful non-swimmers for about a year and was never more proud than when she was given a certificate for swimming the width of the pool. Then she gave up. No way, she said, was she going to be bobbing about in the Atlantic or, worse, trapped in a cabin as the waters rose.

I could have spent more time persuading her of the unlikelihood of a modern-day Cunard cruise encountering an iceberg—they tend to sail when they know the weather conditions will be favourable and, of course, there hadn't been a disaster similar to the *Titanic*, involving a great ocean liner, for nearly a hundred years. But, of course, I didn't. I just laughed at her silliness and failed to be the advocate Dad needed. I could have volunteered to be his companion, but I knew there was no point. There was no way he would set off on something so enjoyable without her. It would have been tantamount to setting sail without his right arm.

I spend hours of my time looking through the old photograph albums I've brought from my parents' home. I can't yet begin to think of putting the house on the market and sorting through the remains of the bilberry pie and minty biscuits Dad has left in the fridge or the mountain of my mother's shoes dating back to the year dot. She always believed they would come back into fashion and quite frequently they did. The thought of rifling through their things now fills me with despair. But a photo can take me back in an instant and brings nothing but pleasure and happy/sad memories.

Here I am sitting on the swing my dad made in Grandma and Grandpa's garden, wearing the white fairy frock designed for the street party for the Queen's coronation. My mother was a little ashamed at her lack of skill with a needle and had had it specially made. She begged me not to tell anyone as everybody else's child was wearing something run up by a more dexterous parent. I can tell from the defiant grin on my face that she's shouting at me to come and get my wings and crown on and not 'under any circumstances to get that dress dirty'. Getting dirty was what I always

did best.

I hated that frock and the pristine white socks and the sensible Clark's sandals. 'We don't want you having your feet ruined like your father's were, wearing shoes handed down from his brothers that never fitted him properly,' she'd say to me. Mine were measured and checked endlessly and the shoes were horribly old-fashioned . . . and, sorry, Mum . . . I have terribly troublesome feet, despite her best efforts.

There's Mum and me on holiday in the Isle of Wight. I have the pigtails of which she approved and am wearing the school blazer of which she was so proud. Why she insisted I wear the wretched thing on holiday I'll never know. Nevertheless I must have just done something to displease her. She's wearing her 'wait till I get you home, you naughty girl' expression. I smile sweetly into the camera for Daddy—he rarely appears in family snaps as he was always the one wielding the camera. At least with my mother there's no

pretence of 'happy snaps'—when she was furious she showed it, in front of the camera or otherwise. And he's caught perfectly her 'just sucked vinegar' look.

The only picture in which Mum looks completely content—she's grinning like a Cheshire cat—is the one where we're leaning on her new Mini. She's just passed her driving test. I must be around twelve or thirteen and I am wearing her idea of what a good daughter should sport— exactly the same as her. We have the same brown ski pants, identical pink-checked shirts—mine distinguished from hers only in the length of the sleeves and the fact that I've done up the button at the neck. We hold sweaters laboriously knitted by her from the same pattern in the same wool, we're wearing the same bracelet, the same watch and my hair is pulled back in the Alice band I loathed and of which she so approved. She must have managed to bully me into rollers the night before as my hair is kinking at the bottom in an entirely uncharacteristic manner. I can feel myself leaping

from the black and white picture, seething with resentment.

There are two pictures of me and my dad. In one I'm a surly teenager, sitting between his knees on the beach at Blackpool, wearing the shortest of shorts and Roy Orbison sunglasses and glowering at my mother, who, no doubt, had made a lot of fuss about which button she should press, being unused to taking photos. The continued presence of the Alice band would not have lightened my mood.

The only photo in which I look entirely relaxed is one which was taken by David soon after we met. The four of us had gone out to lunch. It was a beautiful summer's day. I'm wearing a crisp, cool summer frock and leaning on Dad as he crouches and I sit on the grass. It's how I always want to remember him—smiling, dependable, with those big warm hands held out in front, always ready to catch me should I ever fall.

There is no photo of the one incident in my relationship with my parents that I can look back

on with absolute pride and delight. Soon after I joined *Woman's Hour*—in 1989—my parents were to celebrate their fortieth wedding anniversary. My father was the greatest fan of the Last Night of the Proms and he and Mum would never go out on the night it was broadcast. The concert would be a little later in the year than the actual anniversary, but, if I could swing it, it would be the best present ever. Getting tickets is, as David put it so elegantly, like finding rocking-horse shit, but I happened to know that the then controller of Radio 3, John Drummond, was a fan of *Woman's Hour*. I called him. He could manage just the two tickets and sent them straight over.

I told my parents I'd arranged to take them to the opera and gave them the date. Neither was particularly impressed, but feigned delight and probably were quite pleased that I'd thought about it at all. To be a good liar you have to be very well prepared, and when they arrived for the weekend in London it didn't take Mum long to rumble me. She'd checked what operas were on that weekend. Foolishly, I hadn't. When she asked what we were going to see I told her *Carmen*. She fired back that *Carmen* wasn't on, so I had to tell her the truth, swearing her to absolute secrecy.

Unusually for her, she managed to keep it to herself. We set off in the car at around six thirty (the men in the front, the women in the back . . . gggrrr!) and, happily, Dad knew little of the geography of the capital so he didn't notice we were not heading for the West End. He turned round at one point during the journey.

'You know, love,' he hazarded rather wistfully, 'it's very nice of you to take us out like this, but you did choose a bad night. It's the Last Night of the Proms tonight and I've never missed it, except when we were abroad.' Even my mother managed to keep a straight face.

As the Albert Hall came into view, he turned again, eyes agog with astonishment.

'You haven't, you haven't! Oh my God, I don't believe it. You little so-and-so.' It's not often my father wept, but that night he did. We bought them a Union Jack each and some streamers and gave them their tickets for the best seats in the house.

David and I sat outside in the car, listening to the concert on the radio. I have never seen such radiant faces as they were wearing when they finally emerged. We went to dinner at Prue Leith's and drove home singing 'Land of Hope and Glory'. It was the best thing I ever did.

Postscript

The treatment is over, apart from a five-year course of aromatase inhibitors, daily tablets designed to repress the production of oestrogen and, it's hoped, prevent any return of the cancer. They do terrible things to muscles and joints and I walk like a woman of advanced years, but my hair is back and thick, my skin seems radiant and I've acquired a little dog who, when he's a bit bigger and the weather is warmer, will force me out for long walks and help me to lose weight.

My friends in the Breast Cancer Club continue to insist on delicious lunches at great restaurants (not good for the weight loss regime). Professor Lisa Jardine, two years ahead of me, assures me there *is* life after breast cancer and when I hear of women who have died young from the disease— the wife of my financial adviser died just this week—I grieve for their families and force myself to put my own fear out of my mind.

The reconstruction is done. I chose not to go for the full monty with muscle taken from my back or stomach—it felt too invasive—but instead opted for an implant. I'm still lopsided, but the prosthesis I put into my bra to even things up is small and light.

My parents' house is sold and I don't pick up the phone to call them any more, but I miss them more than I ever thought possible. But when I look back over the year or people ask me how on earth I got through it, I realize I just did. It's what being human is all about. There are good times and there are bad times and what happened to me was what happens to thousands of others. We all just cope.

343

There was, though, one further drama which happened in September when, uninterrupted by chemotherapy treatments, I was ready to take myself back to work. I asked my cleaner to go to my London flat, Wuthering Depths, and give the place a good going over before my return. He rang me on the Thursday morning before I was due back on the Monday.

'I'm so sorry, Jenni,' he said. 'The window in the front has been broken and we didn't want to go in in case there's been a burglary. We wouldn't want to disturb a crime scene. Sorry.'

I really didn't want to leave things till the Monday and arrive there on my own. David agreed we should drive down on the Friday morning, sort things out and make the place secure. We arrived around lunchtime to find glass scattered all over the ground at the entrance to the basement. David busied himself with photographing the scene while I unlocked the door.

The sitting room was a minefield of shattered glass. There was a bath towel thrown over the back of the sofa which I doubted I had left, but couldn't be sure—I do go out very early in the morning when I'm barely awake—but nothing seemed to be missing. Radio, stereo, phones, all in their rightful place. David carried on taking pictures and I said I'd go through to the bedroom to see if the computer was still there.

In my room, a young man in his early thirties, bespectacled, cleanly but casually dressed, was stuffing things into a large black holdall. The bed was in disarray. For a split second I thought it must be the cleaner, braving the crime scene. Then I took a breath. 'What the hell do you think you are

344

doing?' I screamed.

In broken English—it turned out he was Polish—he answered. 'I very sorry, madam, I have nowhere to stay—I only here one night—please let me go.'

'Dave, call the police and guard the front door.' My voice had risen by several more decibels. 'And you—don't you dare move.'

He obeyed and I checked out the kitchen. There were several dirty pans and plates and numerous empty bottles of strong cider (his) and wine (mine) in the bin. He'd clearly been squatting for several days, cooking for himself—most of my pasta and sauces were gone—and using the bathroom. His shaving kit and toothbrush were on the basin. It explained the rogue bath towel in the sitting room.

I stormed back to the bedroom where he was still stuffing his bag.

'Right,' I yelled, 'into the kitchen and make sure you do all those dirty dishes.'

He did.

Next, I shoved a dustpan and brush into his hands. He was on his hands and knees sweeping up the broken glass when the police arrived.

My squatter was eventually taken away in handcuffs. He admitted to breaking in through the window and would be charged with unlawful entry and criminal damage, although he remembered to ask the coppers if they minded fetching his toothbrush and shaving gear from the bathroom.

The police officer who stayed with us was a good-looking character, burly and reassuring. It was rather like being in an episode of *The Bill*. He took our statements, but paused when he came to the end of mine.

'I would normally, at this stage, ask if you'd like a visit from Victim Support, but I think that someone who has made an intruder clear up the mess he's created probably doesn't need it.'

It was then I recognized the harshly furious voice that had emanated from me earlier and imperiously issued the orders about what needed to be done.

So it's true, I thought. We really do all turn into our mothers in the end.